THE NATIVE LABOR PROBLEM
OF SOUTH AFRICA

THE
Native Labor Problem
OF
SOUTH AFRICA

By

J. M. TINLEY

Chapel Hill

THE UNIVERSITY OF NORTH CAROLINA PRESS

1942

COPYRIGHT, 1942, BY
THE UNIVERSITY OF NORTH CAROLINA PRESS

O wad some Power the giftie gie us
To see oursels as ithers see us!

FOREWORD

DURING the past two decades there have been adopted in many nations of the world measures designed to stabilize or rehabilitate the domestic economy or to improve the status of particular groups within their society. Most people in the United States are familiar with the broader aspects of the measures developed in this country since 1930 to stimulate economic recovery although there is disagreement as to the necessity for, and the effectiveness of, some of these measures. Experience does seem to indicate, however, that in the long run the economic interests of all important groups within the economy are closely interrelated and that all programs for improving the status of particular groups must, if they are to attain the ends sought, be in harmony with general welfare.

Such information as has been readily available indicates that many foreign countries have faced problems similar to those in the United States and have adopted corrective measures that resemble those adopted in this country. Little is known, however, as to the details and effectiveness of such measures. Much of the information relative to the reasons for, the nature of, and the results of, policies and programs introduced in other countries is fragmentary and often biased in favor of, or against, particular programs. Seldom are there available comprehensive studies that fit particular policies or programs into their broad economic setting and that evaluate objectively the economic effects of such policies in relation to general welfare. Such information would be of considerable value to policy makers in the United States in evaluating the probable results and effectiveness of policies and programs advocated or in operation in this country.

The Giannini Foundation of Agricultural Economics, of the University of California's College of Agriculture, has undertaken during recent years several studies of state and federal policies relating to this country's agricultural industry and of various aspects of the farm labor problem. As part of its broad program of research, the Foundation plans, whenever funds and personnel are available, to make studies of certain economic aspects of agriculture in foreign countries. The purpose of such studies would be to determine whether, and to what extent, the lessons from the experience of other countries throw light on similar problems confronting the United States.

The Union of South Africa was selected as a suitable country for study because its agriculture resembles in many respects that of the United States. Dr. J. M. Tinley, who had spent many years in South Africa, was detailed to undertake an analysis of the government control policies and farm labor problems of that country. The Carnegie Corporation of New York, which had in the past financed several studies of social problems in South Africa, made a liberal grant to the University for traveling and other expenses connected with this study.

This book presents a study of the Native labor problem of South Africa, with special emphasis on the farm labor aspects thereof. It is anticipated that one or more monographs dealing more specifically with that country's agricultural control policies will be published later.

C. B. HUTCHISON

INTRODUCTION

THE ORIGINAL purpose of this investigation was to analyze the farm labor question of South Africa. Soon after my arrival in that country (August, 1939), I found that a report, *Farm Labour in the Orange Free State*, had just been released by the Institute of Race Relations, attached to the University of the Witwatersrand in Johannesburg, and that another and more comprehensive investigation of Native (Bantu) farm labor by a committee appointed by the Parliament of the Union of South Africa was nearing completion. This report was published in the latter half of 1939.

An analysis of the scope and objectives of these two valuable documents indicated that they focused attention more largely upon actual working conditions in agriculture and upon the more immediate reasons for the alleged existing labor shortage in that industry. The report of the Institute of Race Relations approached the question mainly from the standpoint of the workers (the supply side) whereas the Parliamentary committee report tended to place primary emphasis upon the farmers' needs for labor (the demand side). Although some of the broader social and economic aspects of the question were analyzed in both reports, these matters appeared to receive only incidental attention.

After reviewing these reports and other available literature and discussing the subject with various persons acquainted with the problem, I decided that, in order to avoid unnecessary duplication, it would be best to focus attention on the wider economic and social aspects of the farm labor problem, using the above-mentioned reports as a starting point. As the investigation progressed, it became apparent that the farm labor problem was, in reality, only one phase of the larger problem of unskilled Native labor and that it had its roots in the economic and social development of the country as a whole. The question seemed to be complicated still further by the impact of a modern wage and monetary economy upon the primitive economy of tribal life. As the past and present status of Native wages has been considerably influenced by the policies of successive governments and of the organized labor unions, it was deemed advisable to give some attention to the interrelations between Native and European or white labor. Both preceding and during the writer's visit to South Africa, several conferences were held dealing with nutritional conditions in that country. As much attention was devoted at these conferences to the subject of malnutrition among the Native peoples, it was felt that the picture would not be complete without some consideration of the interrelation between Native labor and the nutritional problems.

In view of all these facts it appeared that the most logical procedure would be to widen the scope of the investigation in order to place the Native labor question in its wider economic and social setting, but at the same time to emphasize the farm labor aspects of the problem.

In few countries is the student of social and economic principles confronted with so many interesting and intricate problems as in the Union of South Africa. These arise out of the fact that there are, in reality, several distinct strata of laborers with widely different wage levels, with widely different standards of living, and with different social and ethnological backgrounds. First of all there are the skilled and "white-collar" European workers, next the unskilled European workers, then the Asiatic and Colored workers, and finally the large body of unskilled Native (Bantu) workers.[1]

The labor question has emerged as a distinct problem in South Africa only since 1870, coincident with the development

---

[1] For a definition of racial groups see the glossary and also page 10.

of the mining industry. The expansion of diamond mining from 1870 onwards, and particularly of the Witwatersrand gold mines from 1886 onwards, has had a profound influence upon the subsequent economic development of South Africa. The immigration of considerable numbers of miners and artisans from Europe, the United States, and elsewhere, was necessary to supply the needs of the mines for skilled workers. The large need for unskilled workers was supplied but with some difficulty, mainly by the Native population of South Africa and surrounding countries. Several cities sprang up in a country which up to 1870 had been mainly rural. The railway system was developed rapidly to provide the mining areas and inland cities with food and supplies. The agricultural industry was transformed within a decade or two from a system of self-sufficient farms to a commercialized basis. Later came the establishment of manufacturing industries.

All of these events, together with subsequent changes in the political and economic structure of South Africa, and especially the measures taken by the government since the end of the first World War to guide the economy of that country in the direction of greater self-sufficiency, have contributed to making the Native labor question the interesting and baffling problem it is today.

Some of the questions confronting the investigator of the Native labor problem of South Africa are whether the difficulty of agriculture and of other industries in securing adequate supplies of Native labor is chronic and likely to become even more acute; whether the gold mining industry is likely to continue operating at the high level of output maintained during the years 1930 to 1939; if not, what will be the effect on the total demand for Native labor, and, perhaps even more important, what will be the effect upon the whole domestic economy of South Africa; whether a further expansion in secondary industries is feasible and under what conditions; what changes in the organization of farming and other industries are necessary in order to permit of a more efficient use of Native labor; and will it be possible for farmers so to increase farm wages (in cash and in kind) and improve working conditions on farms as to make farm work more attractive. These questions are directed at the demand side of the problem.

On the supply side the investigator is interested in learning whether and to what extent the non-European labor supply of South Africa is likely to expand in relation to a possible increased labor demand of primary and secondary industries; whether there is any foundation to the assertion made by both Native leaders and Europeans that the conditions developing in the Native areas are likely to cause a decline in the vitality of the Native population and thus to decrease both their numbers and their efficiency as workers; whether an improvement in the general standard of living of non-Europeans is likely to increase their efficiency as workers.

Although all these questions have an economic bearing, some of them are more within the province of the anthropologist and the sociologist than of the economist. An answer to even the strictly economic questions is far from simple. They involve prognostications as to the future of the gold mining industry, round which the whole of the domestic economy of South Africa revolves, and as to changes in the attitude of the economically and politically dominant European population toward the non-European population. The whole question is still further complicated by the dearth of quantitative information on wage levels in certain industries, on total and seasonal labor requirements, on standards of living, on the extent of malnutrition among both Europeans and non-Europeans, and on numerous other important aspects of the labor problem. The whole of the following analysis is based on the assumption that the present war will not bring about too radical a change in the internal economy and the cultural attitudes of the people of South Africa. If it does, the problem becomes still more complicated and the future even less predictable.

There is no pretense that the answers offered to some of the questions posed above will afford a final solution to the problem; at best they indicate possible lines of policy and action for the future. If the analysis presented in the following pages shows anything at all, it is that efforts of politically powerful pressure groups to obtain special privileges and of the government to maintain a favorable "status quo" for such groups are likely to result in growing maladjustments and to undermine the capacity of a country's domestic economy, as a whole, to adjust itself to changing local and world conditions.

No attempt has been made in this book to draw attention specifically to aspects of the Native labor problem of South Africa which may have a bearing upon similar problems in the United States. Many of the problems are peculiar to South Africa and in other countries may be encountered, in modified form, only where primitive aboriginal groups are brought into contact with a modern exchange economy. In a wider sense the Native labor problem of South Africa is a problem common to all countries, namely that the continued existence of an important underprivileged group in any country is apt to undermine ultimately the economic structure of that country. The solution of this broad problem appears to lie in adjustments which will result in a more efficient utilization of human and physical resources and a more equitable distribution of buying power.

The information on which this investigation is based was gleaned from numerous official and other reports and publications, from interviews with public officials and numerous other persons interested in or connected with the Native labor problem of South Africa. I had considerable difficulty in making contacts with public officials in South Africa throughout the whole of my eight months' stay in that country. Two weeks after my arrival in Capetown, the present war broke out. So great was the internal turmoil and dissension over the question of South Africa's status in the conflict that it was feared for a while that the investigation would have to be abandoned. Even after the country had adjusted itself somewhat to the changed conditions, difficulty was still experienced in getting into contact with public officials. This was due not to any unwillingness on the part of such officials to supply advice and information but to the fact that nearly all government agencies found themselves with new and pressing problems resulting from the war. Although I was given relatively free access to government documents and departmental files, I was handicapped in my interpretation of forces and motives behind certain policies and programs. Individual and group motivation does not usually appear in written form and yet knowledge of such motivation is invaluable for a proper and balanced evaluation of the forces at work.

J. M. TINLEY.

University of California
Berkeley, California
April 15, 1942.

ACKNOWLEDGMENTS

NUMEROUS persons and institutions, both in the United States and in South Africa, contributed to making this study possible. Limitation of space does not permit of specific mention of all such persons and institutions.

The study would not have been possible in the first place had it not been for the interest and encouragement of the late Dr. C. L. Alsberg, Director of the Giannini Foundation, and of Dean C. B. Hutchison of the College of Agriculture, University of California. The matter of finances was solved by generous grants from the Carnegie Corporation of New York towards both traveling and publication expenses.

I want especially to thank Dr. J. F. W. Grosskopf, Chief of the Division of Economics and Markets, Department of Agriculture, Pretoria, and the members of his staff for their courtesy and invaluable advice and assistance. The Division of Economics and Markets placed at my disposal both office accommodation and clerical assistance during the whole of my eight months' stay in South Africa. Professors S. H. Frankel and C. S. Richards of the University of Witwatersrand, Professors R. Leslie, W. H. Hutt, and H. M. Robertson of the University of Capetown, and Professor Raymond Burrows of the Natal University College gave freely of their time and indicated many fruitful sources of information and lines of investigation. I am deeply grateful to Dr. Ray E. Phillips of the American Board Mission in Johannesburg for his help in arranging meetings with Native leaders and with numerous persons concerned with Native affairs. Much useful advice in regard to political and other aspects of the Native question was given me by the Honorable E. H. Brookes and the Honorable J. D. Rheinnallt Jones of the South African Senate and by the Honorable V. M. L. Ballinger (Mrs.) and the Honorable D. B. Molteno of the South African Legislative Assembly.

The Institute of Race Relations attached to the University of the Witwatersrand supplied me with copies of their numerous publications on the racial question and permitted access to their very complete files of newspaper clippings on this subject.

I also wish to thank Professor E. W. Gifford (Department of Anthropology), University of California, for his advice and criticism on the sections of this book dealing with Native tribal customs; Miss Hilda Faust, Specialist in Agricultural Extension, University of California, for similar aid on the sections dealing with nutrition; and Dr. Beatrice M. Mirkowich, Associate in Agricultural Economics, also of the University of California, who assisted me in numerous ways in the preparation of the manuscript.

To all others to whom I am indebted for advice and assistance, I extend my sincere thanks.

Regardless of the sources of information used and the advice given, the author assumes full and sole responsibility for the views and conclusions expressed in this book.

J. M. TINLEY

CONTENTS

CHAPTER	PAGE
FOREWORD	vii
INTRODUCTION	ix
ACKNOWLEDGMENTS	xv

Part I. The Background of the Problem

1.	HISTORICAL AND POLITICAL FRAMEWORK	3
2.	THE ECONOMIC FRAMEWORK	16

Part II. The Supply of Non-European Labor

3.	SUPPLY AND REGIONAL DISPOSITION OF UNSKILLED LABOR	27
4.	SOCIAL AND CULTURAL FACTORS	39
5.	LAWS GOVERNING EMPLOYMENT OF NATIVES	57

Part III. The Demand for Native Labor

6.	THE AGRICULTURAL INDUSTRY	65
7.	THE AGRICULTURAL INDUSTRY: LOCATION OF TYPES OF FARMING	85
8.	THE MINING INDUSTRY	99
9.	THE MANUFACTURING INDUSTRY	121
10.	TRANSPORTATION, COMMERCE, GOVERNMENT AND DOMESTIC SERVICE	136
11.	WORKING CONDITIONS FOR NATIVE LABOR	145
12.	TOTAL DEMAND FOR NATIVE LABOR	171

Part IV. South Africa's Economic Policies

13. WAGE POLICIES	179
14. TAXATION POLICIES	189
15. PROMOTION OF THE MANUFACTURING INDUSTRY	199
16. SUBSIDIZATION OF THE AGRICULTURAL INDUSTRY	210

Part V. Effects and Remedies

17. HEALTH AND EFFICIENCY OF NATIVE LABOR	231
18. WHENCE AND WHITHER	243
APPENDIX	255
BIBLIOGRAPHY	272
GLOSSARY	275
INDEX	277

TABLES

NUMBER		PAGE
I.	Increase in Population of Union of South Africa, 1904-1936	12
II.	Distribution of Population by Provinces, 1936 Census	12
III.	National Income of the Union of South Africa	22
IV.	Value of Agricultural Products, 1934-1935	23
V.	Distribution of Natives in the Various Areas, 1936 Census	28
VI.	Age Distribution of Non-European Population, 1936 Census	30
VII.	Non-European Population of Union of South Africa, 1936	35
VIII.	Distribution of Native Rural Population in Union of South Africa	38
IX.	Number of Principal Types of Livestock in Union of South Africa, 1904-1938	68
X.	Production of Principal Crops in Union of South Africa, 1904-1937	71
XI.	Number of Vines and Fruit Trees in Union of South Africa (European-Occupied Farms)	76
XII.	Output of Corn (Maize) Per Acre for Selected Countries, 1934-1937	82
XIII.	Output of Sugar Cane Per Acre in Selected Regions	83
XIV.	Number and Size of European-Occupied Farms, 1936	86
XV.	Distribution of Field Crops, 1936	87
XVI.	Distribution of Fruit Production, 1936	88
XVII.	Distribution of Livestock by General Agricultural Areas, 1936	89
XVIII.	Value of Output of Mining Industry, Union of South Africa, 1884-1938	101
XIX.	Quantity and Value of Minerals Produced, Union of South Africa, 1938	105

List of Tables

XX. Employees in Mining Industry of Union of South Africa.................................... 107
XXI. European and Non-European Wages in the Mining Industry.................................... 114
XXII. Index Number of Retail Prices and Wages in the Mining Industry, 1910-1938.................. 118
XXIII. Location of Mining Concerns in Union of South Africa, 1938............................... 120
XXIV. Manufacturing Production in Union of South Africa, 1910 to 1936-1937....................... 123
XXV. Establishments by Classes of Industry, 1936-1937.... 127
XXVI. Number of Employees and Wages Paid in Manufacturing, 1915-1916 to 1936-1937............. 128
XXVII. Classification of Employees in Industrial Establishments, 1936-1937........................ 129
XXVIII. Average Salaries and Wages Paid in Private Manufacturing Establishments, 1936-1937........ 130
XXIX. Location of Privately Owned Factories and Number of Employees, 1936-1937.................. 134
XXX. Number of Employees on South African Railways, 1917-1918 to 1937-1938.................... 139
XXXI. Employees on Urban Tramway and Bus Systems of the Union of South Africa, 1916 to 1937-1938..... 140
XXXII. Native Affairs Department: Wages of Regularly Employed Natives, 1939-1940................. 143
XXXIII. Population and Employment in Selected Industries, 1911-1938............................. 174
XXXIV. Revenue and Expenditure: Union Government, 1937-1938................................. 190
XXXV. Mining and Total Revenue, Union of South Africa.. 192

FIGURES

NUMBER		PAGE
1.	Union of South Africa..............................	6
2.	Location of Non-European Rural Population..........	34
3.	Trends in Livestock Production....................	69
4.	Trends in Production of Field Crops................	72
5.	Trends in Numbers of Fruit Trees..................	77
6.	Distribution of Farms by Agricultural Regions and Areas	87
7.	Distribution of Field Crops by Main Agricultural Areas..	88
8.	Distribution of Fruit Trees by Types and Agricultural Areas..	89
9.	Distribution of Cattle.............................	90
10.	Distribution of Sheep and Goats...................	90
11.	Value of Output of Minerals.......................	102
12.	Number of Persons Employed in Mining............	106
13.	Annual Wages of Europeans and Non-Europeans in Mining..	113
14.	Number of Manufacturing Establishments............	124

APPENDIX TABLES

NUMBER		PAGE
1.	List of Commercially Produced Crops and Pastoral Products with Recent Volume Data	257
2.	Principal Agricultural Products in each Region, 1936-1937	258
3.	Number and Size of Farms and Holdings Occupied by Europeans, 1936-1937	263
4.	Regional Distribution of Principal Types of Livestock, Owned by Europeans and Natives, 1936-1937	264
5.	Regional Distribution of Principal Groups of Field Crops in Union of South Africa, 1936-1937	265
6.	Regional Distribution of Principal Classes of Fruits in Union of South Africa, 1936-1937	266
7.	Employees in the Mining Industry of Union of South Africa, 1910-1938	267
8.	Trend of European Wages in Mining Industry, 1911-1938	268
9.	Number of Non-European Employees and Cash Wages in Three Mining Industries, 1910-1938	269
10.	Detailed Classification of Industries	270
11.	Government Assistance to Farmers in Union of South Africa, 1931-1932 to 1938-1939	271

Part I

The Background

of the Problem

CHAPTER 1

HISTORICAL AND POLITICAL FRAMEWORK

THE NATIVE LABOR PROBLEM, as it exists in South Africa today, has its roots in the distant, as well as the near, past. The concentration of Native population in the eastern half of the country is due to the fact that the southward migrations of the Bantu tribes from Central Africa took place along the east coast of Africa. The settlement of the country by Europeans from 1652 onwards, the discovery of minerals, and the economic and political changes of more recent times have all had their share in shaping the present problem. A kaleidoscopic picture of these developments would, therefore, appear to be a prerequisite to a proper understanding of the complex Native labor question.

Discovery and Settlement of the Cape.[1]—The Cape of Good Hope was discovered in 1486 by a Portuguese mariner named Bartholomew Diaz, but it was not until 1652 that the first settlement at what is now Capetown was made.[2] At that time the Netherlands East India Company sent out Jan van Riebeeck with a small garrison of soldiers to establish a victualing station at which the ships of the company engaged in the Indian trade could obtain fresh water, meats, and vegetables. The country surrounding Capetown was gradually settled. In 1688 the settlement was greatly expanded by the arrival of numbers of French Huguenot refugees. From then on until 1806, when the Cape finally came under British rule, the white population

[1] Most of the data in this section are summarized from the *Official Yearbook of the Union of South Africa* (Nos. 1-20, Pretoria, Government Printer), No. 20 (1939). The *Official Yearbooks* are published annually by the Director of Census and Statistics.
[2] Several landings along the coast were made by Vasco de Gama in 1497.

of the country grew, and the occupied territory spread both north and eastward. When the Cape was first occupied by the Dutch, the inhabitants were found to be yellow or brown peoples, the most important of which were Hottentots and Bushmen. As these were very shy and wary of the European interlopers, it was necessary to import slaves from West Africa; the first 400 arrived in 1658. Later, importations were made from the Malayan Archipelago. With the slaves and Hottentots there was always an adequate supply of unskilled labor, although several devastating smallpox epidemics greatly decreased the numbers of Hottentots. The Bushmen have never been civilized and have never constituted an important labor force.

Although explorers and hunters in the interior of the country had on numerous occasions come into contact with Native or Bantu tribes, it was not until the last quarter of the eighteenth century that the eastward expansion of European settlement brought about violent conflicts of interest between Europeans and the Native tribes which were occupying the eastern portions of what is now the Cape of Good Hope. The first Kaffir war took place in 1779, and thereafter ensued periodic clashes between the Europeans and Native tribes.

Although the Cape was finally occupied by the British in 1806,[3] it was not until 1820 that the first important immigration of British settlers took place. In that year some 5,000 British landed at Port Elizabeth and settled largely in what are now Albany and Bathurst districts and in territory already occupied by the Bantu tribes. Incessant strife resulted, and many settlements and farms were wiped out from time to time. Meanwhile settlers were moving into the more sparsely populated central parts of the Cape, and as early as 1818 land was settled north of the Orange River.

Settlement of Interior by Europeans.—In 1836 began what has come to be known as the Great Boer Trek. Large numbers of Dutch settlers (known as "Boers"—farmers), dissatisfied with the British Native policies, with the manner in which the

[3] A temporary occupation took place in 1795 and ended in 1803.

slaves had been liberated in 1834, and with British rule in general, migrated northward into the country now known as the Orange Free State and Transvaal and from thence moved eastward into what is now the Province of Natal, where a small number of English traders had settled at Port Natal (Durban) in 1824. The Boers came into violent and frequent conflict with Native tribes in the Orange Free State and Transvaal and especially in Natal, where large numbers of settlers were massacred in 1838 by Dingaan, the treacherous chief of the warlike Zulu tribe. Later in the same year the Zulus were soundly defeated and Dingaan overthrown by a punitive expedition. Some of the Native tribes were driven north of the Limpopo, the present northern boundary of the Transvaal; others were broken up and subdued, and were allowed to remain in scattered settlements in the Transvaal and Orange Free State. Large numbers of Native families were allowed to settle as squatters or as laborers on European-occupied farms.

Several disconnected and unorganized small republics were established in the Transvaal, Orange Free State, and Natal. In 1843, after conflict between the British and the Natal Republic, Natal was brought under British sovereignty, and large numbers of Boers withdrew into the Orange Free State and the Transvaal. It was not until 1852 that the British recognized the independence of the Boers in the Transvaal. The South African Republic (Transvaal) was formed in 1853, and in the following year the Orange Free State Republic also was recognized as a separate republic. The final union of all the republics in the Transvaal took place in 1859. Responsible government was granted by the British Parliament to the Cape Colony in 1872 and to Natal in 1893.

Meanwhile there had been considerable shifting back and forth of the boundaries of the two colonies (Cape Colony and Natal) and the two republics (the Orange Free State and the South African Republic) and also of the sovereignty over the various territories occupied by Native tribes and not settled by Europeans. These questions were settled gradually at several conventions between the republics and representatives of the

British government, and by 1899, when the Anglo-Boer war broke out, the boundaries of the four separate government units and the three native protectorates (Basutoland, Swaziland, and Bechuanaland) were established essentially as they exist today. (See figure 1.)

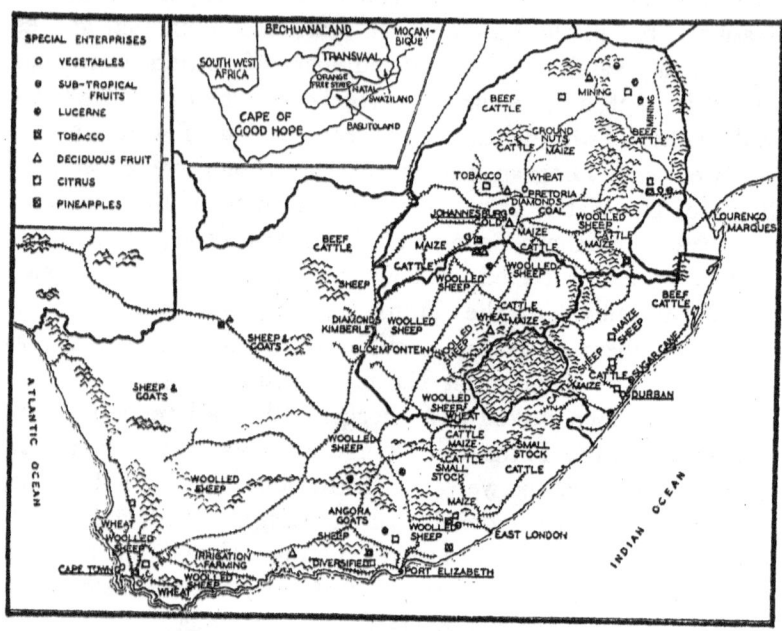

FIGURE 1. Union of South Africa.

The Anglo-Boer war (1899-1902) saw the ultimate defeat of the two Boer republics, which became British crown colonies, known as the Orange River Colony and the Transvaal. In 1906, however, the British Parliament extended responsible government to both the erstwhile republics so that there were then four separate, self-governing colonies. As far back as 1859 and later in 1875 abortive efforts had been made to federate the four European-governed areas of southern Africa. It was not until 1910 that this dream was realized. In that year came into being the Union of South Africa, one of the British Dominions and later one of the members of the British Commonwealth of

Nations. The four colonies became provinces—the Cape of Good Hope,[4] Natal, Orange Free State, and Transvaal.

During the whole of the eighteenth century there were sporadic wars between the Boers and Natives, between the British and Natives, and between various tribes. Fortunately, although there were several serious uprisings which were suppressed only with considerable loss of life, there was no concerted and simultaneous action on the part of a number of the larger tribes, mainly owing to tribal jealousies and the scattered nature of the country. Most of the so-called Kaffir wars thus were fought between the European population and Native tribes occupying particular territories. As these uprisings were suppressed, the areas occupied by the conquered tribes were brought under the rule of either the two republics or the two colonies, or were proclaimed as separate protectorates governed directly from England. It is interesting to note that there are at the present time three such protectorates, Basutoland, Swaziland, and Bechuanaland, which, although in or virtually surrounded by the Union of South Africa, are still administered from England.

In the four provinces certain areas known as territories, locations, and reserves have been set aside for exclusive occupation by the Natives. In these areas the land is owned either by individual Natives, by tribes, or by the Native Affairs Department in trust for individual Native tribes. There are also large numbers of Natives who live permanently, either as individual families or as tribes, in the areas occupied by Europeans. In most of the Native territories the chiefs still exercise a certain amount of control over the members of their tribes, and Native tribal laws and customs which do not conflict with what are regarded as principles of decency and humanity are recognized. In most of the areas, however, supervision over Natives and administration are delegated to Native commissioners, who are European officials of the Native Affairs Department. These

[4] The Cape of Good Hope is also known as the Cape Province. These two names will be used interchangeably in this manuscript.

Native commissioners are assisted by and often work through the tribal chief or headman in areas where such exist.

Government.—The constitution of the Union of South Africa, which, with the exception of a few sections, is entirely flexible,[5] in effect vested full executive and legislative powers in the central government. The four provincial governments (each with an administrator and an executive council) were granted certain specified powers, which are usually subject to amendment or modification by act of the central government.[6] The executive power of the central government is vested in the Governor-General-in-Council, the Governor-General being appointed by the British crown as its representative, but usually after consultation with and the approval of the South African government. The council, or cabinet, consists of members of the majority party in Parliament. All cabinet members must be members of either of the two Houses of Parliament—the Senate or the Assembly. The real executive head, as in England, is the Prime Minister, the leader of the majority party. The legislative functions are vested in Parliament, consisting of the King (acting through the Governor-General, whose powers are largely nominal), a Senate of forty-four members, eight elected by each province, eight appointed by the Governor-General, and four elected by Natives (see below), and a House of Assembly of one hundred and fifty-three members, three of whom represent enfranchised Natives in the Cape of Good Hope. All members of Parliament have to be Europeans. The legislative capital is Capetown (Cape of Good Hope), and the administrative, Pretoria (Transvaal).

Each cabinet member heads one or more of the eighteen Departments of State, with the title of Minister. There may, however, be one or more ministers without portfolio. The government departments are Prime Minister, Agriculture and Forestry, Commerce and Industries, Defense, External Affairs,

---

[5] That is, its provisions may be changed by a bare majority in both the Upper and Lower Houses of Parliament.

[6] The chief powers of the provincial governments are exercised over hospitals, roads, lower education, and other purely local government functions.

Education (Union) and Child Welfare, Finance, Interior, Justice, Labour, Lands, Mines, Native Affairs, Post and Telegraph, Public Health, Public Works, Railways and Harbours, and Social Welfare.

For purposes of administration, each of the four provinces is divided into a number of magisterial districts, in each of which the magistrate (or in Native areas, the Native Commissioner) is the local representative of the central government. The magistrate administers laws, collects taxes, supervises census enumeration, etc. Census data on population, agriculture, and mining are thus prepared on a basis of local political or administrative units which, as in other countries, seldom correspond with economic subdivisions.

There is universal white suffrage in the Union of South Africa, with certain minimum property or income, and educational qualifications. Prior to Union, Colored persons and Natives in the Cape of Good Hope had enjoyed the franchise on much the same basis as Europeans. In the colony of Natal it was also possible for detribalized Natives,[7] under somewhat onerous conditions, to obtain franchise. Asiatics did not have the franchise in any of the provinces, and neither Natives nor Colored in the Transvaal and Orange Free State. After Union, these franchise privileges or limitations were continued. Provision was made in the South Africa Act of 1909 (which established the Union) for four of the eight senators appointed by the Governor-General (see above) to be selected "on the ground mainly of their thorough acquaintance, by reason of their official experience or otherwise with the reasonable wants and wishes of the colored races." In actual practice the word and spirit of the act has not always been observed in making such appointments, the appointees often being political stalwarts who had lost their seats. The knowledge of and interest in problems of native welfare of some of the appointees were questionable.

[7] A detribalized Native is one who no longer belongs to a particular tribe or is no longer subject to the jurisdiction of a tribe. Large numbers of Natives living permanently in cities or on European-owned farms are detribalized.

In the Representation of Natives Act of 1936 an important change in Native representation and franchise took place. Natives who were qualified to vote in the Cape of Good Hope were transferred to a special electoral roll. The Cape of Good Hope was divided into three Native electoral circles[8] which elected one member each to the House of Assembly; such member, however, had to be a European. It was the intention of Parliament eventually to extend similar privileges to Natives in the other three provinces. The Representation of Natives Act also made provision for the election of four additional senators (European) by, and to represent, Natives in four Native electoral colleges, (1) the Province of Natal, (2) the provinces of the Transvaal and Orange Free State, (3) the Transkeian territories, and (4) the Province of the Cape of Good Hope, excluding the Transkeian territories. The elected members of the assembly and senate hold office for five years and have the same privileges as all other elected members of these two houses.

Population.—The population of the Union of South Africa is usually classified into four racial groups: European (persons of pure European descent); Natives (pure-blooded aboriginals of the Bantu race); Asiatics (natives of Asia and their descendants, mainly Indians); Colored (chiefly Cape Colored, but includes also Cape Malays, Bushmen, Hottentots, and all persons of mixed race). Prior to 1904, each colony or republic conducted its population censuses at different times. In 1904, however, each of the four colonies conducted a simultaneous population census for both Europeans and non-Europeans. Complete population censuses were conducted in 1911 (first year after Union), 1921 and 1936 (table I). Censuses of the European population alone were conducted in 1918, 1926 and 1931. The earlier censuses probably greatly understated the actual numbers of Natives. With improvements in enumeration in each succeeding census and with the opening up of the more inaccessible parts of the country, the later censuses have shown a more nearly complete coverage of the Native population. Even

[8] And two electoral divisions each electing one member (a European) to the Cape Provincial Council.

Historical and Political Framework

in 1936, however, enumeration in some areas was not 100 per cent complete.[9]

For these reasons caution must be exercised in interpreting long-time trends among the different racial groups. Between 1904 and 1939 (estimates), the total population of South Africa just about doubled, the rate of increase being somewhat greater for Natives than for Europeans. Part at least of this apparent more rapid increase in Native population can be ascribed to underenumeration in the earlier censuses. The less rapid increase in European population between 1911 and 1921 can be ascribed largely to the absence of immigration during the World War (1914-1918) and to deaths during the influenza epidemic of 1918. The influenza epidemic took an exceptionally heavy toll among the Colored race. The remarkably low rate of increase for Asiatics was due to the fact that between 1911 and 1921, large numbers of Indian males migrated back to India. It is difficult to account for the very low rate of increase among the Native population. Faulty enumeration (in 1911) may account for part of the discrepancy as well as a heavy death rate during the influenza epidemic.

According to the 1936 Census, Europeans constituted 20.9 per cent, Natives 68.8 per cent, Asiatics 2.3 per cent, and Colored 8.0 per cent of the total population. The Immigration Quota Act of 1930 (repealed by the Aliens Act of 1937) has tended to restrict the rate of accretion of European population by immigration.

The Transvaal and the Cape Province each has somewhat over one third of the total population of the Union of South Africa, Natal about one fifth, and the Orange Free State only 8.1 per cent (table II). The Transvaal slightly exceeds the Cape of Good Hope in number of Europeans, these two provinces having about 80 per cent of the European population. The Orange Free State slightly exceeds Natal in European population, each having about 10 per cent of the total. The Transvaal has about 37.0 per cent of the Native population, the Cape 31.0

[9] *Sixth Census of the Union of South Africa,* 1936, *Population* (Pretoria, Government Printer, 1938), Vol. I, p. vii.

The Native Labor Problem of South Africa

TABLE I

INCREASE IN POPULATION OF UNION OF SOUTH AFRICA, 1904-1936

Race	Census 1904	Census 1911		Census 1921		Census 1936		Per cent* increase 1936 over 1904	Estimated mean population 1939
		Number	Average annual rate of increase since 1904	Number	Average annual rate of increase since 1911	Number	Average annual rate of increase since 1921		
European	1,116,806	1,276,242	1.93	1,519,488	1.76	2,003,857	1.86	79.1	2,116,500
Native (Bantu)	3,491,056	4,019,006	2.03	4,697,813	1.57	6,596,689	2.29	87.8	6,997,500
Asiatic	122,734	152,203	3.12	165,731	0.86	219,691	1.90	79.0	231,200
Colored	445,228	525,943	2.41	545,548	0.37	769,661	2.32	72.9	814,800
Total	5,175,824	5,973,394	2.07	6,928,580	1.49	9,589,898	2.19	85.3	10,160,000

*Estimated by author.
Source of data: *Official Yearbook of the Union of South Africa*, No. 20 (1939), pp. 1035, 1036.

TABLE II

DISTRIBUTION OF POPULATION BY PROVINCES, 1936 CENSUS

Province	NUMBERS					PER CENT*				
	European	Native	Asiatic	Colored	Total	European	Native	Asiatic	Colored	Total
Cape of Good Hope	791,574	2,045,570	10,508	682,248	3,529,900	39.5	31.0	4.8	88.7	36.8
Natal	190,549	1,553,629	183,661	18,629	1,946,468	9.5	23.6	83.6	2.4	20.3
Transvaal	820,756	2,444,380	25,493	50,841	3,341,470	41.0	37.0	11.6	6.6	34.8
Orange Free State	200,978	553,110	29	17,943	772,060	10.0	8.4	0.0	2.3	8.1
Total	2,003,857	6,596,689	219,691	769,661	9,589,898	100.0	100.0	100.0	100.0	100.0

*Calculated by author.
Source of data: *Official Yearbook of the Union of South Africa*, No. 20 (1939), pp. 1038-1040.

per cent, Natal 23.6 per cent, and the Orange Free State only 8.4 per cent. On the other hand, Natal has over four fifths of the Asiatic population and the Cape of Good Hope nearly nine tenths of the Colored population.

There is a slight preponderance of males over females among all racial groups, the disparity being greatest for Asiatics. In the urban areas there is a slight excess of female Europeans over males, but the reverse situation holds true in the rural areas. For non-Europeans there is a considerable excess of males in urban areas and a considerable excess of females in rural areas, owing to the fact that large numbers of Native

males migrate annually to cities to work in the various industries and as domestic servants. According to the 1936 Census nearly two thirds (65.24 per cent) of the European population was urban; on the other hand, over three fourths (77.56 per cent) of the non-European population was rural. For all races the percentages are 31.38 urban and 68.02 rural. The density of population for the Union as a whole is 20.29 persons per square mile, the figures for the four provinces being Natal 55.19, Transvaal 30.25, Orange Free State 15.55, and the Cape of Good Hope 12.74 persons per square mile. The density of European population only varies from 2.86 persons per square mile for the Cape of Good Hope to 7.43 persons per square mile for the Transvaal, and for non-Europeans from 9.88 persons per square mile in the Cape of Good Hope to 49.79 persons per square mile in Natal. A large part of the urban population is concentrated in a few large cities. The Witwatersrand (gold mining) group of cities (including Johannesburg, Krugersdorp, Randfontein, Roodepoort, Germiston, Boksburg, Brakpan, Springs, and Nigel) had a combined population, according to the 1936 Census, of over 1,000,000 persons, 40 per cent of whom were European; Capetown had a population of 344,000, Durban 260,000, Pretoria 129,000, and Port Elizabeth 110,000. Over 60 per cent of the urban European population is concentrated on the Witwatersrand and these four cities.

About 98 per cent of the Europeans are of South African nationality by birth or by virtue of their being British subjects. Only 2 per cent have acquired South African nationality by naturalization. The predominant racial strains for the Dutch or Boers are Hollanders, French Huguenots, and Germans, with a sprinkling of other races, all of whom are so intermingled that their previous racial identity is largely lost. The English part of the population is composed of persons who came, or whose forefathers came, from the British Isles or other parts of the English-speaking world. South Africa is a bi-lingual country, or, in other words, it has two official languages, English and Afrikaans (modified and expanded from Netherlands Dutch). There are also numerous Native languages and dialects but these are not official languages. Some idea of the relative numbers of English and Dutch can be obtained by a consideration of the languages spoken by families in their homes. The 1936 Census shows that about 56 per cent of all Europeans had Afrikaans as their home language, 39 per cent English, 2.5 per cent both English and Afrikaans and 2.5 per cent other European languages.

Physical Characteristics of the Country.—The Union of South Africa[10] lies roughly between the latitudes 22° and 34° south and between the longitudes 16° and 31°. The total area of the country is 472,120 square miles or about as large as the states of Oregon, California, Nevada, and Arizona combined. The northernmost province, the Transvaal, has an area of 110,450 square miles, the Orange Free State, just south of Transvaal, 49,647 square miles; Natal (north of the Cape Province along the east coast), 35,284 square miles; and the Cape of Good Hope, which touches all the other four provinces on the east and north, an area of 276,739 square miles.

Although the northern part of the Transvaal stretches into the tropics, the country as a whole has a very equable and temperate climate, only the coastal area of Natal and part of the northeastern Transvaal having a climate that may be regarded as subtropical. The climate of South Africa is conditioned by the fact, first, that the country is bounded on the west by the Atlantic Ocean and on the south and east by the Indian Ocean, and second, that a large part of the country has an elevation of 3,000 feet and over.

A more or less continuous belt of mountain ranges stretching from the eastern Transvaal through Natal and the southern and western part of the Cape of Good Hope divides the country

---

[10] The Union of South Africa (also referred to herein as South Africa) should not be confused with British South Africa, which includes, in addition to the Union of South Africa, Southern Rhodesia and Northern Rhodesia, stretching north above the Transvaal, the three British protectorates, Swaziland (between the Transvaal and Natal), Basutoland (between Orange Free State, Natal, and the Cape of Good Hope), and the Bechuanaland Protectorate (between Cape of Good Hope, Transvaal, Southern Rhodesia, and South West Africa), and finally South West Africa (north of the Cape of Good Hope), the former German South West Africa, which was mandated to the Union of South Africa by the Treaty of Versailles.

into two broad regions (figure 1). The first is the coastal region of varying depth between the mountain ranges and sea and the interior plateau with few mountains but with numerous low hills, isolated or in ranges. Differences in rainfall, altitude, soils, and other natural conditions permit the further subdivision of both the interior plateau and the coastal region, each of these subdivisions having somewhat different agricultural characteristics and potentialities.

Rainfall varies greatly in the different parts of South Africa. Broadly speaking, rainfall gradually increases from west to east. The northwest section of the Cape of Good Hope has a rainfall of less than 5 inches a year, the central portion 5 to 10 inches, and the eastern portion and the western parts of the Transvaal and Orange Free State 15 to 20 inches. In most of these two provinces rainfall varies from 15 to 35 inches a year, with a small section of the eastern Transvaal getting from 40 to 75 inches a year. Along the south coast of the Cape of Good Hope rainfall is more irregular, varying from a low of from 10 to 15 inches a year up to 40 to 50 inches. The heaviness of precipitation in this section is influenced greatly by the slope of mountains in relation to prevailing winds. On the east coast, including part of the Cape of Good Hope and Natal, rainfall is generally heavy, from 35 to 50 inches a year. One of the unfortunate peculiarities of rainfall in South Africa is that, over most of the country, rainfall comes mainly in the spring and summer months (September to March) and often in severe thunderstorms. The southwestern section of the Cape Province is the only area receiving winter rainfall.

South Africa can be divided roughly into nine main soil regions,[11] due consideration being given to climate, geology, and topography, although a much greater division can be made if minor variations are considered. Broadly speaking, the soils of South Africa are very deficient in phosphates, especially in the areas of highest rainfall. In the driest regions, soils of alluvial origin are often strongly alkaline.

[11] *South Africa and Science—A Handbook* (Johannesburg, Hortor's Limited, 1929), Chapter IX, pp. 175-178.

CHAPTER 2

THE ECONOMIC FRAMEWORK

Revolution in South African Agriculture.—Until well into the second half of the nineteenth century, the countries comprising the present Union of South Africa had a strictly rural, extensive, self-sufficient economy.[1] The only resource the country had to exploit was agricultural land, taken from the Natives during the northward and eastward advance of settlement. As this resource was plentiful in relation to European population, and as there were no limitations to the appropriation of land, the earlier farms were large, running into tens of thousands of acres. Such large areas were taken up that by 1870, although the European population was still small, little free land was available and there were general complaints regarding the scarcity of land.[2] The population was almost entirely rural, only a few of the seaport towns having moderate urban populations. Except around Capetown and along the coast of Natal, cattle and sheep farming predominated, although wherever climatic and soil conditions permitted, farmers produced grains, vegetables, and fruits to meet family needs. Wool, hides and skins, and ostrich feathers (all pastoral products) were the only saleable products, although the region around Capetown had at one time developed a profitable wine industry, and the coast region of Natal had an incipient sugar-cane industry. The surplus pastoral products were sold or bartered in nearby towns

---

[1] D. Hobart Houghton, *Some economic problems of the Bantu in South Africa* (South African Institute of Race Relations, 1938), Monograph series No. 1, p. 8.

[2] S. Herbert Frankel, *Capital investment in Africa* (London, New York and Toronto, Oxford University Press, 1938), pp. 41-51.

and villages, and the proceeds used to acquire farm and family requirements.

Up to 1870 South Africa's exports consisted largely of pastoral products and some products from hunting. During the five-year period 1865-1869 total value of exports through the Cape Colony was £2,370,000, wool accounting for £1,802,000, hides and skins for £172,000, and ostrich feathers for £342,000. Exports through Natal were more varied, including maize, ivory, and sugar. Out of a total value of exports through Durban averaging £255,000 for the five-year period 1865-1869, exports of wool amounted to £83,000 and ivory to £10,000.[3] Value data are not available for hides and skins and other products exported.

There was no labor problem. Except in the older settled regions around Capetown, employment of labor for monetary wages had not become general. The large number of Native families settled on European farms as labor tenants or as settlers constituted an adequate labor force. As the European economy of agricultural self-sufficiency corresponded largely with the cultural and traditional economy of the Native peoples, the latter were willing to work for the privilege of being allowed to occupy a portion of the European-owned farm, to cultivate a small tract of land, and to graze their cattle.

The opening up of the diamond mines in 1870 and especially the Witwatersrand Gold Mines in 1886 revolutionized South African agriculture and heralded in an agricultural labor problem that promises to become ever more acute. A large influx of population took place from 1886 onwards, and large urban populations grew up around Kimberley and Johannesburg and the seaport towns of Capetown and Durban. The enormous demand of the newly created urban centers for farm products encouraged the rapid transition of agriculture from a self-sufficient to a more specialized basis, although extensive methods of field husbandry were still the rule rather than the exception.

[3] *Official Yearbook of the Union of South Africa*, No. 6 (1910-1922), pp. 705-706.

The introduction of refrigeration, improvements in ocean and land transportation, the development of new and improved varieties of crops, fruits, and animals were a further stimulus to this change. At the same time, as most agricultural land had been appropriated, there was a growing tendency for existing farms to be subdivided among the children of the original occupiers. This revolution in agriculture required more capital and greater skill in the planning of the farm enterprise. Unfortunately, many of the older farmers and their children were unable to adapt themselves to the new techniques and gradually lost their farms. This situation was further aggravated during the Anglo-Boer war (1899-1902), when large numbers of farms were destroyed and left uncultivated for several years.[4]

The Emergence of the Labor Problem.—The great and rapid expansion of mining generated an enormous demand for labor, creating some very complicated labor problems. Because South Africa had up to that time been largely agricultural, she had not developed a white labor force of skilled technicians. White immigrants to South Africa had been persons with little capital, whose chief interest was farming or trading. The country had never attracted immigrants to undertake unskilled labor as was the case with the United States, Canada, Australia, and New Zealand.[5] The requirements of the mines for technicians were met by attracting skilled artisans from England and other countries at very high wages. Relatively high wages were also paid to persons who, although unskilled, were necessary to supervise the work of Natives.

Although an adequate supply of white skilled labor was obtained by the lure of high wages, the securing of an adequate and continuous supply of unskilled labor to work in the mines has always presented difficulties. Traditionally, there was no laboring class among the Natives, and the idea of working for

---

[4] The Carnegie Commission of Enquiry on the Poor White Problem gives a detailed analysis in their report (1932) on the economic factors involved in the development of the "poor white" problem.

[5] S. Hubert Frankel, *Capital investment in South Africa*, p. 38. See also D. Hobart Houghton, *Some economic problems of the Bantu in South Africa*, p. 11.

wages had no part in their social structure. The wage lure alone was thus insufficient to attract a continuous and adequate flow of Native labor to the mines. Various forms of compulsion, such as taxation, were resorted to in order to induce Natives to go out and work for wages.[6] The difficulties of the mines in securing a sufficient supply of low-wage labor are shown by the importation around the end of the last century of indentured Chinese labor and Natives from territories adjacent to the Union. Although Chinese labor was excluded long before Union, the mining industry even to the present day has to supplement its Native labor force by recruiting in adjacent territories.

Gradually economic conditions in the Native reserves forced larger and larger numbers of Natives to seek work in the mines and elsewhere in order to secure sufficient income to support their families and to meet their taxes. The mines were able to secure large numbers of Natives at wages which, although far lower than those paid to Europeans, were yet higher than those which farmers had been able to pay. The result has been that as agriculture expanded and became more commercialized, it experienced increasing difficulty in securing not only seasonal labor but also labor to meet regular needs.

The high level of wages paid in the mines for skilled or supervisory white labor has had a very important bearing upon the level of European wages in other economic undertakings. Although wage levels for Europeans in other industries are generally lower than in the mining industry, special steps such as "colour bar" legislation and trade union restrictions have been taken to boost European wages in other industries more nearly to the level of wages in the mining industry. Still another difficulty exists in the fact that persons who, for one reason or another, have been unable to secure skilled labor positions have found themselves in competition in the unskilled field with low-wage Natives, whose earnings normally are too low to support a European family even on a mere subsistence level. This

[6] *Report of the Native Economic Commission,* 1930-32 (Pretoria, Government Printer, 1932), p. 77.

factor combined with a deep-seated aversion on the part of large numbers of Europeans to undertaking "Kaffir" or hard navvy work gives rise to the permanence of the "poor white problem" with which successive governments have grappled, apparently with only indifferent success. Finally, the disparity between the high level of European wages and the low level of Native wages appears to have been a serious deterrent to the development of secondary industries. The high level of European wages tends to keep up unit costs in industries using much skilled labor. On the other hand, the low buying power of the numerically predominant non-European element of the population tends to restrict the market for manufactured products.

Present Economic Situation in South Africa.—From 1886 onwards a number of secondary industries were established to meet the growing needs of a greatly augmented population and to supply certain requirements of the mining industry. The most important of these earlier industries were those for the manufacture of cement and of explosives. Later followed the manufacture of boots, shoes, and furniture. During the first World War (1914-1918), when it was difficult for South Africa to obtain supplies of certain simple manufactured goods, several new local industries were established to provide domestic needs for such products. Considerable impetus was given to the development of secondary industries by the high protective policy on which the country embarked in 1924. The Electricity Act of 1922 provided for the control of the production of electric power and for the establishment of the Electricity Supply Commission (a corporation under government supervision) to undertake the production of power. In 1928 was passed the Iron and Steel Industry Act which provided for the formation of a government-controlled corporation to undertake the production of iron and steel products. Several secondary industries have developed around the iron and steel industry.

No reliable data are available relative to the number of factories and output prior to 1915-16. In that year there were just under 4,000 manufacturing establishments in South Africa. By 1920-21 the number had increased to 7,000, and by 1936-37 to nearly 10,000, with a gross output of £175,765,000 and employing 140,000 Europeans and 193,000 non-Europeans.[7] With few exceptions, most of these manufacturing industries, because of bulkiness or perishability of product handled, would tend to become established in a country even without tariff protection. Few manufactured goods are exported from South Africa.

The country has a well-run government-owned system of railways linking the important interior mining and farming centers with coastal ports (figure 1). In many parts of the country the South African Railways has a road motor service for goods and passengers to link up more thinly populated areas with the railway system. The South African Railways also operates an air transport service. It is the proud boast of South Africans that the government has never defaulted on a single penny of the capital invested in railways and that the passenger and goods rates compare favorably with those in other countries with much denser populations. As in other countries the expansion of the railway system assisted in and was assisted by the development of mining, agricultural, and other resources.

A rough estimate of the relative importance of various types of economic activity in South Africa is shown by the estimates of total national income. Unfortunately, satisfactory comparable data covering a period of years do not exist. An attempt was recently made by Frankel and Neumark of the University of the Witwatersrand to estimate the total national income for the years 1927-28, 1932-33, and 1934-35.[8] The authors admit that their estimates are a rough first approximation and leave room for considerable refinement which may mean some changes in the totals and the relative contributions by the various groups to such totals. Their estimates indicate that the total national income in 1934-35 was £327,674,000, which was higher than for the other two years (table III). Mining, manufacturing, and services each contributed about 17 per cent of the total in 1934-35, commerce about 21 per cent of the total, and agriculture just under 13 per cent. In

[7] *Official Yearbook of the Union of South Africa*, No. 20 (1939), p. 901.
[8] S. H. Frankel and S. D. Neumark, *The national income of South Africa* (mimeo.). Report issued in 1940. 45 pp.

TABLE III
NATIONAL INCOME OF THE UNION OF SOUTH AFRICA

Group	Income in £1,000's			Per cent of total		
	1927-28	1932-33	1934-35	1927-28	1932-33	1934-35
Agricultural, pastoral and fishing	50,418	33,104	41,656	17.24	12.86	12.71
Services	48,894	43,030	56,324	16.72	16.71	17.19
Commerce	59,250	48,570	68,960	20.26	18.86	21.05
Manufacturing	44,609	41,599	56,562	15.26	16.15	17.26
Transport	18,845	18,010	23,600	6.44	6.99	7.20
Mining	50,091	56,043	58,397	17.13	21.76	17.82
Rent	20,329	17,175	22,175	6.95	6.67	6.77
Total	292,436	257,532	327,674	100.00	100.00	100.00

Source of data: S. H. Frankel and S. D. Neumark, *The national income of South Africa.*

1927-28 agriculture's share was 17 per cent, but in 1932-33 only 13 per cent. The biggest increase took place in the share contributed by manufacturing, largely owing to the output of the government-controlled iron and steel industry. It is more than probable that some change has taken place in the relative position of the various economic groups since 1934-35. The contributions of the various branches of the agricultural industry to the total national income in 1934-35 are shown in table IV which gives some idea of the wide range of farm commodities produced in South Africa.

Another comparison which gives a picture of the place of agriculture in the economy of South Africa is afforded by an examination of the trend of exports. Agricultural products (mainly pastoral) account for over 90 per cent of the total average annual exports from the Cape Colony during the period 1865-1869. During the five-year period 1880-1884 exports of agricultural products (still largely pastoral) amounted to £3,666,000, or only 47 per cent of the annual total of £7,742,000. Exports of diamonds amounted to £3,417,000, copper to £364,000, and gold to £18,000, or altogether to over 49 per cent of the total. In the five years preceding Union (1905-1909) combined exports from the Cape Colony and Natal amounted to £44,820,000 annually. Exports of pastoral products increased absolutely to £5,447,000, but their relative importance had de-

TABLE IV
VALUE OF AGRICULTURAL PRODUCTS (1934-35)

Product	European production	Native production	Total production
	£1,000	£1,000	£1,000
Maize	5,561	1,322	6,883
Wool	5,532	279	5,811
Dairy products (milk, butter, etc.)	4,782	300	5,082
Wheat	4,810	...	4,810
Cattle and calves	4,111	100	4,211
Sheep, lambs, and goats	2,679	400	3,079
Poultry and poultry products	2,071	428	2,499
Sugar cane	2,295	146	2,441
Timber and firewood	1,594	50	1,644
All local fruits, flowers, and vegetables	1,491	...	1,491
Potatoes (ordinary and sweet)	1,056	12	1,068
Citrus fruit (export)	853	...	853
Oats	780	...	780
Fisheries and game	680	100	780
Pigs	392	300	692
Wattle bark and other tanning materials	631	10	641
Kaffir-corn	221	412	633
Deciduous fruit (export)	579	...	579
Pumpkins	400	40	440
Dried fruit (farm produce)	412	...	412
Tobacco	380	25	405
Grapes (export)	398	...	398
Peas and beans	285	8	293
Rye	249	...	249
Barley	244	...	244
Minor crops	93	100	193
Onions	169	...	169
Mohair	121	8	129
Groundnuts* (unshelled)	65	18	83
Grapes for distilling	73	...	73
Honey and wax	60	...	60
Cotton	51	...	51
Lucerne and manna (seed)	38	...	38
Ostrich feathers	35	...	35
Horses, mules and donkeys	25	...	25
Tea (green leaf)	22	...	22
Total	43,238	4,058	47,296

*Peanuts.
Source of data: Summarized from . H. Frankel and S. D. Neumark, *The national income of South Africa*, 1940, p. 45.

clined to just over 13 per cent of the total. During the three-year period 1935-1938, the total annual average value of all exports amounted to £112,336,000. Exports of all agricultural products amounted to £22,607,000, or 20 per cent of the total; pastoral products to only £13,186,000 or less than 12 per cent of the total. Exports of products of the mines amounted to £86,-356,000 during the three-year period, or 77 per cent of the total, gold exports alone totaling £77,754,000 (on a realized value basis).[9]

These figures indicate the dominant importance of the mining industry, and especially of gold mining, in the economy of the Union of South Africa. The mining industry not only provides a market for a large part of the products of agriculture and industry but also contributes an important share of the revenue of the country. Nevertheless, the agricultural industry of South Africa is still important because of the large number of persons dependent upon it both directly and indirectly, making its welfare important to the welfare of the country as a whole.

[9] In 1929 output of gold amounted to 9,980,713 ounces valued at £42,395,000; production in 1938 amounted to 11,839,000 ounces, the realized value being £84,373,000. Forty-ninth Annual Report (Transvaal Chamber of Mines, 1938), p. 103.

Part II

The Supply of Non-European Labor

CHAPTER 3

SUPPLY AND REGIONAL DISPOSITION OF UNSKILLED LABOR

ALTHOUGH this study is primarily concerned with Native labor, it is necessary to give some consideration to the Asiatic and Colored populations as well in assessing the total supply of unskilled labor. In some parts of Natal, Asiatics constitute an important supplementary supply of labor for agriculture, mining, and manufacturing. In most of the central and western Cape Province, on the other hand, the Colored population provides the main supply of agricultural and industrial labor. Very few Europeans are employed as laborers in agriculture anywhere in South Africa. Although many of the larger farms have one or more hired Europeans, other than members of the farmer's family, they are employed mainly as managers, foremen, or skilled technicians. It is possible that in some areas there may be small numbers of white farm laborers, but their position is likely to be temporary. They may accept employment as farm laborers until such time as they can obtain more permanent and more satisfactory employment elsewhere. In mining, manufacturing, and transportation Natives also provide the bulk of unskilled labor.

The Total Non-European Labor Supply.—According to the 1936 Census 82.69 per cent of the Native population was classified as rural in contrast to 33.73 per cent of the Asiatic and 46.09 per cent of the Colored populations. If permanent domicile and not place of residence at the time the census was taken is considered, well over 90 per cent of the Native population would be found to reside in rural areas. This is shown by census enumeration of the number of Natives in different areas (table V). According to these data 2,196,000 Natives

TABLE V

DISTRIBUTION OF NATIVES IN THE VARIOUS AREAS—1936 CENSUS

Area	Males	Females	Total	Per cent of total
Urban (residential areas and townlands)	234,156	156,239	390,395	5.9
Urban locations	165,520	189,647	355,167	5.4
Rural suburbs	6,545	4,760	11,305	0.2
Rural townships	19,444	16,401	35,845	0.5
Native townships	14,655	17,094	31,749	0.5
Farms owned or occupied by Europeans	998,850	1,054,590	2,053,440	31.1
Asiatic or Colored persons	12,817	14,129	26,946	0.4
Companies	42,986	58,431	101,417	1.5
Government	8,025	5,907	13,932	0.2
Native areas:-				
Crown reserves or locations	1,005,915	1,414,433	2,420,348	36.7
Mission reserves or stations	49,524	64,611	114,135	1.7
Tribally-owned farms	55,996	78,428	134,424	2.0
Native-owned farms	61,461	81,649	143,110	2.2
Crown lands	63,404	86,975	150,379	2.3
Alluvial diggings	14,883	9,749	24,632	0.4
Mine compounds	371,323	15,535	386,858	5.9
Industrial compounds (including sugar, wattle, etc. estates)	102,832	10,904	113,736	1.7
Municipal compounds	34,231	1,819	36,050	0.6
Construction gangs	41,414	1,781	43,195	0.7
Other areas	8,670	956	9,626	0.1
Total	3,312,651	3,284,038	6,596,689	100.0

Source of data: *Sixth Census of the Union of South Africa*, 1936, *Population*, Vol. I (U. G. November 21, 1938).

lived on farms (mainly European-owned or -operated) and 2,962,000 lived in Native areas, or together about 78.2 per cent of the total Native population. Another 824,000, or 12.5 per cent of the total, were shown to be in urban residential areas and locations, rural suburbs and townships, and Native townships. The balance, 613,000 or 9.3 per cent, were on alluvial diggings, in industrial compounds (including wattle and sugar estates), municipal compounds, construction gangs, and miscellaneous areas. The great bulk of the 613,000 Natives, however, can be regarded as living only temporarily in the areas specified, having been recruited for work from Native areas. On the other hand, the permanently urbanized Natives would be found almost entirely in the 824,000 living in urban areas. A substantial proportion of Natives in this classification, however, would also be Natives working only temporarily in urban areas as domestic servants or in other urban occupations.

In parts of the Orange Free State and the eastern part of the Cape Province many Native females are engaged in domestic service. In all parts of the country, where there is a substantial Native population, Native females may also engage temporarily in harvesting crops. As far as the country as a whole is concerned, however, Native females constitute only a small part of the total supply of Native labor. Similarly only very small numbers of Asiatic females engage in wage occupations. Large numbers of Asiatics are engaged in trade, truck gardening, or as hawkers, working on their own behalf, and thus cannot be regarded as constituting part of the total labor supply. On the other hand, a considerable proportion of the Colored females in the Cape Province and elsewhere engage in domestic service and work in manufacturing establishments. Substantial numbers of Colored males, moreover, are engaged in trade or farming on their own behalf, or work as skilled laborers.

With these qualifications in mind it may be stated that non-European males between the ages of 15 and 65 would constitute the upper limit of the unskilled labor supply. On this basis it is found that in 1936 there were 1,442,000 Native males, 66,000 Asiatic males, and 178,000 Colored males between the ages of 15 and 65 or a total of 1,686,000 (table VI). Native males alone constitute about 85 per cent of the total figure. If allowance is made for the number (unknown) of Asiatics and Colored persons engaged in trade or farming on their own behalf or in skilled occupations, the importance of the Native population as the chief source of unskilled labor is still further magnified. In addition to manpower in the Union itself, some 200,000 Natives are brought in each year from surrounding territories for work in the Union.

TABLE VI
AGE DISTRIBUTION OF NON-EUROPEAN POPULATION—1936 CENSUS

Age Group	Asiatics		Colored		Natives	
	Males	Females	Males	Females	Males	Females
0–4	17,832	18,469	61,318	61,860	455,101	497,636
5–9	17,501	17,339	55,232	55,108	459,266	456,721
10–14	14,790	13,858	46,373	44,776	420,703	385,412
15–19	12,757	11,256	36,783	37,686	343,754	320,175
20–24	10,810	9,476	33,645	37,490	269,920	283,696
25–29	8,414	7,542	30,155	30,848	291,451	253,929
30–34	6,084	5,522	24,520	23,440	236,360	237,650
35–39	5,759	4,529	21,718	20,317	218,405	189,584
40–44	4,514	3,296	16,986	16,024	164,810	165,473
45–49	5,129	2,881	15,679	14,081	128,484	112,576
50–54	4,906	2,318	13,079	11,549	94,184	108,350
55–59	3,745	1,433	9,085	7,803	65,069	68,740
60–64	3,363	1,173	7,711	6,862	56,677	77,989
65–69	1,728	593	5,998	5,646	40,775	43,592
70–74	901	362	4,173	3,965	30,701	38,075
75–79	396	146	2,263	2,044	15,185	16,858
80–84	207	100	1,278	1,276	10,817	15,196
85+	144	87	996	1,044	9,178	11,195
Unspecified	171	160	440	411	1,811	1,191
	119,151	100,540	387,431	382,230	3,312,651	3,284,038
	219,691		769,661		6,596,689	

Source of data: *Official Yearbook of the Union of South Africa*, No. 20 (1939).

Another approximation of the total Native labor force available in the Union can be obtained from the number of payers of the general tax (Natives). All Native males of 18 years and over, except indigents, are required to pay a tax of £1 a year per person. In 1935-36 the total revenue received from this source was £1,275,000, indicating a like number of payers.

The Native Farm Labour Committee (1937-1939) made the following estimate of Natives available in 1937 for labor in the Union of South Africa:[1]

(a) *Taxpayers*

Transvaal	409,000	
Natal	340,000	
Cape Province	522,000	
Orange Free State	133,000	1,404,000

[1] *Report of the Native Farm Labour Committee*, 1937-1939 (Pretoria, Government Printer, 1939), pp. 7-9.

(b) Alien Natives, including those from Protectorates employed in labor districts as indicated in returns of Director of Native Labour, December 1937.................................... 193,000
(c) Clandestine immigrants from northern territories (estimated on basis of information available to Committee)........................... 25,000
(d) Natives employed in Union, outside labor districts, from Bechuanaland Protectorate, Basutoland and Swaziland, placed on a conservative estimate at.................................. 10,000

Total................................. 1,632,000
Add juveniles from 16 to 17 years of age (supplied by Department of Census and Statistics)   132,000

1,764,000

These estimates likewise must be regarded as indicating the upper limit of the total potential supply of all unskilled Native labor. From these figures must be deducted the numbers (unknown) of Native squatters on European farms, Natives farming on their own behalf, rich Natives, and idle Natives. To complete the picture it is necessary to consider how efficiently that labor force is organized and utilized.

Organization and Use of Non-European Labor.—The Province of Natal had a total Native population of 1,558,000 in 1936, or about 23 per cent of the total Native population of the Union. The importance of Natal as a source of Native labor is, however, not nearly as great as these figures would indicate. In 1938 Natal supplied only 12.2 per cent of all Native labor (from the Union only) employed in the mining industry. In addition, employers in Natal recruit Natives each year in other parts of the Union and in adjacent territories. Some of these Natives from outside Natal are from areas in which Natives are immune or resistant to malarial fever and are required for work in the sugar-growing areas of parts of

Zululand where malaria is rife. The coal-mining and wattle-growing areas, however, also recruit Natives from outside Natal. The extent of recruitment of Native labor is given by the following statement made by the Native Farm Labour Committee:

> Thus employers of labour in Natal employ collectively 38 labour agents to recruit within the Province and 157 to recruit beyond its borders. The evidence given to us was to the effect that in places upwards of 60 per cent of the labour employed came from beyond the border of the province.[2]

There are apparently two main reasons for the relatively inadequate utilization of Native labor in Natal. In the first place, Natives in this province occupy some of the most fertile country in South Africa. In the early days after European occupation, Natives in Zululand and on the reserves in Natal were able to procure an adequate livelihood from farming operations alone. Thus there was not the same incentive, as in some other parts of South Africa, for Natives to supplement their income from cash wages, although pressure in this direction has become stronger within recent years. But perhaps an even more important reason was the attitude of successive Natal governments before Union and to a certain extent the attitude of Europeans in this province since Union. The policy has been to conserve the Native population of Natal for labor in the province. To this end numerous difficulties were placed in the way of recruitment of Natives for work outside of Natal. Moreover, employer groups in Natal appear to have made little effort to mobilize effectively the local labor supply; on the contrary, special efforts seem to have been made to recruit outside Natives. It seems clear that the Native labor supply of Natal is still utilized very inadequately.[3]

Another factor that tends to decrease greatly the number of effective man-hours of work performed by Native labor generally, is the conditions inherent in the methods of employ-

---

[2] *Ibid.*, p. 56.   [3] *Ibid.*, pp. 54-57.

ment in both agriculture and industry. Under the labor-tenancy system, which will be explained more fully later, Natives living on European farms in most parts of Natal and the Transvaal and to a lesser extent in the Orange Free State perform from three to nine months' service each year on the farm where they are resident, in exchange for the privilege of running a certain number of head of cattle, cultivating a certain area of land, and erecting the necessary family dwellings. During the rest of the year these Natives are free to cultivate their own land or to seek work in cities. In either event considerable time is lost by the Natives either through idleness or in traveling to and from cities and in searching for work. The same is true, to perhaps a lesser extent, of Natives from Native areas, who either go to the cities or are recruited for work in the mines or in other urban occupations.

One other aspect of this problem, which will also be discussed more fully later in this book, is the fact that up to the present time there has been little incentive for Natives to develop special skills. As a result the preponderance of Native labor can be classified as being unskilled. Hence it is not uncommon for the same Native to work in half a dozen different occupations in the same number of years. The output per man-hour of Native labor is thus kept at a very low level.

Regional Distribution of Non-European Labor Supply.—The labor problem of South Africa is complicated by the fact that the centers of Native population do not coincide with the important agricultural, mining, and industrial centers. It is thus necessary for hundreds of thousands of Natives to leave their homes each year for work in the important mining and industrial centers and to a lesser extent for work in agriculture. This situation does not obtain as far as the Asiatic and Colored populations are concerned.

In order to present the picture more clearly the Union of South Africa has been divided into 23 regions, 12 of which are in the Cape Province, 3 in Natal, and 4 each in the Transvaal and Orange Free State. Each of these regions represents an area in which agricultural production and types of farming are

34   The Native Labor Problem of South Africa

more or less uniform.[4] If provincial barriers and less important differences in agricultural conditions are ignored, the 23 regions can be still further combined into 7 broad agricultural areas. The agricultural region is used throughout this book as the basis of comparison because it is better adapted for classification of types of farming and shows relative concentrations of Native population. Mining activity is concentrated largely in the central portions of the Transvaal with lesser concentrations at Kimberley (diamonds) and in Natal (coal). Industrial activity likewise is concentrated largely in four centers, Capetown and Port Elizabeth in the Cape Province, Johannesburg in the Transvaal, and Durban in Natal. The geographic distribution of non-European population in 1936 is shown in table VII and of non-European rural population in figure 2.

About 90 per cent of the 220,000 Asiatics in South Africa

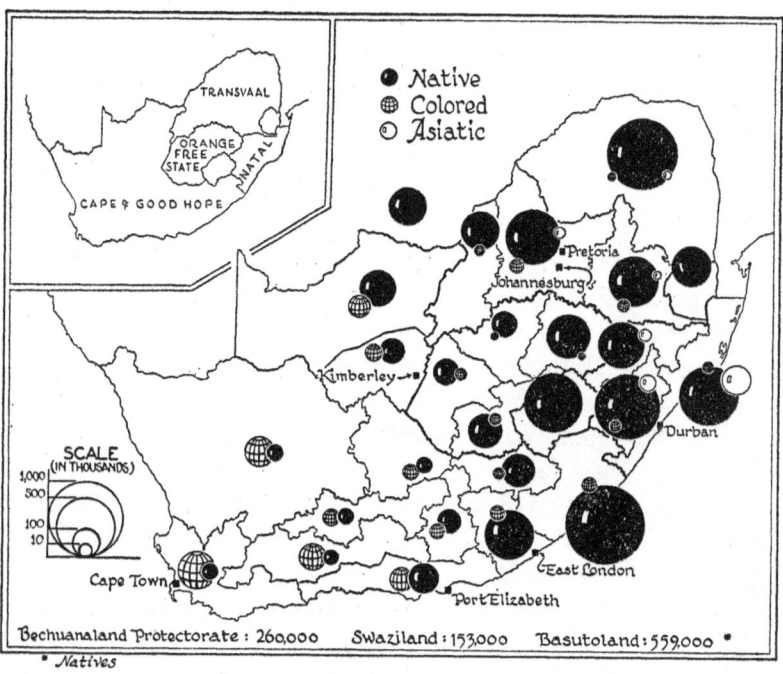

FIGURE 2. Location of non-European rural population.

[4] These regions were selected on the advice of members of the Division of Economics and Markets, Department of Agriculture, Pretoria.

TABLE VII
NON-EUROPEAN POPULATION OF UNION OF SOUTH AFRICA—1936
(IN 1,000'S)

	Region*	URBAN			RURAL		
		Native	Asiatic	Colored	Native	Asiatic	Colored
1.	Southwest (C)	17	4	212	9	..	113
2.	Northwest (C)	3	..	17	8	..	57
3.	South Coast (C)	53	3	49	69	..	33
4.	South Karroo (C)	3	..	19	8	..	42
5.	Central Karroo (C)	6	..	11	9	0	12
6.	North Karroo (C)	4	..	6	9	..	9
7.	East Karroo (C)	9	..	5	28	..	9
8.	Bechuanaland (C)	6	..	5	112	..	22
9.	Griqualand West (C)	21	1	12	44	..	11
10.	Border (C)	65	1	12	304	..	6
11.	Northeast (C)	17	..	4	86	..	4
12.	Transkei (C)	13	..	4	1,141	..	8
13.	Highveld (N)	23	5	1	227	5	..
14.	Middleveld (N)	26	11	3	670	8	3
15.	Coast (N)	79	97	8	528	57	3
16.	East Highveld (T)	26	1	1	315	1	3
17.	Central Highveld (T)	630	19	35	423	2	7
18.	West Highveld (T)	12	1	1	117	..	2
19.	Lowveld (T)	23	1	1	898	1	1
20.	Northeast (O)	34	..	1	212	0	1
21.	Northwest (O)	16	..	1	85	0	1
22.	Southeast (O)	19	..	2	105	0	3
23.	Southwest (O)	35	..	4	47	..	4
1.–12.	Cape of Good Hope	218	10	360	1,836	..	326
13.–15.	Natal	128	114	12	1,426	70	6
16.–19.	Transvaal	691	22	38	1,754	4	13
20.–23.	Orange Free State	104	..	8	449	..	10
	Total Union	1,141	146	418	5,465	74	355

*Abbreviations: (C) = Cape Province; (N) = Natal; (T) = Transvaal; (O) = Orange Free State.
Source of data: *Sixth Census of the Union of South Africa*, 1936, Population table 7, Vol. I, 6-29.

were in the three Natal regions, the Coastal region alone having about 70 per cent of the total. Outside of Natal only the Central Highveld region of the Transvaal showed any large number of Asiatics, 19,000 urban and 2,000 rural. About 40 per cent of the Asiatics in Natal are rural. It is possible that many Asiatics living in the smaller towns are engaged in agricultural work, largely on the sugar plantations and on small subtropical fruit farms. In the urban areas Asiatics are engaged principally in trade and as waiters in hotels and restaurants.

Some 543,000, or about 70 per cent of the 770,000 Colored

population of South Africa, are concentrated in four regions of the Cape Province, the Southwest, the Northwest, the South Coast, and the North Coast regions, the Southwest region alone having about 50 per cent of the total for South Africa. The rest of the Cape Province has an additional 144,000 Colored population, which brings the Colored population of the Province up to 89 per cent of the total in the Union. The Central Highveld region of the Transvaal and the Coast region of Natal together have another 53,000 Colored persons or 7 per cent of the Union's total. Of the 414,000 persons classified as being in urban areas, some 300,000 are in the Southwest and South Coast regions of the Cape Province and in the Central Highveld region of the Transvaal. In most of the other regions the rural Colored population exceeds or equals the urban.

The Native urban population exceeds the rural in only 2 of the 23 regions. In the first, the Southwest region of the Cape Province, which includes Capetown and several fairly large towns, the Native population is small, only 27,000, of which 9,000 are rural. In the second, the Central Highveld region of the Transvaal, which includes the Witwatersrand gold mines and important coal mines, a large part of the Native urban population is engaged temporarily in mining and other activities.

If a line were drawn north from Port Elizabeth through Kimberley (see figure 2) it would be found that practically the entire Native population is to the east of the line. An even better idea of the easterly concentration of Native population can be gathered from the fact that only seven regions, the Border and Transkeian regions in the Cape Province, the three Natal regions, and the East Highveld and Lowveld regions of the Transvaal, all on the eastern fringe of the Union, together contain 4,083,000 rural Natives, or about 75 per cent of the total rural Native population. If the Native populations of the two protectorates, Basutoland and Swaziland, which are almost entirely rural, are included, the extreme easterly concentration of the Native population is still further accentuated.[5] In con-

---

[5] Basutoland has a Native population of 559,000 and Swaziland 153,000. The Bechuanaland Protectorate between the Transvaal and the Orange Free State has a Native population of 260,000 Natives. Its population, however,

trast, the most important mining and industrial areas are in the Central Transvaal and some of the most important agricultural areas in the Central Transvaal and Orange Free State; hence the annual mass migrations of Natives to and from work in the urban areas.

Excluding the Transkeian territories, there were only 695,000 rural Natives in the whole of Cape Province, or just under 13 per cent of all rural Natives in the Union. Of these 571,000 were in four regions, the South Coast, Bechuanaland, Northeast, and Border, all in the eastern section of the province. Again excluding the Transkeian territories it is found that 317,000 Natives were on farms (mostly European owned or controlled) and 339,000 in Native areas, the balance being on alluvial diggings, construction gangs, and so on (table VIII). In the Transvaal and Orange Free State there were 1,414,000 Natives on farms and a further 612,000 in Native areas. The Natives living on farms would constitute an adequate supply of agricultural labor for these two provinces, were it not for the fact that even in the central and western portions large numbers of Natives are drawn off annually from three to nine months to work in urban occupations. Large numbers of Natives living in Native areas in these two provinces would also tend to move to the cities for like periods, thus limiting the possibility of farmers augmenting the supply of regular and seasonal labor. In Natal, including Zululand, there were 437,000 Natives on European farms and 904,000 in Native areas, also a seemingly more than adequate supply of agricultural labor. For the reasons explained above, however, the Native labor supply of Natal is poorly mobilized, and in addition, Natives are drawn off, as in the Transvaal and Orange Free State, for work in urban areas. In Natal, the Transvaal, and the Orange Free State, farmers situated near Native reserves or locations usually experience less difficulty in securing adequate supplies of permanent and seasonal labor than do farmers who are not so fortunately situated.

---

is scattered over a wide semi-arid area, almost as extensive as the Cape Province. A very small proportion of the population of the Bechuanaland Protectorate usually goes to work in the Union of South Africa.

TABLE VIII

DISTRIBUTION OF NATIVE RURAL POPULATION IN UNION OF SOUTH AFRICA—1936

Area	Number on farms occupied by						Numbers in Native areas					Total number on farms and in Native areas
	Europeans	Asiatic and Colored persons	Companies	Government	Total	Crown reserves and locations	Mission reserves and stations	Tribally-owned farms	Native-owned farms	Crown lands	Total	
Cape Province (excluding Transkeian territories).....	309,348	2,039	3,624	2,253	317,264	311,672	8,916	....	10,283	7,966	338,837	656,101
Transkeian territories......	25,463	730	23	1,325	27,541	1,081,015	5,203	4,174	15,775	934	1,107,101	1,134,642
Cape Province total.....	334,811	2,769	3,647	3,578	344,805	1,392,687	14,119	4,174	26,058	8,900	1,445,938	1,790,743
Natal (excluding Zululand)....	395,568	19,558	8,094	1,180	424,400	410,203	69,658	10,169	79,747	16,049	585,826	1,010,226
Zululand.................	10,958	19	1,178	736	12,891	282,624	4,108	....	1,283	30,289	318,304	331,195
Natal total...............	406,526	19,577	9,272	1,916	437,291	692,827	73,766	10,169	81,030	46,338	904,130	1,341,421
Transvaal total............	902,774	4,204	87,712	7,360	1,002,050	319,731	25,407	120,081	32,417	95,141	592,777	1,594,827
Orange Free State total......	409,329	396	786	1,078	411,589	15,103	843	....	3,605	....	19,551	431,140
Union total..............	2,053,440	26,946	101,417	13,932	2,195,735	2,420,348	114,135	134,424	143,110	150,379	2,962,396	5,158,131

Source of data: *Sixth Census*, 1936, Population, table 13, Vol. I, 86-107.

CHAPTER 4

SOCIAL AND CULTURAL FACTORS

THE SOCIAL and cultural background of the aboriginal and other non-European groups in South Africa affords a fascinating study. For the purpose of this study, however, attention will be focused only on such aspects of the subject as appear to have a direct bearing upon the willingness of these groups to work for wages and upon their present and probable future efficiency. Although the Asiatic and Colored populations fall into a different category from that of the Natives, certain characteristics of these two groups also are distinctly related to the Native labor problem.

The Asiatic Population.—The term Asiatic is applied to all persons born in, or whose forefathers came from, the continent of Asia and the islands adjacent thereto, with the exception of descendants of the early Malay slaves, who are now grouped with the Colored population. The Asiatic population is predominantly Indian, that is, persons from India. The 1911 Census, the first after Union, showed that 98.3 per cent of the Asiatics were Indians, the balance being Chinese and Japanese.[1] The relative proportion of Indians to all Asiatics has not diminished since 1911, for under the Immigration Act of 1913 the further immigration of Asiatics was almost entirely stopped.

Prior to Union, each province had its own laws regulating immigration of Asiatics, their property rights, and their franchise rights. These laws, with certain modifications, were continued after Union, except that further immigration into the

---

[1] M. Nathan, *The South African Commonwealth* (Johannesburg and Capetown, The Specialty Press of South Africa, Ltd., 1919), p. 253.

Union was governed by the Immigration Act of 1913. Movement between the four provinces, however, was still regulated by the older colonial laws. It is differences in the old colonial laws, reflecting differences in policy, which account for the fact that three of the provinces have such small Asiatic populations. Indians are British subjects. In South Africa even Indians born in that country are regarded as subjects rather than as citizens. Only in the Cape Province do Asiatics have voting privileges, provided that they are British subjects by birth or naturalization. Several pre-Union and post-Union acts define the property rights of Indians. Ironically enough it was the English traders in Pretoria, themselves not citizens of the Transvaal Republic, who agitated for the first laws restricting property rights of Indians.[2] The Boers under the Transvaal Republic were primarily engaged in farming and were not unduly interested in what nationalities carried on trade. The accumulative property legislation against Asiatics appears to be based partly upon racial, partly upon economic, and partly upon social grounds. Asiatics, as is well known, are keen traders, and, with their willingness to accept a low standard of living as measured by Europeans, are able to provide very destructive competition for European traders. Moreover, they have introduced into South Africa social, cultural, and religious customs differing from both those of the Europeans and the aboriginal peoples. The fear is that this may still further complicate an already complicated problem arising out of the fusion of, or interrelation between, modern and primitive cultures.

The purpose of the old Cape colonial laws regarding Asiatics was definitely to restrict immigration. The Orange Free State laws having the same purpose were even more rigid. In the earlier days of the Transvaal Republic there were no restrictions on Asiatic immigration and large numbers of Indians from Natal and India settled in the Republic mainly as hawkers and traders. Only in Natal were there systematic efforts to introduce Indians into the country, a policy not abandoned until 1911, after Union.

[2] *Ibid.*, p. 255.

Social and Cultural Factors 41

The Asiatic question in Natal is closely related to the development of the sugar industry of that province. In the early days of the establishment of this industry, around 1860, considerable difficulty was experienced by planters in securing farm labor, although the industry was located in an area with a large Native population. The Natives, however, were unaccustomed to working for wages and showed little interest in going out as laborers. Moreover, they did not work satisfactorily without supervision. In 1860, under agreement with the government of India, a number of Indians were brought into Natal under indenture to work on the sugar and tea plantations. So satisfactory was this source of labor that, with the exception of an eight-year period (1866-1874), the introduction of indentured Indians continued until 1911, when it was finally abandoned. Later, indentured Indian labor was also used in the coal mines and in other occupations. In the beginning the period of indenture was five years, after which individual Indians were free to return to India or to settle in the colony as "free Indians." Large numbers of them chose the latter alternative and engaged in farming, market gardening, hawking, and other pursuits. In addition to the indentured Indians, there was also a constant dribble of Indian traders, priests, and others who entered the country at their own expense.

The large numbers of Indians who were settling in Natal eventually caused considerable alarm to the government, and delegations were sent to India to arrange for a new basis of indenture.[3] In 1895 a new law was passed in Natal requiring that the initial period of indenture be five years as heretofore, and that the period of indenture could be extended for a further period of years. At the end of the extended period of indenture, Indians were either to be returned to India or, if they elected to remain in Natal, they were required to pay an annual tax of £3 a year. It was considered that such a heavy tax, in the light of their low earnings, would effectively discourage further settlement in Natal. In spite of this restriction considerable

---

[3] Even as late as 1904 there were 123,000 Indians in Natal as compared with only 97,000 Europeans.

numbers of Indians still elected to remain in Natal at the end of their period of indenture.[4] This tax continued in effect until 1914, when it was abolished.

The Indian question in South Africa has caused the government a great deal of trouble. As can be expected, the Indian community suffered and continues to suffer under many disabilities. In 1913 the problem became so acute that a widespread strike of Indians in Natal took place, a part of the strike policy being an attempted march of several thousands of Indians from Natal into the Transvaal. After much violence and some bloodshed, the strike, which was led by the now world-famous Mahatma Gandhi, was put down.

When the indenture system was first introduced only male Indians were brought into Natal. Indians who had settled in Natal were afterwards permitted to bring in their families, male children over 16 years of age being excluded. A surplus of males over females, however, continued right up to the present time (1940), although this disparity is being reduced rapidly. In 1904 there were only 48 females to each 100 males; in 1921 there were 70; and in 1936 there were 84.

In the Transvaal, Orange Free State, and Cape Province, Asiatics are engaged mainly in trade, as hawkers, or as waiters in hotels and restaurants. It is generally agreed that Indians are hardworking and more efficient than Natives for certain types of work, especially work where the individual laborer cannot be kept under constant supervision. Unlike the Native population, the Asiatic population is largely stationary, individuals and families living permanently where they work. Although from a broad social viewpoint the assimilation of an additional large group of people with different physical, religious, and social characteristics adds to the racial problem of South Africa, these differences do not detract from the importance of Indians as laborers in both the skilled and unskilled fields.

The Colored Population.—This group, according to the

[4] South African Indian Enquiry Commission, *Report of the Indian Enquiry Commission* (London, H.M. Stat. Off., 1914), 40 pp. (Great Britain Parliament. Papers by Command. Cmd. 7265.)

designation in the *Official Yearbooks of South Africa*, consists chiefly of Cape Colored but also includes Cape Malays, Bushmen, Hottentots, and all persons of mixed race.

For many years after the first European settlement in and around Capetown, the only aboriginal tribes encountered were Hottentots and Bushmen, who probably inhabited most of the western half of southern Africa stretching up into what is now South West Africa—the more arid regions of the country. The Bushmen were barbaric, nomadic hunters inhabiting much of the upland country of the west.[5] They have never been civilized and still exist in small numbers of detached family units in parts of the northwestern Cape Province and in South West Africa. Their numbers at present are small, and still smaller is the number that has entered service of any kind. More important were the Hottentot tribes, a semi-civilized, pastoral people in the coastal belt to the south and southeast of the Cape Province. Their numbers were greatly depleted by a succession of smallpox epidemics in the early days after settlement, and the tribes were largely broken up and scattered. Hottentots still exist in scattered communities in several parts of the Cape Province. Most of them, however, combined with other races, are grouped broadly in what is known as the Cape Colored population. The Cape Malays are largely descended from slaves introduced in the early days by the Dutch East India Company from the Malay Peninsula and the Malay Archipelago. Although the Cape Malays still retain the physical characteristics and religious observances of their forefathers, they have become an integral part of the Colored population of South Africa, both in language and in habits of ordinary life.[6] The final group included in the Colored population is persons of European and non-European unions, and persons of mixed non-European unions.

As there is practically no immigration of persons who would

---

[5] Raymond A. Dart, *The natives of South Africa: an ethnographic review.* In *Official Yearbook of the Union of South Africa*, No. 7 (1910-1924), pp. 877-884. The writer of this article was professor of anatomy at the University of Witwatersrand.

[6] M. Nathan, *The South African Commonwealth*, p. 253.

be included in this group, the accretion of Colored population is from natural increase. The Colored population of South Africa increased from 445,000 in 1904 to nearly 770,000 in 1936, the ratio of males to females being about one to one. Although Colored persons are found in all parts of the Union, about 88.6 per cent of them are in the Cape Province and in this Province mainly in the Southwest and South Coast regions. Except in and around Capetown and a few other large towns, the Colored population is largely rural and constitutes the chief agricultural labor supply over most of the western half of the Cape Province. In the cities many of the Colored people have acquired a high degree of manual skill. They constitute a large part of the labor force in the furniture and building trades. Large numbers of Colored women enter domestic service. In the Cape Province Colored persons have practically all the privileges that are enjoyed by Europeans, but in other provinces they are subject to certain restrictions. Colored laborers, like Indians, are not migratory. Individuals and families live permanently where they work, except that in the Southwest region large numbers of Colored men, women, and children move from the cities into the immediately surrounding country each year to assist in the harvesting of crops—a situation not unlike that in certain parts of the United Kingdom and the United States. Wages paid to Colored laborers, both rural and urban, are usually appreciably higher than those paid to Natives.

Cultural Background of the Bantu.[7]—The origin of the Native peoples, or Bantu, like that of the Hottentots and Bushmen, is still somewhat obscure although recent research has thrown much light on the subject. The Bantu is of Negroid stock; his more immediate ancestors probably came from central or west Africa above the Equator. Arabic records indicate that migrations of the Bantu tribe into southeastern Africa had been taking place since the earlier centuries of the Christian era. Probably both prior to and subsequent to the Bantu migrations,

[7] Much of the information in the next few pages is summarized from the *Official Yearbook of the Union of South Africa*, No. 7 (1910-1924), pp. 877-884, "The natives of South Africa; an ethnographic review," by Raymond A. Dart.

there were invasions of the eastern coastal belt by peoples of Asiatic origin. There are still distinct traces of Semitic infiltrations in many of the Rhodesian, northern Transvaal, and east African tribes.

The Bantu tribal laws and customs show the influence of two predominant basic cultures, the Hamitic and Negro hoe cultures, and probably also of some more recent cultural influences. Typical of the Hamitic culture are the round beehive huts, generally constructed of skins or grass over supple poles; the absence of any kind of bed in the huts; the kaross (blanket made of tanned animal skins) forming a mantle by day and a bed and covering by night; the storage of grains, where cultivated, in underground receptacles, usually in the cattle kraal or enclosure. In general it is a culture in which pastoral habits predominate. On the other hand, the typical features of the Negro hoe culture are rectangular huts with gable roofs, or cylindrical huts with conical roofs; a tendency to build on piles, especially true of the grain storehouse; the dress is often of bark cloth rather than of skins; and the dominant interest is in grain culture and not pastoral pursuits. The tendency of the Hamitic culture is towards nomadism, that of the hoe culture towards settled habitation and continuous occupation of the same land. The former is warlike; the latter peaceful and docile.

Nowhere among the Bantu tribes of South Africa are there distinct lines of cleavage between these two basic cultures. Thus among the coastal tribes the Hamitic cultural elements predominate in type of hut, dress, grain receptacle, and so on; whereas with the Bantu of the more central parts of the Union, the cylindrical huts and raised grain receptacles show the influence of the Negro hoe culture. All tribes, however, show similarity of dress and shield, all tribes do some cultivation of grains, and all tribes hold cattle in great esteem.

Some of the tribes of the central part of the country (the Bechuana and Basuto groups) have the remains of a tribal totemism, in that each independent section of the people, which may at one time have represented a "sib,"[8] has a "siboko" or

---

[8] A "sib" is a social structure which holds together all families claiming a

praise name taken from some animal or natural phenomenon. Nowadays the main division of the people is into patrilineal groups, and the mere possession of a common praise name is no bar to marriage, as would be the case in true totemic societies. In the coastal areas there are few traces of totemism. In its place is found a strongly developed, patriarchal family structure in which the tribal authority is supreme. All persons belong to the chief, and all members of the family to the head of the family. Any injury to individual members of a tribe is an injury to the chief, and compensation for injury or death must be paid to him. These are the first signs of central authority concerning itself with crimes in the modern sense.

The three principal elements in the tribal system were the family, land, and cattle. Under primitive conditions the family unit was one of the most stabilizing and salutary influences in tribal life. In a sense, the tribe itself is merely an extension of the family. The head of the family rules over and supervises all its members, allocates work, and represents the family in dealings with other families. If a young Native in one family wants to marry the daughter of another family, all arrangements are conducted through the family heads. Under this system no individual member of a family could be destitute unless the whole family was in a similar state. All the members of a family worked together on a cooperative basis to supply all common needs, and all members of the family shared in the common pool of family resources. As work was done by the family for the family, there was no wage-earning class and no monetary or exchange system. There were no skilled artisans and no manufacturing, except such primitive handicrafts as were necessary for family and tribal needs. In effect each family was a self-contained economic unit.

Essential to the continued existence of the family was adequate land, both for cultivation and for grazing. Under conditions where people lived largely on a subsistence level and where transportation facilities simply did not exist, it was es-

---

common descent from some remote ancestor, either along patrilineal or matrilineal lines.

sential that each family and each tribe have adequate land for grazing and cultivation. All land was held on a communal basis, each family being allocated its share by the tribe. Grazing land was usually common to all members of the tribe. Native agriculture was of a very primitive and extensive type; crop rotation was not practiced, nor was any attention given to selective breeding of livestock or of conserving the fertility of land. As arable land was exhausted, new and virgin fields were brought under cultivation. Little consideration was given to the problem of overgrazing; land was generally so plentiful that families and tribes could migrate to new regions in search of pasture. Constant tribal warfare, forays for cattle and grain, and periodic famines were important factors preventing overpopulation.[9]

Cattle in the Tribal Economy.—Cattle play a peculiarly symbolic and practical role in native tradition. Not only do they form the chief source of wealth, and as such determine the importance of an individual and a family in the tribe, but they have a deep religious significance. In many tribes cattle are regarded almost as part of the family. The acquisition of a wife usually involves the transfer of cattle from one family to another. Cattle, however, are not regarded as a medium of exchange but partly as a symbol of wealth and partly as an integral function of the society to which they belong, linked up with its good and evil fortune. They are more than mere possessions or property; they are at the very least the medium through which man is bound as an important entity to his tribe and through which he communes with his gods.

Thus among the Zulu and Pondo tribes if a Native drinks the milk from cattle in another "sib," he is regarded as having pledged blood-brotherhood with that "sib" and henceforth is debarred from marrying into it. Although details of the "lobola" or "ukalobola" system differ somewhat from tribe to tribe, the essential feature of the custom is the transfer of so many head of cattle from the family of the groom to the father

[9] D. Hobart Houghton, *Some economic problems of the Bantu in South Africa*, p. 4.

of the bride-to-be. Women play an important role in family life. Much of the hard work in connection with the cultivation and harvesting of crops was done by the women, the men being concerned chiefly with hunting and fighting, and the young Natives or "umfaans" with tending the cattle. A sizable number of women in a family was thus desirable. The transfer of "lobola" cattle in effect represents the compensation of the bride's father by the groom for the loss of a valuable worker and at the same time a pledge on the part of the groom that he will treat his wife well. Under certain circumstances, for example, if a woman proves barren, dies within a certain period, or deserts her husband, all or some of the cattle may be returned by her father to her husband. As the Bantu practices polygamy, a Native's standing in his tribe is determined jointly by the number of wives and cattle he possesses. It is the main objective of a young Native to acquire cattle. To this he bends all his energies. On the other hand, any decrease in the number of cattle owned or limitation to the ownership of cattle is regarded as a diminution of social status.

The institutions of land, cattle, and the family are thus closely interrelated; they govern and condition each other. The acquisition of cattle is a prerequisite to the establishment of Native family life. But cattle require adequate land for grazing. As a result, influences which are likely to modify the one are likely, sooner or later, to modify the other two institutions as well.

European Influence on Native Customs.—The expansion of European occupation and civilization in South Africa has had a profound and not altogether beneficial influence upon the welfare of the Native peoples of that country. Although there is much to deplore in primitive Native life, such as intertribal warfare and the practices of witch doctors, for example, many of the Native customs were beneficial and essential to the continuance of tribal and family life. Much damage has been done to the moral, and perhaps also the physical, fiber of the Native peoples by foisting upon them European customs and habits before they were in a position to benefit from them, and by removing certain of the checks and balances involved in tribal life. Europeans have taken much away from Natives and, so far, have given little in return.

It will not be possible in this treatise to inquire into all the social and cultural effects of this impact of European civilization upon the well-being of the Bantu. Attention, however, will be concentrated on the economic significance, from both the standpoint of the Native and of the European, of changes under European influence in the traditional status of land, the family, and cattle.

Before European settlement land was plentiful and the safeguard against overpopulation and overstocking was ever present in intertribal warfare, forays, and famine. Since European settlement, however, Natives have been either confined to certain areas set aside specifically for their occupation or have been allowed to settle, as independent family units, on European-occupied farms. Their numbers have increased greatly, the increase between 1904 and 1936 alone being about 87 per cent. Although much of the land now occupied by Natives is some of the best farming land in South Africa, poor cultural methods and overstocking are resulting in the depletion of the fertility of these areas. The situation is excellently summarized in the *Report of the Native Economic Commission, 1930-1932*:[10]

> ... The Native system postulates plenty of land for grazing and for cultivation. The Europeans put limits to the factors which diminished the pressure of both population and animals on land. At the same time they created new conditions which increased this pressure. Tribal war was succeeded by peace, enforced by the power of the white man, better transportation relieved famine, measures against human and animal diseases increased numbers. At the same time the white man, accustomed to a higher standard of living, occupied large territories on which the Natives had hitherto fallen back in case of need.

The solution of this problem does not appear to be in making more land available to the Native, for within a decade or

[10] *Report of Native Economic Commission*, 1930-1932 (Pretoria, The Government Printer, 1932), p. 10.

two population and cattle numbers will again have increased to the extent of overtaxing the carrying capacity of the new and old Native-occupied territories. It must not be presumed that this is an argument against further cession of land to Natives. Considerations of equity and justice would seem to demand this —a principle fully recognized by most enlightened Europeans in South Africa. Native agricultural practices, however, are still notoriously poor. An improvement of such practices is highly important for the better utilization not only of the lands already occupied, but also of such additional lands as may from time to time be set aside for Native occupation.

The necessity for an improvement in cultural practices is well recognized. In 1925 a Director of Native Agriculture was appointed in the Department of Native Affairs. He has under him a staff of agricultural experts and Native agricultural demonstrators. In addition to this activity, the numerous schools and missions are concentrating a great deal of attention on agricultural education among Natives. The work encounters much difficulty in overcoming ignorance, superstition, and the suspicion among Natives of new-fangled ideas foisted upon them by Europeans. Furthermore, the benefits of such educational work are not readily available to the large numbers of Natives residing as labor-tenants on European farms. In view of the gravity of the situation and the difficulty involved in getting Natives to adopt better cultural methods, the educational work in agriculture would appear to be woefully inadequate.

From a national viewpoint the situation is very serious and likely to have results even more serious in the not too distant future. Confining attention to conditions in the Native territories, it is found that not only is much good agricultural land being ruined by soil erosion and the spread of noxious and inedible weeds, but that the actual volume of production in the Native areas is inadequate to supply food needs in those areas. As a consequence, large numbers of Natives are forced each year to seek work temporarily on nearby farms and in the urban areas. The agricultural, mining, manufacturing industries and many other branches of economic activity are vitally dependent upon such labor, and it is difficult to see how this movement can be reversed without seriously impeding the economic development of the country. One of the problems of South Africa is that the chief concentrations of mining are located at a considerable distance from the chief centers of supply of unskilled labor. A rapid mass movement of this labor force more nearly to the centers of employment would undoubtedly raise social and economic problems even more difficult than now exist.[11]

This difficulty, however, should not blind the people of South Africa to the serious economic and social consequences of the present situation. In the first place, the Native areas are deprived each year of a large number of the able-bodied men, whose services are necessary if the Native areas are to be fully developed. In the second place, there is a tendency towards the breakdown of family life. Serious moral and physiological problems have arisen from the prolonged separation each year of men and women. In addition, Native children are deprived of paternal authority at a time when they most need it. Some of the youths who go to the cities often break away completely from their families and their tribes and tend to become urbanized. Finally, even with the augmented cash income from urban employment, the resources of Natives are inadequate to insure basic food needs. If, as some medical authorities and persons familiar with living conditions in Native territories claim, there is evidence that Native physique is being undermined as a result of long periods of inadequate nourishment, the already low efficiency of the skilled labor force of South Africa will be still further impaired.

Natives on European Farms.—Turning to conditions of Natives living on European farms, an equally disquieting condition is found. It was stated earlier that as European occupation was extended into what is now the Orange Free State, Transvaal, and Natal, the warlike Native tribes were subdued

[11] It would mean the merging of tribes, the greater urbanization of Natives, the abandonment of much land by Natives in some areas, and the procurement of land in areas already densely settled by Europeans.

and dispersed. Large numbers of Native families were permitted to settle on European farms as squatters and as labor-tenants. These Natives have become almost completely detribalized in that they are no longer subject to tribal authority. During the past few decades laws[12] have been passed with the object of discouraging and eventually eliminating the Native squatter on European-owned farms, such Natives being moved to lands elsewhere which have been set aside for their occupation.

The labor-tenant system, well suited to conditions when European agriculture was still organized on the basis of extensive, self-sufficient farming units, did not involve any radical break with the primitive tribal economy. The essence of the labor-tenant system is a contract, verbal or oral, between the European farmer and the head of the Native family residing on his farm, whereby in exchange for the privileges of running a certain number of head of cattle on the farm, of cultivating a certain area of ground, and of erecting the necessary family buildings, the services of the Native and several stipulated members of his family, females as well as males, would be made available to the farmer for a stipulated period each year. This period usually varies from three to nine months. In the early days no cash wage was involved. The Native family unit was preserved, and the family was assured of adequate land for grazing and cultivation. A close personal interest prevailed between the farmer and the Native families residing on his farm. Bearing in mind the fact that the European farmer himself lived in somewhat primitive circumstances, there was not the great difference in the standards of living of the Europeans and Natives that has since come to exist. In reality, a sort of benevolent feudal economy prevailed.

Although the system was advantageous to both the European farmer and the Native families under the system of agriculture that existed in the early days of settlement, it does not appear to be well adapted to the modern commercialized system of farming that now exists, and the system has outgrown its use-

---

[12] For example, the Native Land Act of 1913 and the Native Land and Trust Act of 1936.

fulness. With the decrease in the size of farms, the emergence of, and rapid increase in, land values, and the introduction of expensive farm machinery and equipment, the farmer is compelled to make a more efficient use of both his available land and labor force. The labor of the Native family is often inadequate and not available when most necessary to meet peak seasonal needs. The poor use made of land, both for grazing and cultivation, has caused the farmer more and more to restrict the number of cattle which the Native family is permitted to run, and to deny altogether this privilege to young Native families. In the place of these privileges the farmer has tended to substitute a cash wage, often a liberal substitute from the farmer's standpoint, for the privileges taken away from the Native. The latter, however, tends to regard money as merely a means to an end, the eventual acquisition of cattle, although he now also needs cash to pay his taxes. Any decrease in the number of cattle which a Native may possess is regarded as a deterioration of social status—a loss of face.

Even more serious is the effect upon Native youths, who realize that they will never be able to enjoy the opportunity of owning and running cattle on the farm on which their families reside. As a result, many Native youths leave their families each year, with or without the consent of their parents and the farm owner, to seek work in the cities. By one means or another and in spite of laws to the contrary, a large number of these youths fail to return to their families. For the Natives living on European farms, there is little social contact, poor facilities for education, and, in the absence of opportunity to run cattle, little chance for advancement. Hence Frankel's statement that, "Broadly speaking, farm labour owing both to custom and legislation, has become the most immobile in the country."[13] In contrast, although conditions in cities are far from attractive measured by European standards, the city Native has opportunity for social contacts, some chance of an education, some entertainment, and higher cash wages than can be earned on European farms.

[13] S. H. Frankel, *Capital investment in Africa* (London, New York and Toronto, Oxford University Press, 1938), p. 125.

In rural areas, both on European-owned farms and in Native territories, the size of the Native family is gradually declining. The inability of Natives to acquire and graze cattle has tended to restrict the number of wives a Native may have. In addition, the introduction of European agricultural implements, requiring considerable manual power to operate, has decreased the value of women as agricultural workers. As Native males have to do more of the heavy manual work, there is less incentive to acquire a number of wives, who still have to be fed, even if their scope as workers is more limited than formerly. Thus economic conditions, as well as the teachings of missionaries, are placing limits on the institution of polygamy.

There requires attention yet one more aspect of the social problem arising from the breakdown of the Native family unit. As the possibility for marriage or early marriage declines, many Native women, deprived of male companionship in Native areas, tend to drift to the cities where many of them enter domestic service. Large numbers of these Native women, however, support themselves in haphazard manner, brewing kaffir beer or living as prostitutes. In many parts of the country the spread of venereal diseases is causing alarm. Numbers of Native women may live with Native men, as man and wife, without having conformed to the rites of a Native marriage. Such unions are not regarded by either party as binding and are often dissolved at the least pretext. What is even more regrettable is that children of such unions are not regarded with the same esteem as children from legally contracted marriages. As a result, many children are abandoned, becoming a burden on the community or joining lawless and idle bands of Native youngsters.

Need for Modification of Cultural Practices.—If the very valuable institution of family life is to be preserved, and if the productivity of land is to be preserved and increased, there must be a modification of the "lobola" system. Interference with traditions and customs is dangerous and difficult—but, as conditions are now, such interference must either come about voluntarily at the present time or will be forced upon South Africa.

The problem appears to resolve itself into one of increased efficiency of production. Natives are interested in quantity, not quality of cattle. The most promising line of attack—one fully recognized and approved by both Europeans and Native leaders—is the substitution of quality for quantity in the "lobola" system.

This, however, is a problem encompassed by numerous difficulties.[14] In the first place, Natives tend to view with misgiving any modification of their customs—especially the "lobola" system. Prolonged education will be necessary to get Natives to accept the idea of replacing quantity by quality. In the second place, they need dual- or even triple-purpose cattle for hauling, for milk, and for meat. As a by-product dung is used most uneconomically for fuel purposes. It will be necessary either to evolve a new breed of triple-purpose cattle or to educate Natives to the use of specialized cattle—milk and meat breeds. In the third place, to be effective, the program of substituting quality for quantity must be carried out on a grand scale. In most Native territories there are no fences—grazing land is commonage. If good cattle are to run indiscriminately with the existing scrub cattle, the task of improving quality will be greatly prolonged, if not made impossible of achievement. Finally, any movement to substitute quality for quantity must be preceded by education of Natives in better methods of both field and animal husbandry. Native leaders point out that their cattle are hardy and inured to conditions existing in Native territories. Cattle of higher quality are likely, in the beginning at least, to be more susceptible to cattle diseases and may deteriorate rapidly if they are subjected to conditions as they exist in these territories at the present time. Moreover, the loss of one high quality cow will be far more severe than the loss of several head of the existing cattle. An improvement in field husbandry will be necessary to provide cattle with supplementary feed during winters and periods of drought.

An improvement in both field and animal husbandry meth-

[14] Much of this information is based upon interviews conducted by the author with Natives and teachers at the Adams Mission School in Natal, supplemented by additional interviews with Natives in Pretoria and Johannesburg.

ods is of vital importance from the standpoint of Natives as well as their cattle. Under primitive conditions leaves and herbs provided part of the essential food elements in their diet. Much of this has been destroyed through overgrazing, and no substitutes have been provided. In addition, the droppings from cattle are put to very uneconomical use. Owing to the fact that the veld has been denuded of trees and shrubs, Natives are hard put to it to obtain sufficient fuel for cooking and other purposes. Cattle dung in many areas has become an important source of fuel, and the ground is deprived of this important revitalizing element. This, again, brings home the point that cannot be too strongly stressed—the paramount necessity of increasing the efficiency, through education, of Natives as agricultural producers. It is a problem that cannot be temporized with, without still more damage to the agricultural, and eventually the social, structure of South Africa.

Although there may be certain highly desirable features in the "lobola" system, under the impact of European civilization and influences it is working to the detriment of both the Native and the European population. Its modification and perhaps eventual elimination may be necessary if South Africa is to take her place as an important industrial nation. The process of emancipation or transition from a primitive to a modern economy is not a simple one and will require several generations. Meanwhile, and until the native population can benefit from the operation of a monetary exchange economy, considerable caution must be exercised in grafting, consciously or otherwise, European ideas and European customs upon the Native population. All that can be said with any assurance is that unless the productive efficiency of Natives in agriculture and in industry is greatly increased, there are very definite limits to the continued progress of the economy of South Africa.

CHAPTER 5

LAWS GOVERNING EMPLOYMENT OF NATIVES[1]

BEFORE PROCEEDING to analyze the extent of employment of Natives in urban occupations and in farming, consideration will be given to some of the more important laws and regulations governing such employment. It should be observed that many of the laws have the effect of safeguarding the labor supply of agriculture.

The Pass Laws.—The most important laws governing Native employment are what are known as the pass laws, under which Natives are required to carry traveling passes or permits when moving from one area to another. Pass laws and requirements, however, are not uniform for the country as a whole. Those in force in each separate colony prior to Union (1910) were carried over after Union, although some of the laws (in the Transvaal and Orange Free State) have since been amended. Natives in the Cape Province are not required to carry traveling passes when journeying in that province, except that Natives entering or leaving British Bechuanaland and the Transkeian territories (Native areas) are required to do so. Similarly, Natives in Natal are not required to carry passes when traveling in that province but under Law No. 48 of 1884 (Natal) must present them when entering or leaving the province.

The earlier pass laws of the Transvaal and Orange Free State were consolidated in Pass Proclamation No. 150 of 1934.

[1] Information in this section, except where otherwise stated, is summarized from the *Official Yearbook of the Union of South Africa*, No. 20 (1939), pp. 465-475, and from the *Report of the Native Farm Labour Committee, 1937-1939* (Pretoria, Government Printer, 1939), pp. 15-21.

Section 3 provides that no Native shall enter, travel within, or leave a pass area unless he is in possession of a pass (on prescribed form) issued by a duly authorized officer, the pass to have a duration not in excess of thirty days. A Native in employment, however, need not have one if he leaves his place of employment to lodge a complaint against his master or a member of his family. Section 5 provides further that a Native residing on a farm or private property may be granted a pass by his employer for travel within a pass area on business for his employer or for the purpose of visiting. Such a permit, however, must bear the date of issue and disclose the purpose for which it is issued, and be for not more than thirty days. Natives living in locations and reserves are not required to carry passes in the reserves but must do so when entering or leaving the reserves. A fine of £2 or imprisonment, with or without hard labor, for a period not exceeding one month is provided for contravention of the pass-carrying provisions, and still heavier penalties are imposed for forging or falsifying such documents. Provision is made for the exemption of certain classes of Natives, such as clergymen and educated Natives of good repute, from carrying passes. Up to 1938, however, only about eight thousand exemptions had been granted.

The reasons for the enforcement of the pass laws are that it affords a protection of the rural Native who comes into surroundings which are new and strange to him; that insofar as the pass represents a service contract, it affords a further protection of the Native; the pass is a means of identification; it helps to prevent crime and tends to prevent wholesale entry of Natives into towns where they will have no employment and where they will tend to loaf and live by their wits.[2] Whatever may be the merits of the pass system, there can be no doubt that both the laws and the manner of their enforcement are one of the prime grievances of the Native peoples of South Africa, who feel that the laws place them in an inferior and invidious position.

[2] *Report of Native Economic Commission,* 1930-1932 (Pretoria, Government Printer, 1932), pp. 105-106.

The Native Service Contract Act.—Many of the provisions of the Native Service Contract Act, No. 24, of 1932, tie in closely with the existing pass laws. One of the purposes of this law was to amend the Transvaal and Natal laws relating to masters and servants. The act has no application in the Cape Province and only minor application in the Orange Free State. This act, as it applies to the Transvaal and Natal, prohibits the employment of any male Native living in the Union or the issue of a pass to such a Native to proceed to a place other than his home, unless he can produce a document of identification. It also makes it illegal to employ a Native domiciled in the Transvaal and Natal on land outside a Native location unless the Native can produce a labor-tenant contract between himself and the owner of such land, or unless he has a statement from the owner that he is not obliged to render the owner service during such period. No male Native under eighteen years of age may be employed unless he has the consent of the owner of the land on which his family lives, and unless he also has the permission of his guardian. The latter is given the right to contract with the owner for the services of his children under eighteen years of age. The objectives of these provisions are to bolster up Native parental authority and to insure that Natives observe their labor-tenant obligations. Section 5 of the Native Service Contract Act provided that no labor-tenant contract, whether verbal or written, shall be binding for a period in excess of three years. If no period is expressly stated, the contract is presumed to be for one year, but is automatically renewed from year to year unless notice is given by either party at least three months before the date of termination.

Taxation of Natives.—Although taxation is not regarded in most countries as having a bearing on labor problems and conditions, in South Africa taxes are levied upon Natives, *inter alia*, to induce them to seek employment.[3] Under the Native Taxation and Development Act, No. 41, of 1925 (subsequently amended), every male Native of eighteen years and over is re-

---

[3] *Report of the Native Economic Commission,* 1930-1932 (Pretoria, Government Printer, 1932), pp. 123-124.

quired to pay a personal tax, known as the General Tax, of £1 a year. In addition, every occupier of a hut or dwelling in a Native location is required to pay a Local Tax of 10/- a hut a year, up to a maximum of £2 a year. In many parts of the Union, Natives occupying land are required to pay a "Quitrent," or "Squatter's" tax, which exempts the payer from the Local Tax, or hut tax. A number of Native tax offices and suboffices are established in all parts of the country. Each district has a register of Natives in that district liable to pay taxes. At the time the Native pays his tax, he is issued a receipt showing his district, suboffice, and his own personal number. This receipt thus becomes an important document identifying a Native, and its presentation is required if a Native seeks employment.

Most of the revenue from these Native taxes is earmarked for improvement of conditions in Native areas and for Native education. One of the criticisms of this use of the revenue from these sources is that roads, hospitals, and educational facilities in Native areas are not generally available to Natives living on European farms, who are thus required to pay taxes from which they derive little direct benefit.

Recruitment of Native Labor.—In order to insure an adequate supply of Native labor for the mining and other industries, a system has been developed for the recruitment of Natives in various parts of the country. This activity is governed by the Native Labour Regulation Act, No. 15 of 1911, which is administered by the Director of Native Labour with headquarters in Johannesburg. The law provides for the licensing of recruiting agents and for the conditions of employment of recruited Natives. Recruitment of Natives in certain areas of the Union (usually where there is a marked shortage of farm labor) is prohibited, but no obstacle is placed in the way of Natives in such prohibited areas from entering at their own expense unrestricted areas or employment centers in search of work. A number of labor districts (working districts) have been established in the Union, practically none of which are in areas having a dense rural Native population. Seventeen of these labor districts are in the Transvaal (mainly mining areas), three in the Orange Free State, four in the Cape Province, and two in Natal. At one time most of the Natives were recruited for service in the mines; within recent years, however, other industries, including agriculture, have made considerable use of this device for securing their unskilled labor needs. As a general rule, Natives not conforming to certain standards of physical fitness or suffering from social diseases are rejected. In 1938 some 571,000 Natives were shown as employed in labor districts. Of these, 144,000 were from the Cape Province (mainly Transkeian territories), 72,000 from Natal, 130,000 from the Transvaal, 26,000 from the Orange Free State, 85,000 from the Basutoland, Bechuanaland, and Swaziland Protectorates, and 117,000 from Mozambique and other areas.

Other Laws Regulating Employment.—In addition to the Native Service Contract Act and the Native Labour Regulation Act, the employment of Natives is also governed by the general Masters and Servants Laws carried over after Union in the various provinces and by Act No. 26 of 1926 (Union) amending the Transvaal and Natal laws. These laws, which apply to Europeans and non-Europeans, set forth the basis by which contracts can be made and provide penalties for nonfulfillment of such contracts. As a general rule, contracts of service can be oral or written and, if no time limit is stipulated, are subject to one month's notice on either side. Contracts are not binding for a longer period than twelve months, nor are they binding unless it is stipulated that service should be commenced within one month from the date of agreement. If, however, a contract is entered into before a Magistrate (Cape Province and Transvaal) or Justice of the Peace (Natal and Orange Free State), such contract may be for a longer period of time, ranging from two years in the Orange Free State to five years in the Cape Province and Transvaal.

The employment of Natives in urban areas is governed also by certain provisions of the Factories Act of 1918, the Mines and Works Act of 1925, and the Wages Act of 1937. Most of the provisions of these acts, in so far as they relate to labor conditions, apply to Europeans and non-Europeans alike, except that under the Mines and Works Act of 1926 Natives are precluded from acquiring certificates of competency to fill certain positions in the mining industry, so-called "Colour Bar" legislation. In actual practice, however, there is a "Colour Bar" which is enforced by labor unions and which in effect excludes Natives from certain grades of work in other industries as well.[4] It should be noted, also, that since 1920 under what is known as the "Civilized Labour Policy," advocated generally throughout the Union by the government, labor unions, and other European agencies, a consistent attempt has been made to encourage the employment, wherever feasible, of unskilled Europeans in place of Native labor.

[4] *Op. cit.*, pp. 123-125.

Part III

The Demand for Native Labor

CHAPTER 6

THE AGRICULTURAL INDUSTRY

General Characteristics.—The agricultural industry of the Union of South Africa has played and continues to play an important role in the economic and political life of the country. This industry in normal (nondepression) years accounts for from one fifth to one fourth of the total national income, and both directly and indirectly provides a living for over one third of the European population. The bulk of the Native, and a large part of the Asiatic and Colored, populations are likewise wholly or partially dependent upon agricultural pursuits, either as producers or as laborers. Moreover, a large part of the European urban population is of rural origin and with rural sympathies. The desires and aspirations of the European farm population thus loom large in the general economic policies of the country. In fact, it can be said that successive governments have always shown a distinctly rural or agricultural bias.

The great variation in rainfall, climate, and soils in the different parts of South Africa makes possible the production of a wide range of farm products, including those found in both tropical and subtropical climates. Livestock production is widely dispersed throughout the country, but production of most field crops and horticultural products is highly localized.[1] For this reason there are wide variations in the permanent and seasonal labor requirements of farmers in the different parts of the country.

The most comprehensive and reliable source of data on the agricultural industry of South Africa is that provided by the

[1] For a list of farm products see table 1 in the Appendix.

Office of Census and Statistics. The Statistics Act of 1914 provided, *inter alia*, for (1) complete periodic censuses of agriculture, (2) annual censuses of the more important items of agricultural and pastoral production, and (3) the centralization of all agricultural statistics in the Office of Census and Statistics. For various reasons the agricultural provisions of the Statistics Act did not come into force until 1917-18, when the first complete agricultural census was taken.[2] Since then complete censuses have been taken in 1920-21, 1925-26, 1929-30, and 1936-37. Partial censuses were taken in all intervening years, with the exception of the period 1930-31 to 1932-33, when, for reasons of economy, the work was temporarily discontinued. The results of these censuses are published in reports of the Director of Census and are summarized in the *Official Yearbooks of the Union of South Africa*, published by the same office. In these publications distinction is usually made between data for European-occupied farms,[3] data for Natives on European-occupied farms, and data for Natives in reserves and locations.

According to the 1936-37 Agricultural Census there were 104,554 European-occupied farms[4] in the Union of South Africa covering a total area of 99,912,000 morgen (a morgen = 2.11654 acres), or 211,500,000 acres (table 3 in Appendix). As South Africa covers a total area of 472,000 square miles, or 302,000,000 acres, just over two thirds of the country is under European farms. The area under cultivated crops was 5,576,000 morgen, under orchards and vineyard 141,400 morgen, under banana and pineapple plantations 8,600 morgen, and under wattle and other timber plantations 418,100 morgen. About 458,000 morgen are under irrigation. Some 69,500 of the European-occupied farms were owned by the occupier, 20,900

---

[2] In the General Census of 1911 and in the 1904 Census, taken simultaneously in the four colonies, data were collected on certain phases of the agricultural industry. The data collected in the various colonial censuses, prior to 1904, were taken in different years and hence are not comparable with subsequent data.

[3] Data for farms occupied by Asiatics and Colored persons are included with data for European-occupied farms.

[4] Information is not available relative to the number of farms occupied by Natives because over most of South Africa Natives do not occupy farms as individuals but as tribes.

were rented, 7,300 occupied on a share basis, and 6,800 were under a manager. The owner-occupied farms averaged 970 morgen in size, the rented farms 815 morgen, the share-rented 640 morgen, and the managed farms 1,540 morgen. About 38,000 farms were in the Cape Province, 10,000 in Natal, 32,000 in the Transvaal, and 23,000 in the Orange Free State. In the Cape Province farms averaged 1,600 morgen in size, as compared with 500 morgen in Natal and 600 morgen in the Transvaal and Orange Free State. In each of the four provinces the average size of the managed farms exceeded that of the owner-occupied farms, and the latter, in turn, the average size of the cash and share-rented farms.

Trends in Production.—Significant shifts have taken place in the relative importance of the various branches of the agricultural industry of South Africa since the turn of the century. In assessing the importance of these long-time shifts, it is necessary to bear in mind that, while the production of certain products, particularly livestock, is widely dispersed throughout the country, the production of most field and horticultural products is highly localized. Such shifts, therefore, are likely to have an important bearing upon the profitability of agriculture in different parts of South Africa and also upon regional demands for farm labor.

Attention should also be drawn to the fact that certain classes of livestock and certain field crops are owned or produced both by Europeans and Natives, whereas others are owned or produced almost entirely by Europeans. Separation is made of such data wherever possible in tables IX and X and figures 3 and 4. In the 1904 and 1911 general censuses only total figures of livestock and field crops for all races are available. The 1918 census showed livestock under two subdivisions: (1) on farms occupied by Europeans, including livestock owned by Natives on such farms, and (2) on locations, reserves, and Native farms. The 1926, 1930, and 1937 censuses showed livestock owned (1) by Europeans, (2) by Natives on European-occupied farms, and (3) by Natives on locations, reserves, and Native farms. Field crops were divided in the four censuses

68   The Native Labor Problem of South Africa

on a basis similar to that for livestock. The data in the various censuses have been regrouped in tables IX and X for purposes of comparison.

Livestock.—Between 1904 and 1911 the number of all types of livestock, except mules, increased considerably (table IX and figure 3). Since 1911, however, the numbers of non-woolled sheep, angora goats, other goats, and ostriches have declined, the decline being most marked in the case of angora goats and ostriches. In 1937 there were only 696,000 angora goats as compared with 4,275,000 in 1911, and only 40,000 ostriches as

TABLE IX
NUMBER OF PRINCIPAL TYPES OF LIVESTOCK IN UNION OF SOUTH AFRICA—1904-38 (IN 1,000's)

Year*	Cattle	Horses	Mules	Donkeys	Pigs	Woolled sheep	Non-woolled sheep	Angora goats	Other goats	Ostriches
On farms occupied by Europeans† (including non-Europeans on such farms)										
1904	Separate data not available									
1911										
1918	5,172	678	83	474	661	22,775	4,122	2,570	2,703	314
1926	7,021	685	124	622	614	32,008	3,142	1,712	3,449	104
1930	6,668	646	127	529	630	39,748	3,935	1,661	3,074	32
1937	7,558	575	124	623	685	32,635	4,736	642	2,884	40
Owned by Natives on European-occupied farms (included in above)										
1904	Separate data not available									
1911										
1918										
1926	1,475	205	2	131	146	324	257	88	1,092	0
1930	1,496	228	2	131	135	328	205	87	998	0
1937	1,361	170	1	125	147	139	167	32	827	0
Natives in locations, reserves, and Native farms										
1904	Separate data not available									
1911										
1918	1,680	103	2	81	382	2,283	733	161	2,584	0
1926	3,316	171	3	133	295	3,261	447	113	2,674	0
1930	3,906	190	3	170	311	4,164	511	139	3,079	0
1937	3,630	176	2	200	313	3,200	462	54	2,530	0
Total (both European and non-European)										
1904	3,500	450	135	142	679	11,821	4,502	3,393	6,378	361
1911	5,797	719	94	337	1,082	21,842	8,814	4,275	7,488	747
1918	6,852	781	85	554	1,043	25,059	4,855	2,731	5,288	314
1926	10,337	856	127	755	909	35,269	3,589	1,825	6,122	104
1930	10,574	836	130	700	941	43,912	4,446	1,801	6,154	32
1937	11,188	751	126	822	999	35,835	5,199	696	5,414	40

*Data for 1904 and 1911 pertain to general censuses. Data for other years pertain to complete agricultural censuses.
†"Farms occupied by Europeans" include also farms occupied by Colored and Asiatics.
Source of data: *Reports of Agricultural and Pastoral Production,* Agricultural Censuses of 1930 and 1937 (Pretoria, Office of Census and Statistics, Government Printer), Nos. 13, 17.

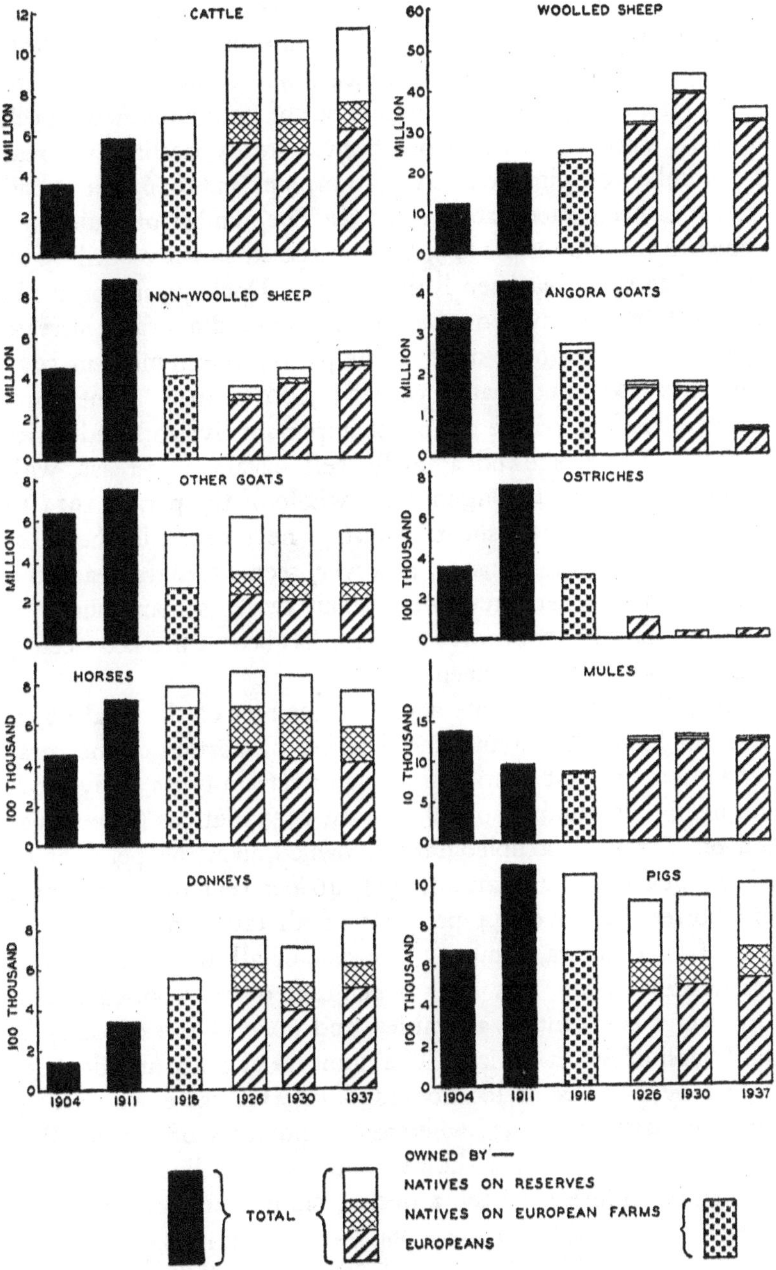

FIGURE 3. Trends in livestock production. Data from table IX.

compared with 747,000 in the earlier year. The number of horses and pigs was practically the same in 1937 as in 1911, although the two types of livestock showed opposite fluctuations in the intervening years. The number of horses reached a peak in 1921, since when there has been a steady decline, whereas the number of pigs reached a low point in 1926, the trend thereafter being moderately upward. The number of mules continued to decline until 1919, then increased steadily until 1930, since when there has been little change. Donkeys, important in transportation in much of the country, showed a steady increase in numbers throughout most of the period, the number in 1937 being 822,000 as compared with 337,000 in 1911. The number of cattle, one of the two most important livestock industries in South Africa, showed a fairly well sustained increase, with minor fluctuations, throughout the whole of the period 1911 to 1937.[5] The woolled sheep industry, next to cattle the most important livestock industry, however, seems to have reached a peak in 1930, when there were about twice as many sheep as in 1911. Since 1930, however, there has been a marked decline in numbers of woolled sheep.

Natives, who constitute about 70 per cent of the total population of South Africa and a still larger proportion of the rural population, own substantial numbers of certain types of livestock and negligible numbers of others. In 1937 Natives (in reserves and on European-occupied farms) owned about 62 per cent of all the goats (other than angora), 46 per cent of all the pigs and horses, just over 44 per cent of all cattle, nearly 40 per cent of all donkeys, about 12 per cent of all angora goats and non-woolled sheep, just over 9 per cent of all woolled sheep, just over 2 per cent of all mules, and none of the ostriches in the Union of South Africa. The numbers of cattle and donkeys owned by Natives in locations and reserves increased greatly between 1918 and 1937, whereas the numbers of non-woolled sheep and angora goats showed a marked decline. It is significant that there has been a decline since 1926 in all types of

[5] The 1937 census showed that Europeans owned 2,170,000 cows and heifers two years and over. Data, however, are not available to indicate what proportion of these are of dairy breeds.

The Agricultural Industry

livestock, except donkeys, owned by Natives on European farms. This seems to bear out the fact (see p. 53) that European farmers are curtailing the labor-tenant system prevalent in much of the Transvaal and Orange Free State.

Field Crops.—Turning attention to the field crops, one finds that wheat and maize production increased greatly since 1904, and sugar cane production since 1918 (table X and figure 4). Data on cane production prior to 1918 are not available, although the sugar cane industry is one of the oldest field crop

TABLE X

PRODUCTION OF PRINCIPAL CROPS IN UNION OF SOUTH AFRICA—1904-37

Year*	Wheat	Barley (grain only)	Oats (grain only)	Kaffir-corn	Maize	Potatoes	Raw cotton	Tobacco	Green leaf tea	Sugar
					Million pounds					1,000 tons
	On farms occupied by Europeans† (including non-Europeans on such)									
1904	Separate data not available									
1911										
1918	587	97	335	93	1,943	220	1	13	7	1,258
1926	541	53	174	64	1,698	200	25	15	4	2,311
1930	638	106	301	165	3,759	355	16	12	3	2,798
1937	941		230	192	5,042	357	4	18	3	3,808
	Natives on European-occupied farms (included in above)									
1904	Separate data not available									
1911										
1918										
1926				38	161					
1930				87	307					
1937	5			81	460	2				
	Natives in locations, reserves, and native farms									
1904	Separate data not available									
1911										
1918	22	2	10	267	585			2		
1926	12		2	87	486			2		
1930				189	718			1		
1937	18			120	594	3		1		
	Total (both Europeans and non-Europeans)									
1904	142	49	131	188	722					
1911	362	61	309	310	1,727	184		15	7	
1918	609	99	345	360	2,528	235	1	15	7	1,258
1926	553	53	176	151	2,184	203	25	17	4	2,311
1930	638	106	301	354	4,477	355	16	13	3	2,798
1937	959	59	230	311	5,636	360	4	19	3	3,808

*Data for 1904 and 1911 were obtained as a part of the general censuses taken during those years; data for the remaining years were obtained in complete agricultural censuses.
†"Farms occupied by Europeans" include also farms occupied by Colored and Asiatics.
Source of data: *Reports of Agricultural and Pastoral Production*, Agricultural Censuses of 1930 and 1937, Nos. 13, 17.

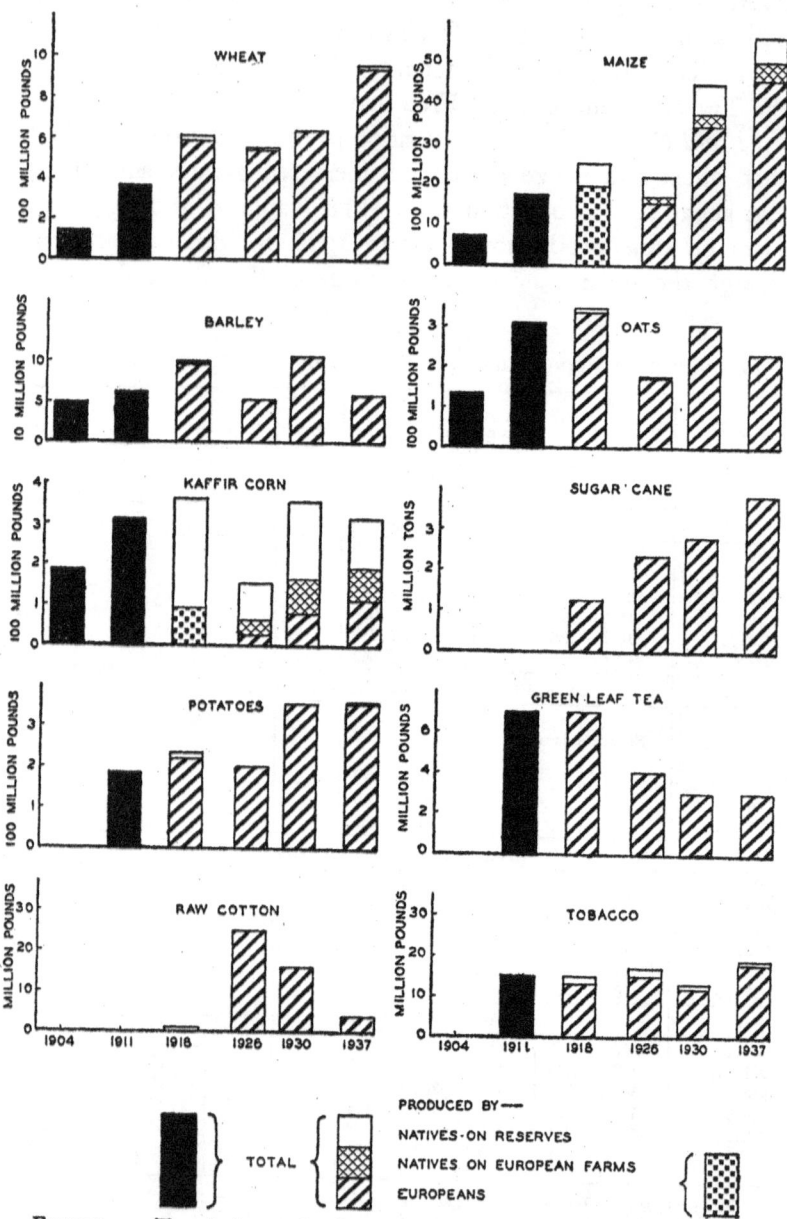

FIGURE 4. Trends in production of field crops. Data from table X.

industries in South Africa. Although the output of barley, oats, and kaffir-corn increased considerably between 1904 and 1911, and although there have been large fluctuations in output since then, there has been no significant trend. For all three of these cereals, the output in 1937 was either below, or substantially the same, as that of 1911. Production of potatoes and tobacco has shown a steady growth since 1911, the first figures available on these two crops. On the other hand, output of green-leaf tea has declined from seven million pounds in 1918 to about four million pounds in 1937. Cotton production is unique. Practically no cotton was grown prior to 1918. In that year about 800,000 pounds of raw (unginned) cotton was produced. Eight years later (1926) production had increased to around twenty-five million pounds, but thereafter declined rapidly to under four million pounds in 1937. At one time it was hoped to establish cotton production as an important field crop in South Africa, but unfavorable production conditions and low prices of cotton have caused this industry to decline to a position of minor importance.

An examination of the yearly figures on production of field crops shows very wide annual fluctuations in the case of the cereals and potatoes.[6] For example, maize production by Europeans only declined from 3,153 million pounds in 1923 to 1,666 million pounds in 1924, increased to 4,188 million pounds in 1925, and again declined to 1,698 million pounds in 1926. Similar, although less violent, fluctuations occurred for the other cereals and for potatoes.

For only three crops, kaffir-corn, maize, and tobacco, does the production by Natives constitute an important share of total production. In 1937 Natives in reserves and locations produced nearly 39 per cent of all kaffir-corn, and Natives on European farms another 26 per cent. Natives thus produced about 65 per cent of all kaffir-corn, an important food for Natives. Natives in the reserves and locations produced nearly 11 per cent of all maize, and Natives on European farms another 8

---

[6] *Report on Agricultural and Pastoral Production*, 1936-1937, Agricultural Census No. 17, Table 12.

per cent, or together about 19 per cent of all maize produced in South Africa. Natives in reserves and locations and on European farms produced somewhat under 1 million pounds out of 19 million pounds of tobacco in 1937. The data given in table X for sugar cane apply to European production only. According to a statement in the *Agricultural Census* of 1937, non-Europeans produced 372,422 tons of cane in 1936-37, of which 38,996 tons were produced by Natives.[7] The total production of sugar cane in 1936-37 was 4,180,000 tons, the production by Natives being just under 1 per cent of the total.

Fruit Trees.—The determination of shifts in number of fruit trees is complicated by the fact that there have been important changes in the basis on which the various censuses were conducted. All censuses are confined to fruit trees owned by Europeans, including Asiatics and Colored. The number of fruit trees owned by Natives in locations and reserves or on European farms is insignificant. Prior to 1921 trees in urban areas were not enumerated. From 1926 onward only trees, the fruits of which were produced for sale, were enumerated. This would include fruit trees in urban areas, provided the fruit was produced for sale, but would not include fruit trees on farms, the fruit of which was not intended for sale. As large numbers of farms in all parts of the country have small orchards for domestic use, this fact is no doubt in large part responsible for the marked decline in the number of certain types of fruit trees, for example, peaches, after 1925. For these reasons the expansion in fruit trees between 1911 and 1921 is not as great as the figures in table XI indicate, and the expansion since 1921 is greater than the figures indicate.

Bearing these qualifications in mind, the data in table XI and figure 5 nevertheless indicate a very marked expansion since 1911 in the number of orange trees and, since 1918, in the number of mango trees. It is probable that a similar great increase has taken place in grapefruit trees, the number of which prior to 1926 was so unimportant as to be grouped with other trees. The number of vines just about doubled between 1918

---

[7] *Op. cit.*, Summary table No. 3.

and 1937. There has also been steady expansion in the number of apple, apricot, pear, plum, and prune trees since 1911. The census data indicate a marked decline in the number of peach, nectarine, lemon, and naartje (tangerine) trees since 1918. It is impossible to tell, however, whether this represents an actual decline or whether the lower figures are due to the fact that fruit trees, the fruit of which is not grown for sale, were excluded from later censuses. In any event the decline would not be as severe as is indicated in the figures in table XI.

Significance of Shifts.—These long-time shifts in the production of the various pastoral and agricultural products are important because they indicate changes in the labor needs in the different branches of agriculture and also have a bearing upon the regional needs for labor. The expansion in the production of field and horticultural products is particularly significant because these products require considerably more labor than do pastoral products. Moreover, the production of these products is more highly localized than is the case with pastoral products. An important factor influencing shifts in production is the relative profitability of various types of products. The profitability of production in turn influences farmers' ability to pay wages high enough to attract sufficient competent labor. Perhaps even more important in their effects upon the profitability of different types of farming, upon the level of income of laborers, and upon the number of persons employed, are the very marked fluctuations in annual production of certain crops, particularly the cereals, owing to exceptionally favorable or unfavorable weather conditions. For example, although there may be a long-time shortage of labor in the maize-growing areas, there may actually be a localized surplus of such labor in years of crop failure. As Natives are likely to experience a similar failure in their crops, the decline in real income of Native laborers is thus doubly great.

Efficiency of Agriculture in South Africa.—To be complete, an analysis of the demand for and supply of agricultural labor must give some consideration to the efficiency of agricultural production. The determination of efficiency involves an analysis

TABLE XI

NUMBER OF VINES AND FRUIT TREES IN UNION OF SOUTH AFRICA—(EUROPEAN-OCCUPIED FARMS)—IN 1,000's

Year*	Number of vines	Apple	Apricot	Mango	Nectarine	Peach	Pear	Plum and prune	Lemon	Orange	Naartje (tangerine)	Grapefruit	Other fruit trees	Total excepting vines
1911	....	1,430	1,025	....	99	5,902	651	636	173	986	404	†	‡	....
1918	87,840	2,171	1,161	97	206	5,770	788	1,144	248	1,826	442	†	1,316	15,169
1921	102,108	2,471	1,454	134	78	5,446	838	1,422	161	1,811	376	†	2,024	16,215
1924	....	2,707	2,169	156	78	6,147	1,073	1,740	226	2,950	321	†	1,595	19,162
1925	....	2,976	2,387	170	106	6,842	1,156	1,812	271	3,559	342	†	1,853	21,474
1926	....	2,438	2,039	189	†	†	998	1,552	193	3,633	307	195	4,947	16,491
1930	....	2,464	2,191	231	76	3,591	1,010	1,379	197	3,883	272	244	1,481	17,019
1936	150,633	2,572	1,787	233	101	3,894	1,076	1,148	158	4,149	271	292	1,475	17,156
1937	164,766	2,677	1,940	267	92	4,056	1,111	1,198	181	4,409	296	321	2,220	18,768

*Trees in urban areas were not enumerated until 1921. As from 1926 the census was confined to trees, the fruit of which was produced for sale.
†Included in other fruit.
Source of data: *Official Yearbook of the Union of South Africa*, No. 20 (1939), pp. 762, 767.

The Agricultural Industry

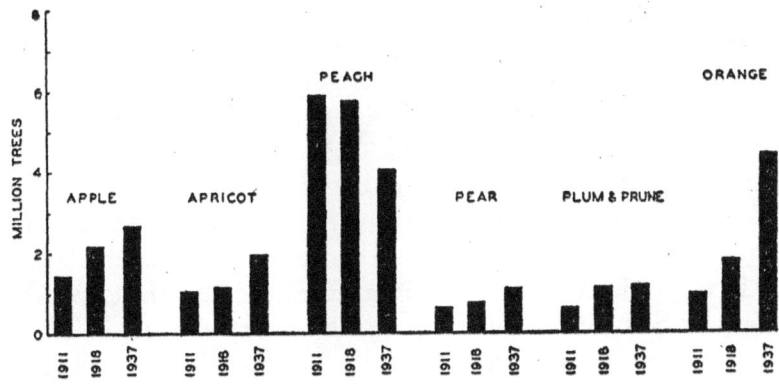

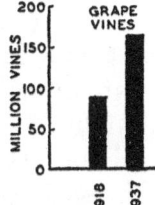

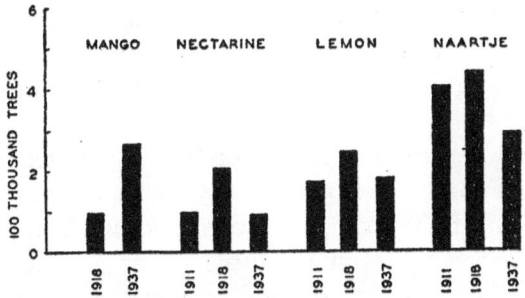

FIGURE 5. Trends in numbers of fruit trees. Data from table XI.

of output in terms of input factors, or when input factors are likely to be similar (so much land or labor or capital) comparisons of output in different countries may serve as a useful guide. Such comparative measurement of efficiency as between countries is a problem of extreme difficulty. To be reliable, it must be based on average output over a number of years in order to eliminate year-to-year fluctuations due to variations in climatic conditions. Consideration must also be given to certain factors which are difficult to measure quantitatively, e.g., quality of product and the extent to which soils are being maintained in a condition of productiveness. Another difficulty is that for many countries only fragmentary data are available as to output of a particular product per acre, per man-hour, or per unit of capital invested. Frequently such data as are available refer only to production of a crop in a selected area, which may or may not be typical of production of a country as a whole.

For these reasons an analysis of the efficiency of agricultural production in South Africa must be predicated partly upon a consideration of climate, soils, disease, and other factors governing production in that country, and partly upon comparisons, where such are possible, of output in South Africa and other countries. Unfortunately, data in man-hours devoted to a particular line of agricultural production are not readily available by countries; nor is it possible in most countries to obtain data on the amount of capital invested in particular lines of agricultural production. It is necessary, therefore, to place chief reliance upon comparative data on output per acre, even though such data are not entirely satisfactory, because output per acre is a product of several factors such as amount and cost of labor, amount and cost of capital, as well as of efficiency of techniques employed.

In South Africa the population of 10,000,000 persons is small in relation to the size of the country, 472,000 square miles. Much of the country, however, is semi-arid and is thus suitable only for the most extensive form of pastoral production and, in the absence of mineral resources, can provide profitable occupation for only a very small population. There have been frequent references in the press and government publications to the problem of overgrazing. The fact that the number of sheep has tended to decline since 1930 and production of cattle has increased only ten per cent would indicate that South Africa with its present extensive methods of production has reached its peak in carrying capacity of livestock. Further increase in total numbers of livestock will be dependent upon the more intensive use of cereals (mainly maize), and cultivated fodder grasses and root crops as feed supplementary to natural pasture. Qualitatively, too, there is much room for improvement, by substitution of high-grade beef and dairy cattle for the scrub cattle that constitute such a large part of the numbers, especially in Native areas. Such a development must await a realization that Native agriculture is not separate and distinct from, but complementary to, European production and that Natives must be more fully trained in field and animal husbandry.

Even in the more thickly settled regions of South Africa, where rainfall is more plentiful, the human population per square mile, outside areas with large urban population, is small. Farms are comparatively large and only a small proportion of the land in farms is under cultivation. Because of the low wages paid to non-European workers, the high wages paid to skilled European workers, and the relatively high cost of agricultural machinery and fuel power, extensive methods of production are practiced over most of South Africa. Only in a few areas, outstandingly suitable for the production of particular crops, is agriculture on a more intensive basis. For example, a fairly high degree of intensiveness exists in vegetable production in areas adjacent to large cities, in the limited sugar cane area in Natal, and in those areas engaged in commercialized production of deciduous and citrus fruits, pineapples, and bananas. Even in such areas more human labor and less capital are used than in most other countries producing similar products.

Even more important than low average rainfall in part of the country, is variability in rainfall from year to year and time of precipitation within the year. Most of the interior plateau (outside the coastal belt) has a spring and summer rainfall. Although superficially the average rainfall over a period of years may appear adequate in much of this area, there are very marked fluctuations in rainfall from year to year and in some years rainfall, which usually starts in September and October, may be so late that farmers are unable to cultivate their usual acreage. Early and plentiful rainfall usually means large acreages sown to crops and vice versa. Then, too, if rain later in the season is delayed or is inadequate much of the acreage sown will not be harvested. It is very seldom that the interior of South Africa experiences plentiful rainfall well dispersed throughout the planting and growing year. When this happens, bumper crops result. Because of the variability of the rainfall, South Africa experiences extreme annual fluctuations in the total volume of production and also in the output per acre.

South Africa's mild and equable climate is not an unmixed blessing. Although most of the country is suitable for European habitation, the absence of severe winter weather over most of the country is conducive to the survival and spread of pests and diseases, which have caused considerable loss among animals and to crops and fruits. Eradication and control of such diseases and pests involve the country annually in very great expenses. The Department of Agriculture has an extensive and efficient staff of technicians engaged in the investigation and eradication of plant and animal diseases and pests.

Agricultural development is retarded not only by variable and limited rainfall and by numerous diseases and pests, but also by the farming practices which prevail over much of the country. In the pastoral areas overgrazing is having serious results. In addition to widespread erosion, the depletion of edible bushes and grasses encourages the spread of noxious or inedible plants and weeds. For example, in many parts of South Africa and especially in the eastern Cape Province jointed cactus and prickly pear infestation has necessitated the temporary abandonment of much land that once provided excellent grazing. In other areas, the spread of other types of noxious or inedible plants is becoming more and more serious. Vigorous but costly steps have been and are being taken by the government and farmers to eradicate or at least prevent the spread of such infestations.

In much of the wheat- and maize-growing territory, the

absence of practices involving suitable rotations of crops or the combination of field and animal husbandry is resulting in a depletion of the chemical constituents and productivity of the soils, and that in spite of a growing use of chemical fertilizers.

Many prominent persons, well acquainted with agricultural conditions in South Africa, informed the author that if agriculture is to expand or even to survive on its present scale, radical changes in farming practices must take place in the near future, changes which must be based upon considerations of the long-time carrying capacity of grazing land, the widespread adoption of crop rotation systems and the combination of animal and field husbandry. As will be shown later, the problem is particularly acute in the Native territories. Unfortunately, the problem is complicated by the necessity of developing markets overseas for certain products. For example, the expansion of the beef cattle industry and the utilization of maize for animal feed rather than for export, are dependent upon the extent to which South African beef can penetrate the European market. Regrettably, too, the South African government appears to have given very inadequate consideration to the effect of its various agricultural control policies on the output of farm products in South Africa. As will be shown in a separate manuscript, some of these control policies have encouraged an expansion in production of certain types of commodities, which, from the standpoint of the most efficient utilization of South Africa's agricultural and other resources, should rather have been contracted. There is also evidence that some of the control policies have tended to encourage "one-cropping" of land and the extension of production of certain crops into areas not well adapted to such production.

Comparable data are not available relative to the output per acre of all important agricultural commodities produced. The United States Department of Agriculture has, however, presented comparable data for a number of countries relative to the production of wheat and corn. These data indicate that during the period 1925-29 only 4 countries (Mexico, Guatemala, Algeria, and Tunisia) out of 48 countries had a lower output of wheat per acre than the Union of South Africa.[8] During the period 1930-34, only 1 country (Tunisia) had a lower output per acre. During the latter period output of wheat in South Africa averaged 8.1 bushels per acre as compared with 12.2 bushels in Australia, 13.8 bushels in Argentina, 13.6 bushels in Canada, 13.5 bushels in the United States, and 33.3 bushels in England and Wales. For the three-year period 1936-38 production per acre in South Africa averaged only 7.2 bushels indicating a progressive decline in average output per acre. This conclusion appears logical as, since 1930, wheat acreage in South Africa has expanded greatly into areas not suitable for wheat production.

The United States Department of Agriculture estimates of maize (corn) output per acre for certain selected countries for the years 1934 to 1937 are shown in table XII together with the author's estimates of maize output per acre for South Africa for the same years. These data indicate that output of maize per acre in South Africa is low in comparison with output in other important maize-producing countries. Even more significant is the wide fluctuation in output per acre in South Africa.

TABLE XII
OUTPUT OF CORN (MAIZE) PER ACRE FOR SELECTED COUNTRIES (1934-37)
BUSHELS PER ACRE

Country	1933-34	1934-35	1935-36	1936-37
Mexico	9.6	9.2	9.0	8.7
United States	22.6	15.8	24.0	16.5
Hungary	25.3	29.7	19.6	36.2
Yugoslavia	22.5	30.9	19.5	31.2
Bulgaria	20.8	18.4	22.4	23.5
Rumania	15.0	15.4	16.6	15.1
Brazil	18.6	21.7	22.6	25.8
Argentina	25.3	32.1	30.9	30.1
Union of South Africa*	11.2	9.0	8.6	13.1

*Production by only Europeans in South Africa. South African figures are for morgen reaped and bags (200 lbs.) produced. The following formula was used to convert South African production to a bushels-per-acreage basis:

$$\frac{\text{Bags produced} \times 200}{56 \text{ (pounds per bushel)}} \div \text{Morgen} \times 2.11654 \text{ (acres per morgen)}.$$

Source of data: *Agricultural Statistics* (1937), pp. 42-43; (1938), pp. 46-47; (1939), pp. 48-49.

[8] *Agricultural Statistics* (1939), U. S. Dept. of Agriculture, Table 6, pp. 16, 17.

TABLE XIII

OUTPUT OF SUGAR CANE PER ACRE IN SELECTED REGIONS
(SHORT TONS PER ACRE)

Region	1935	1936	1937
Hawaii	67.8	70.1	69.5
Philippines	12.6	14.6	15.0
Puerto Rico	25.1	23.3	27.1
Louisiana	13.6	17.1	21.4
Florida	34.7	33.2	33.4
Natal (South Africa)*	20.8	18.7	18.8

*Union of South Africa: Calculated by author from data on acreage reaped and total cane reaped appearing in the *Official Yearbooks of the Union of South Africa* (1937 to 1939).
Source of data: Agricultural Statistics, Hawaii, Philippines, Puerto Rico, Louisiana and Florida (1939), pp. 133-134.

The figures in table XIII indicate that although sugar cane production per acre in South Africa is considerably below that in Hawaii and also below that in Puerto Rico and Florida (U. S. A.), it compares favorably with that in the Philippines and in Louisiana (U. S. A.). The sugar industry in South Africa is generally regarded as having reached a high degree of efficiency in the techniques of production. There is some question, however, whether it can be regarded as efficient in terms of the input of capital and labor. The Board of Trade and Industries in its Report No. 66 of the 14th of April, 1926, drew attention to the fact that much cane land had been acquired by city people as a speculation. It went on to add that "Many of the present planters bought sugar land at high prices when labor costs were much lower." In spite of this conclusion, the Board in its recommendations at the end of the report and in subsequent reports recommended forms of control by the industry which have had the effect not only of consolidating high land values, but of encouraging still further increases.

Many economists and business leaders consulted by the author in South Africa claim that, considering the nature of the country and the climatic and other disabilities under which agricultural production takes place in South Africa, the output of most products per acre is satisfactory. They contend, however, that output is not satisfactory when evaluated in terms of input of capital and that much of the difficulty experienced by farmers in South Africa arises from the fact that when measured in terms of output per acre and in prices received for products farm lands generally are overvalued. If the shortage of labor experienced during the years 1930-1939 should continue, agriculture, or certain lines of agriculture, will have to contract or marked changes will have to be made in the techniques of production. These changes will have to involve (1) a more efficient utilization of the Native labor available, (2) a greater use of power-driven agricultural implements and machinery, (3) the concentration on those lines of agricultural production for which the country is best adapted, and (4) adoption of farming practices which involve both animal and field husbandry in order to decrease as far as possible seasonal peaks of production and labor needs and to conserve the productivity of the soil.

Farm Wages.—Data on Native farm wages are unsatisfactory: (1) labor contracts are often between the farmer and the Native family head for all family labor; (2) under the labor-tenant system the members of the Native family work only part of the year and may or may not receive cash wages; (3) full-time workers are often allotted an area of land and its produce. It is hard to set a value for this and other privileges. Available data, gleaned mostly from farm-management studies made by the Department of Agriculture, are summarized in the Native Farm Labour Committee Report (pp. 33-43). These indicate wide variations in cash wages and in total wages (cash and kind) in different parts of the country. The report shows that only in rare instances do total wages per adult worker exceed £35 a year. Farm wages are much lower than those earned by Natives in urban occupations. Although this disparity accords with that in other countries, there are special considerations in South Africa. Native farm workers are spared the expense of traveling to cities for work. Furthermore, as several members of the family work, family income is greater than where the city worker is the sole wage earner. More important, Natives place a high value on the privilege of grazing cattle.

CHAPTER 7

THE AGRICULTURAL INDUSTRY: LOCATION OF TYPES OF FARMING

BECAUSE TYPES of farming in South Africa are so varied as to intensity and location, a proper appreciation of the farmers' needs for Native labor can be obtained only on a broad regional basis. As pointed out before, the Union of South Africa was divided into 23 agricultural regions: 12 in the Cape of Good Hope or Cape Province, 3 in Natal, and 4 each in the Transvaal and Orange Free State.[1] In several of these regions the more important types of farming are similar; separation was made because of minor variations in general agricultural conditions in each region, and because similar regions may fall into different provinces. For the purpose of analyzing regional needs for permanent and seasonal agricultural labor, such a detailed division into farming areas is not necessary. The various regions have thus been regrouped in 7 general areas in which the predominant types of agriculture are roughly similar. The salient agricultural features of each group appearing below are based on information contained in the *Agricultural Census* for 1936-37. The information relating (a) to number of farms and area covered by farms (table XIV and fig. 6), (b) to area under field crops (table XV and fig. 7), (c) to numbers of fruit and nut trees (table XVI and fig. 8), refers to production on European-occupied farms only. The data relative to livestock refer to numbers on European-occupied farms and to those on Native

---

[1] The magisterial districts and farm products in each region are shown in table 2 in Appendix.

TABLE XIV

NUMBER AND SIZE OF EUROPEAN-OCCUPIED FARMS—1936

General Area No.	Number of farms	Area in farms Morgen (acres)	Average size of farms Morgen (acres)	Per cent of total for Union	
				Farms	Area in farms
1............	7,324	4,322,000 (9,148,000)	590 (1,249)	7.0	4.3
2............	22,842	49,905,000 (105,626,000)	2,185 (4,625)	21.8	49.9
3............	11,752	10,236,000 (21,665,000)	871 (1,844)	11.2	10.2
4............	1,526	706,000 (1,494,000)	463 (980)	1.5	0.8
5............	7,538	3,121,000 (6,606,000)	414 (876)	7.2	3.1
6............	47,870	25,373,000 (53,703,000)	530 (1,122)	45.8	25.4
7............	5,702	6,249,000 (13,226,000)	1,096 (2,320)	5.5	6.3
Total for Union .	104,554	99,912,000 (211,468,000)	......	100.0	100.0

Source of data: Summarized from Appendix, table 3.

farms, reserves, and locations (table XVII and figs. 9 and 10). This distinction is made because although Natives produce very minor quantities of field crops (with the exception of maize and kaffir-corn) and very little fruit, they own substantial numbers of livestock.

General Area No. 1 includes only the Southwest Region of the Cape Province. It is the oldest and at the same time one of the most important farming areas in South Africa with Capetown, second largest city in South Africa, as its chief port and industrial center. Although the region is mountainous, its coastal plains and wide sheltered valleys are well adapted to the production of a considerable range of field crops and fruit. On the whole, rainfall is adequate and well distributed. The area is unique in that it has the only winter-rainfall climate in South Africa.

Location of Types of Farming

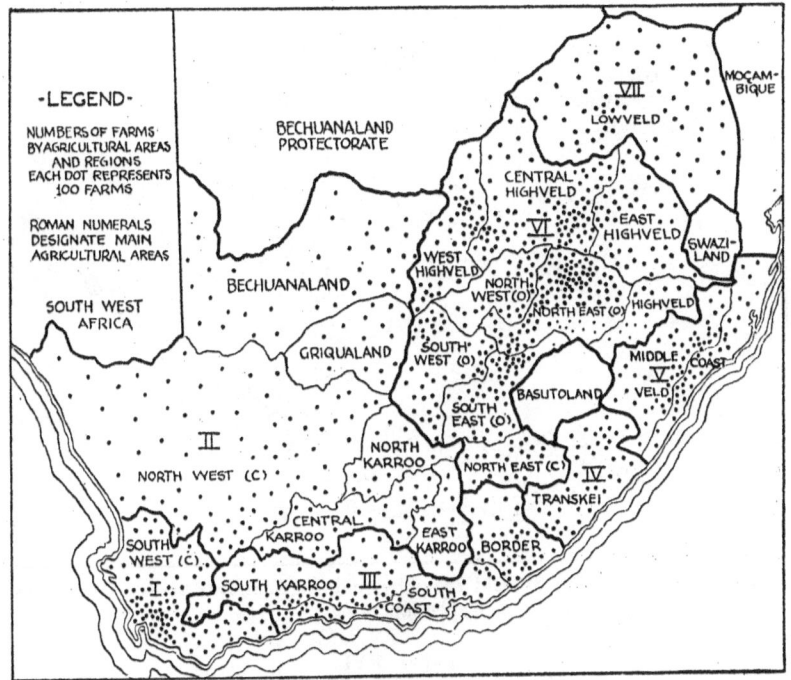

FIGURE 6. Distribution of farms by agricultural regions and areas. Data from Appendix, table 3.

TABLE XV

DISTRIBUTION OF FIELD CROPS—1936

General Area No.	1,000 morgen under					Percent of total for Union				
	Wheat	Barley, rye and oats	Maize and kaffir-corn	Sugar cane	Other crops	Wheat	Barley, rye and oats	Maize and kaffir-corn	Sugar cane	Other crops
1............	361	200	3	0	11	32.8	39.3	0.1	0.0	5.5
2............	175	68	202	0	16	15.9	13.4	6.2	0.0	8.0
3............	66	45	70	0	20	6.0	8.8	2.1	0.0	10.1
4............	13	20	31	0	2	1.2	3.9	0.9	0.0	1.0
5............	1	12	120	170	19	0.1	2.4	3.7	100.0	9.6
6............	469	159	2,703	0	84	42.6	31.2	82.8	0.0	42.2
7............	16	5	137	0	47	1.4	1.0	4.2	0.0	23.6
Total........	1,101	509	3,266	170	199	100.0	100.0	100.0	100.0	100.0

Source of data: Summarized from Appendix, table 5.

88   *The Native Labor Problem of South Africa*

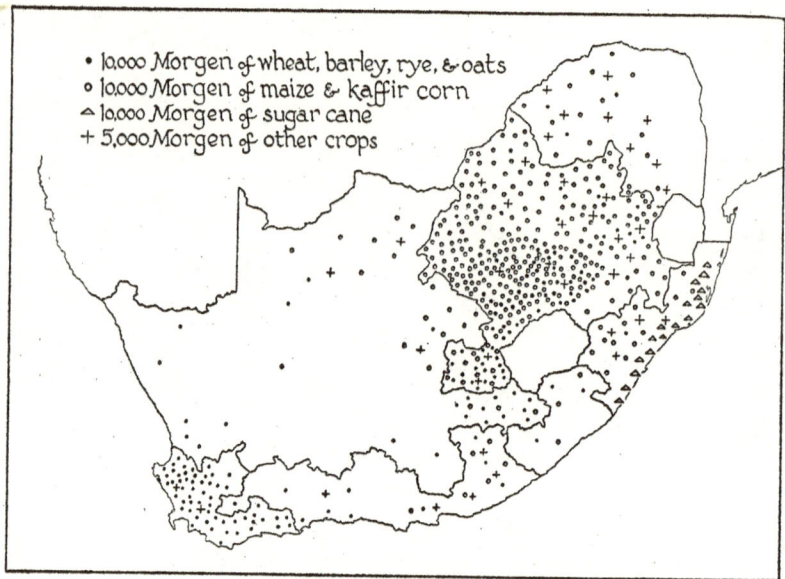

FIGURE 7. Distribution of field crops by main agricultural areas. Data from Appendix, table 5.

TABLE XVI
DISTRIBUTION OF FRUIT PRODUCTION—1936

General Area No.	All citrus 1,000 trees	All deciduous 1,000 trees	Mango, pawpaw, avocado 1,000 trees	Vines 1,000's	Pineapple plantations (morgen)	Banana plantations (morgen)	Percent of total for Union					
							Citrus	Deciduous	Mangos, pawpaws and avocados	Vines	Pineapples	Bananas
1.....	287	5,284	0	119,233	......	......	5.5	43.7	......	72.4	......	......
2.....	533	1,222	0	12,527	......	......	10.2	10.1	......	7.6	......	......
3.....	1,407	1,514	26	32,223	3,379	330	27.0	12.5	2.5	19.5	76.6	7.9
4.....	21	51	4	......	13	49	0.4	0.4	0.4	......	0.3	1.2
5.....	493	143	110	3	958	3,668	9.4	1.2	10.5	0.0	21.8	87.8
6.....	612	3,562	12	780	5	3	11.8	29.5	1.2	0.5	0.1	0.1
7.....	1,854	314	890	......	54	125	35.7	2.6	85.4	......	1.2	3.0
Total..	5,207	12,090	1,042	164,766	4,409	4,175	100.0	100.0	100.0	100.0	100.0	100.0

Source of data: Summarized from Appendix, table 6.

Notwithstanding the fact that the Southwest Region has only 7 per cent of all farms and 4.3 per cent of all land in farms in South Africa, it has 72 per cent of all vines, 44 per cent of all deciduous fruit trees, 33 per cent of the total area

Location of Types of Farming

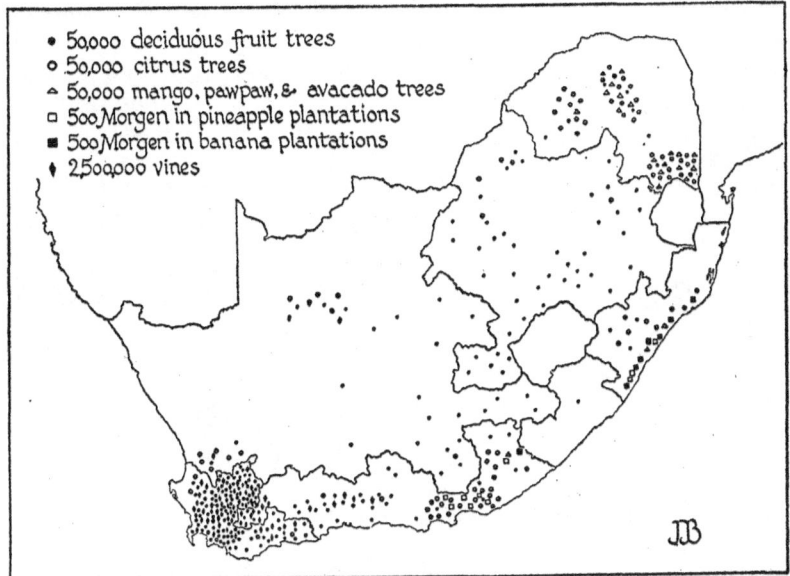

FIGURE 8. Distribution of fruit trees by types and agricultural areas. Data from Appendix, table 6.

TABLE XVII

DISTRIBUTION OF LIVESTOCK BY GENERAL AGRICULTURAL AREAS—1936

General Area No.	Number (in 1,000's)					Percent of total in Union				
	Cattle	Horses, mules and donkeys	Woolled sheep	Non-woolled sheep	Goats (including Angora)	Cattle	Horses, mules and donkeys	Woolled sheep	Non-woolled sheep	Goats (including Angora)
1..........	119	96	1,538	48	156	1.1	5.6	4.3	0.9	2.6
2..........	1,191	450	13,718	3,823	1,896	10.6	26.5	38.3	73.5	31.0
3..........	789	133	4,592	571	1,145	7.0	7.8	12.8	11.0	18.7
4..........	1,731	141	3,041	1	924	15.5	8.3	8.5	0.0	15.1
5..........	1,883	149	733	200	886	16.8	8.8	2.0	3.9	14.5
6..........	4,505	586	11,979	375	590	40.4	34.5	33.4	7.2	9.7
7..........	970	144	234	181	513	8.6	8.5	0.7	3.5	8.4
Total.....	11,188	1,699	35,835	5,199	6,110	100.0	100.0	100.0	100.0	100.0

Source of data: Summarized from Appendix, table 4.

of wheat, and 40 per cent of the total area in barley, rye, and oats in the country. All Turkish tobacco produced in South Africa is raised in this region. Maize production is negligible, but the region also has important numbers of all types of live-

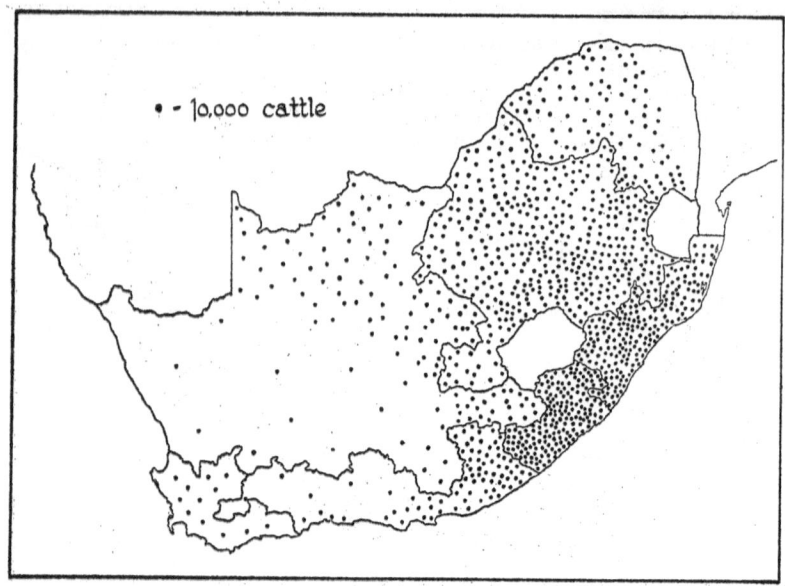

FIGURE 9. Distribution of cattle. Data from Appendix, table 4.

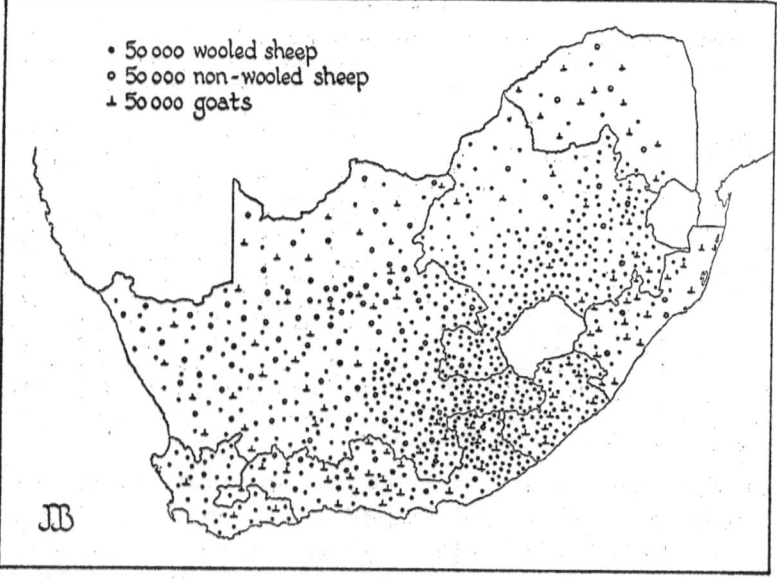

FIGURE 10. Distribution of sheep and goats. Data from Appendix, table 4.

stock, including about 11.3 per cent of all pigs. In the northern section of this region, citrus production is of some importance. The average size farm in the area is 590 morgen or about 1,250 acres.

The Southwest Region has need of a large supply of permanent and seasonal agricultural labor. Its permanent labor force is supplied largely by its Colored population, relatively few Natives being employed in agriculture in this region. Its large seasonal needs for harvesting small grains and fruits are met by temporary migrations of Colored men, women, and children from nearby towns and villages.

General Area No. 2 includes the Northwest, Central Karroo, North Karroo, East Karroo, Bechuanaland, Griqualand West, and Northeast Regions in the Cape Province and the Southwest Region of the Orange Free State, which together cover about one third of the total area of South Africa. It is an area of low rainfall, varying from less than 5 inches a year in parts of the Northwest Region to 15 inches in the more easterly parts. Most of the area has a rainfall of less than 10 inches a year.

This area has just over one fifth of all European-occupied farms in South Africa and about one half of all land in farms. The farms are large, varying from an average of 720 morgen (just over 1,500 acres) in the Northeast Region of the Cape Province to 4,400 morgen (about 9,300 acres) in the Northwest Region of the same Province. In most of the area, the average size farm exceeds 2,180 morgen (slightly over 4,600 acres).

Pastoral production constitutes the chief agricultural activity in this area. Just over 38 per cent of all woolled sheep, 73 per cent of all non-woolled sheep, 25 per cent of all angora goats, 32 per cent of all other goats, and 10 per cent of all cattle in the Union are in this area. The greatest concentration of woolled sheep and angora goats is found in the southern and eastern parts of this huge area. Non-woolled sheep are found mainly in the northwestern part, whereas cattle become of increasing importance in the northeastern sections.

The area taken as a whole is relatively unimportant in regard to production of field crops and fruit, although there are important but limited areas under cultivation. Some citrus fruit and small grains are produced in the southern part of the Northwest Region of the Cape Province; some deciduous and citrus fruit in irrigation settlements along the Orange River; and some maize in the easterly sections bordering on the maize triangle of the Orange Free State and Transvaal.

The permanent and seasonal labor needs of this vast area are light and are supplied mainly by the rural Colored population, although in the northern and eastern sections Native labor tends to augment and even to supplant Colored labor. The northern and easterly sections have relatively small Colored populations and relatively large Native populations.

General Area No. 3 includes the South Coast, South Karroo, and Border Regions of the Cape Province. It is largely mountainous with, however, wide coastal plains and interior valleys. Rainfall, though adequate in most of the area, varies considerably, even in closely adjacent parts. This is due largely to the slope of the mountain ranges in relation to prevailing winds. Rainfall is also less reliable, there being considerable year-to-year fluctuations. As is usual in South Africa, rainfall tends to be heavier in the more easterly sections. This area, especially the South Karroo Region, has considerable areas of land under irrigation. The area has about 11 per cent of all European-occupied farms in the Union and about 10 per cent of all land in farms. The average size of farms for the area was 871 morgen (1,840 acres) varying from around 570 morgen (1,200 acres) in the South Coast Region to 1,440 morgen (about 3,050 acres) in the South Karroo Region.

Because of the wide variation in topography, rainfall, and climatic conditions in this area, it is difficult to regard it as having any predominant type of farming. Generally speaking, it may be considered as a mixed farming area in which livestock and crops, mainly alfalfa, are combined. The western section of the South Karroo Region, however, tends to merge into the Southwest Region of the Cape Province. This section has about 20 per cent of all vines in the Union and is thus the second most important grape-producing area in the country. The western section of the South Coast Region also produces small grains—wheat, barley, rye, and oats. The northern sections of the South Karroo and Border Regions tend to merge into General Area No. 2, in which pastoral production (woolled sheep and angora goats) predominates. The easterly section in turn tends to merge into the semitropical regions of Natal. The South Coast and Border Regions have 77 per cent of South Africa's total area in pineapple plantations, 8 per cent of the total area in banana plantations, and 26 per cent of all citrus fruit trees.

Livestock is raised throughout the whole of the area, but except for the western section of the South Coast Region, General Area No. 3 is not important in production of cereals.

Throughout most of the area, both permanent and seasonal labor needs are light and are supplied by the rural Colored population. In the fruit-growing sections of the extreme western part of the South Karroo Region, seasonal labor needs are met by temporary migrations of Colored persons from nearby towns. The heavy permanent and seasonal needs of the semitropical fruit-growing sections of the eastern South Coast Region and the Border Region are supplied largely by the Native population in these regions and by Natives from the adjacent Transkeian territories.

General Area No. 4 includes only the Transkei Region, in which most of the land is owned by Natives individually or as Native reserves. The region includes some of the best agricultural land in South Africa and has a fairly high rainfall. There are only 1,526 farms occupied by Europeans in this area or less than 1.5 per cent of all European-occupied farms in the Union. The area covered by such farms is only 706,000 morgen or less than 1 per cent of all land in European-occupied farms. The average size of farms occupied by Europeans is only 460 morgen (980 acres). The Europeans in this area engage in mixed farming, grain, livestock, and some fruit. Their total production, however, constitutes a very small proportion of the totals for the Union.

Natives in this area raise considerable amounts of grain,

mainly maize, but their output is insufficient to meet consumption needs in the area, and they have to buy, mainly from the Transvaal and Orange Free State, an important part of their annual needs for cereals. The outstanding agricultural feature of the Transkei is the large number of all types of livestock, which plays an important part in the social, cultural, and religious life of the Natives. Although there are twenty-three agricultural regions in South Africa, the Transkei has 15.47 per cent of all cattle, 16.91 per cent of all horses, 17.72 per cent of all pigs, and 16.53 per cent of all goats, other than angoras. The region also has considerable numbers of woolled sheep, poultry, and angora goats.

Permanent and seasonal labor needs of the small number of European farmers are small and the supply of Native labor is more abundant than anywhere else in South Africa.

General Area No. 5 includes the Coast and Middleveld Regions of Natal. In reality there are marked differences in the rainfall, climatic conditions, and types of farming in the two regions. In most of the Middleveld Region, agricultural conditions parallel closely those in the eastern part of the South Coast and the Border Regions of the Cape Province, but in other sections they correspond more closely to the typically semi-tropical conditions of the Coast Region of Natal. In the Middleveld Region, rainfall ranges from 25 to 40 inches a year, whereas in the Coast Region it ranges from 35 to 50 inches, with small sections having a still higher rainfall. Although much of the area is mountainous, there are large coastal plains and interior valleys.

There are considerable Native reserves in both these regions. Notwithstanding this fact, the two regions together have about 7.5 per cent of all European-occupied farms in the Union and about 3.3 per cent of the land in such farms. The average size farm (European-occupied) in the Middleveld Region is 650 morgen (about 1,370 acres) and in the South Coast Region, only about 180 morgen (about 380 acres).

The entire sugar-cane acreage of the Union is in the Coast Region of Natal. This region also has nearly 88 per cent of the area in banana plantations, over 21 per cent of the area in pineapple plantations, and nearly 10 per cent of the mango, pawpaw, and avocado pear trees. The two regions together have nearly 10 per cent of all citrus trees in the Union. The Middleveld Region has over one third of the total private acreage in timber, mainly in wattle trees, and produces some grains, mainly maize. Both regions have considerable numbers of livestock, a situation usually correlated with a large Native population. Together they have nearly 17 per cent of all cattle in South Africa; over 14 per cent of the poultry; 14 per cent of the goats; 9 per cent of the horses, mules, and donkeys; and 9 per cent of the pigs.

Permanent and seasonal labor requirements are heavy in both these regions. Although Asiatics (Indians) constitute an important part of the permanent labor force in the sugar-cane area, Natives supply most of the permanent and seasonal labor requirements of this area. In spite of the fact that the area has a fairly dense and well-distributed Native population, considerable difficulty is at times experienced in securing sufficient labor, especially seasonal labor. The Native population of Natal, as was pointed out earlier, p. 32, is poorly utilized, and considerable numbers of Natives are recruited outside of Natal for work in agriculture.

General Area No. 6 includes the Highveld Region of Natal, the East Highveld, Central Highveld, and West Highveld Regions of the Transvaal, and the Northeast, Northwest, and Southeast Regions of the Orange Free State. Over most of this area, rainfall, which comes mainly in the spring and summer, averages around 30 inches a year. Most of the area consists of a high, relatively flat, inland plateau, with occasional ranges of low hills.

There are nearly 48,000 European-occupied farms in the seven regions together, covering a total area of 25,373,000 morgen. The area thus has about 47 per cent of all European-occupied farms in South Africa and just over 25 per cent of all land in such farms. The average size of farms varies from about 390 morgen (about 820 acres) in the Central Highveld

Region of the Transvaal to 750 morgen (nearly 1,600 acres) in the Highveld Region of Natal.

These seven regions have in their borders what is known as the "maize triangle" of South Africa. Together they have nearly 83 per cent of all the area under maize in South Africa. The Northeast and Southeast Regions of the Orange Free State are also important in production of the small grains (wheat, barley, and oats), having just over 21 per cent of the total area in South Africa under these crops. Livestock raising, either in combination with cereal production or as a ranching enterprise, is also of considerable importance in these regions. Together they have just over 40 per cent of all cattle in South Africa; nearly 42 per cent of all poultry; 39 per cent of all pigs; 32 per cent of all horses, mules, and donkeys; and 33 per cent of all woolled sheep. Three of the regions in this area, namely, Highveld (Natal) and the East and Central Highvelds (Transvaal), have considerable areas under commercial timber, mainly eucalyptus and wattle trees, and together just over one fourth of all privately owned timber acreage. The Central Highveld Region of the Transvaal is important in the production of citrus and deciduous fruits, having 8.58 per cent of all citrus trees and 14.68 per cent of all deciduous fruit trees in South Africa. The Central and East Highveld Regions of the Transvaal produce most of the non-Turkish types of tobacco grown in the Union and also most of the groundnuts (peanuts).

This general area, as one of the most important agricultural areas in the Union of South Africa, requires a considerable number of Natives for both permanent and seasonal labor. The area has a large Native population which would be adequate, were it not that large numbers of them are drawn off annually for work in the gold and coal mines and industries located principally in the central region. Furthermore, the labor-tenant system, still prevalent in much of this area, results in a very poor utilization of a large part of the Native population living in rural areas. Farming areas adjacent to large urban centers and at a distance from Native reserves usually experience much difficulty in securing permanent labor and still more difficulty in meeting their seasonal labor requirements. The labor shortage of farmers distant from large cities or near to Native reserves is much less acute.

General Area No. 7 includes only the extensive Lowveld Region of the Transvaal. Although, as the name implies, it covers that part of the Transvaal of relatively low elevation, it has a very varied climate. In the northwestern section, rainfall does not exceed 25 inches a year, whereas in the eastern section[2] rainfall is very heavy, exceeding in some small areas 70 inches a year. Much of the area is mountainous, but there are numerous wide, sheltered valleys and low-lying plateaus.

The Lowveld Region has about 5.5 per cent of the European-occupied farms in South Africa, which cover about 6.2 per cent of the total area in such farms. The average size farm is about 1,100 morgen (just over 2,300 acres). The farms are much bigger in the northern than in the eastern section of the region. Although this region has large numbers of all types of livestock, its chief importance lies in its production of semitropical fruits. Nearly 36 per cent of the citrus fruit trees and just over 85 per cent of the mango, pawpaw, and avocado trees of the Union are located in the Lowveld Region.

The Lowveld Region has need for a considerable amount of both permanent and seasonal labor. Its large Native population, however, is more than adequate to supply its needs. Shortage of agricultural labor is less acute in this than in any other part of South Africa, the Transkei excepted.

To summarize: Sheep and goat production predominates over most of the western and central portion of the Cape Province and spreads into the Orange Free State and the southern part of the Transvaal. Cattle production, on the other hand, is concentrated in the eastern third of South Africa, running from the Border Region north through the Transvaal and Orange Free State. Wheat, barley, rye, and oats production is concentrated largely in the Southwest district of the Cape Prov-

[2] The eastern section includes the famous Kruger National Park, an area covering some 8,000 square miles and stretching along the border of Portuguese East Africa or Moçambique. There are very few Natives in this area and practically no agriculture.

ince and the Northeast and Southeast Regions of the Orange Free State along the Basutoland border. Sugar-cane production is all concentrated in the Coast Region of Natal. Crops, other than cereals and sugar cane, are produced mostly in the Southwest district of the Cape Province and in Natal and the Transvaal. The largest concentration of deciduous fruit trees is in the Southwest Region of the Cape Province, which also has the preponderance of vines in South Africa. Lesser concentrations of deciduous fruits are found in the South Karroo Region, the Southwest Region of the Orange Free State, and the Central Highveld Region of the Transvaal. Citrus fruit production is widely scattered—some in the Southwest Cape Province, some in the eastern part of the Coast Region of the Cape Province, in Natal, and in the Lowveld Region of the Transvaal. Semi-tropical fruits, including pineapples and bananas, are found in the eastern part of the South Coast Region, Border Region, Coast Region of Natal, and Lowveld Region of the Transvaal.

CHAPTER 8

THE MINING INDUSTRY[1]

MENTION WAS made earlier of the fact that all industries in South Africa compete for what may be regarded as a common pool of unskilled Native labor. Although large numbers of Natives live permanently on farms and acquire considerable skill as agricultural laborers, they are not debarred thereby from seeking employment in cities whenever they so desire. There are no strong labor unions among Natives in either the city or country. Native labor is regarded as being unskilled whether it is in the city or in the country.[2] It is not uncommon for a Native to work in successive years in two or more different types of occupation, and often in different localities.

No industry has had a more profound effect upon the employment of Natives than mining, which, directly and indirectly, gives employment to more Natives than any other, for, as will be shown later, many manufacturing industries exist merely to supply the needs of the mining industry. Furthermore, this industry, especially the gold mining industry, is more highly localized than any other. Finally, wage policies adopted during the early days of the mining industry have had a profound effect upon the wage structure of the country right up to the present time.

[1] Except where otherwise stated, much of the factual information in this section was obtained from the *Official Yearbooks of the Union of South Africa*, No. 4 (1910-1920), and No. 20 (1939), and from the *Annual Report of the Government Mining Engineer for the Calendar Year Ended 31st. December, 1938* (Pretoria, Department of Mines, Government Printer, 1939).

[2] It should not be inferred that Natives are incapable of acquiring skill. Because of custom and attitudes of Europeans, Natives have come to be regarded as unskilled laborers no matter what type of work they do.

History.—South Africa is a country rich in minerals, especially the precious minerals. There is evidence that gold was mined in South Africa long before the country was settled by Europeans and that the Natives used coal and iron in the manufacture of their crude implements and arms. The commercial use of these minerals, however, did not begin until the last half of the nineteenth century. The first mineral worked on a commercial basis was copper, production of which began in the Namaqualand district of the Cape Colony in 1852. Between 1854 and 1903 nearly 1,200,000 tons of copper ore were exported from the colony. Although copper deposits have been worked in many parts of the country, the most important workings are in Namaqualand and at Messina in the Northern Transvaal. The peak of copper production seems to have been reached in 1914 and 1915, when about 29,000 tons of copper (not ore) were exported. During the period 1934 to 1938 shipments of copper averaged just over 13,000 tons a year.

Coal was used by the early settlers for fuel, but the mining of coal on a commercial scale did not begin until the establishment of the diamond and gold mining industries developed a demand for power. The first important production of coal—16,500 tons—took place in the Cape of Good Hope in 1885. Since then coal mining has expanded rapidly, and by 1904 the total output of the four colonies (now provinces) had reached 3,500,000 tons a year valued at £1,560,000 (table XVIII). By 1920 output had increased to nearly 11,500,000 tons valued at £4,500,000 and by 1938 to 17,500,000 tons valued at £4,700,000. Some coal is mined in all four provinces, but in 1938 the Transvaal alone produced 11,500,000 tons or nearly 66 per cent of the total for the Union. Natal produced 4,500,000, the Orange Free State just over 1,500,000, and the Cape Province only 3,000 tons.

Within a few years after diamonds were discovered in 1870, this industry expanded into the most important single commercial industry in the country. Between 1883 and 1901 over 61,000,000 carats of diamonds valued at £84,000,000 were produced. Up to 1938 the accumulated total value of diamonds

The Mining Industry

produced was about £327,772,000. The most important mining areas are in and around Kimberley in the Cape Province and the Premier Mine near Pretoria, the capital of the Union. There are, however, also extensive alluvial diamond diggings in various parts of the Cape Province, Transvaal, and Orange Free State. The diamond mining industry is subject to sudden and violent fluctuations, associated with changes in world-wide economic conditions. Between 1884 and 1913 the value of output of diamonds increased somewhat irregularly from £2,600,000 to £11,400,000 (table XVIII and figure 11). In 1914, how-

TABLE XVIII

VALUE OF OUTPUT OF MINING INDUSTRY, UNION OF SOUTH AFRICA, 1884-1938
(in £1,000's)

Year	Gold*	Dia-* monds	Coal†	All other‡	Total	Year	Gold	Dia- monds	Coal	All other	Total
1884	10	2,563	‡	......	......	1911	35,041	8,747	1,935	......	......
1885	6	2,229				1912	38,686	10,061	1,999	1,303	52,049
1886	35	3,345				1913	37,273	11,390	2,240	1,400	52,303
1887	169	4,126				1914	35,664	5,487	2,259	1,336	44,746
1888	967	3,689				1915	38,639	400	2,142	1,859	43,040
1889	1,491	4,168				1916	39,491	5,728	2,740	1,988	49,947
1890	1,870	3,837				1917	38,308	7,714	3,276	2,073	51,371
1891	2,924	3,557				1918	35,759	7,115	3,225	1,639	47,738
1892	4,541	3,799				1919	39,280§	11,734	3,416	1,450	55,880
1893	5,480	4,041	322			1920	45,606§	14,763	4,520	1,885	66,774§
1894	7,667	3,510	430			1921	43,082§	3,103	5,072	1,000	52,257§
1895	8,570	3,983	596			1922	32,343§	2,267	3,395	609	38,614§
1896	8,604	4,034	721			1923	41,575§	6,033	3,714	1,311	52,633§
1897	11,654	3,822	826			1924	44,739§	8,033	3,825	1,747	58,344§
1898	16,241	4,128	962			1925	40,768§	8,198	3,862	1,659	54,487§
1899	15,452	3,827	893			1926	42,285	10,684	4,047	1,679	58,695
1900	1,481	3,366	591			1927	42,998	12,392	3,826	1,942	61,158
1901	1,097	5,388	1,059			1928	43,982	16,678	3,673	2,073	66,406
1902	7,297	4,953	1,308			1929	44,229	10,590	3,778	2,306	60,903
1903	12,622	5,248	1,476			1930	45,420	8,341	3,494	2,030	59,285
1904	16,018	7,209	1,561			1931	46,206	4,183	3,033	1,473	54,895
1905	20,848	6,205	1,514			1932	49,098	1,680	2,733	851	54,362
1906	24,606	9,597	1,584			1933	68,687§	1,560	2,918	1,274	74,439§
1907	27,401	9,986	1,737			1934	72,311§	1,438	3,154	1,468	78,371§
1908	29,973	5,407	1,747			1935	76,533§	2,171	3,540	1,827	84,071§
1909	30,988	7,199	1,756			1936	79,495§	2,125	3,950	2,947	88,517§
1910	31,973	8,189	1,867	1,300		1937	82,557§	3,445	4,206	4,084	94,292§
						1938	86,670§	3,496	4,729	3,895	98,790§

*Up to 1901. Includes production for Cape of Good Hope only; 1902 and 1903 include also Transvaal; 1904 onwards, all provinces.
†1893-1896, output of Natal and Transvaal only; 1897-1903, output of Transvaal, Natal and Cape of Good Hope; 1904 onwards, output of all four colonies and provinces.
‡Data inadequate
§Realized value for gold. All other years gold valued at £4.24773 per fine ounce.
Source of data: *Official Yearbooks of the Union of South Africa*, No. 1 (1910-1916), pp. 428-475; No. 20 (1939), pp. 817-888 and *Annual Report of the Government Mining Engineer* for 1938, Sec. III, Tables 11-16.

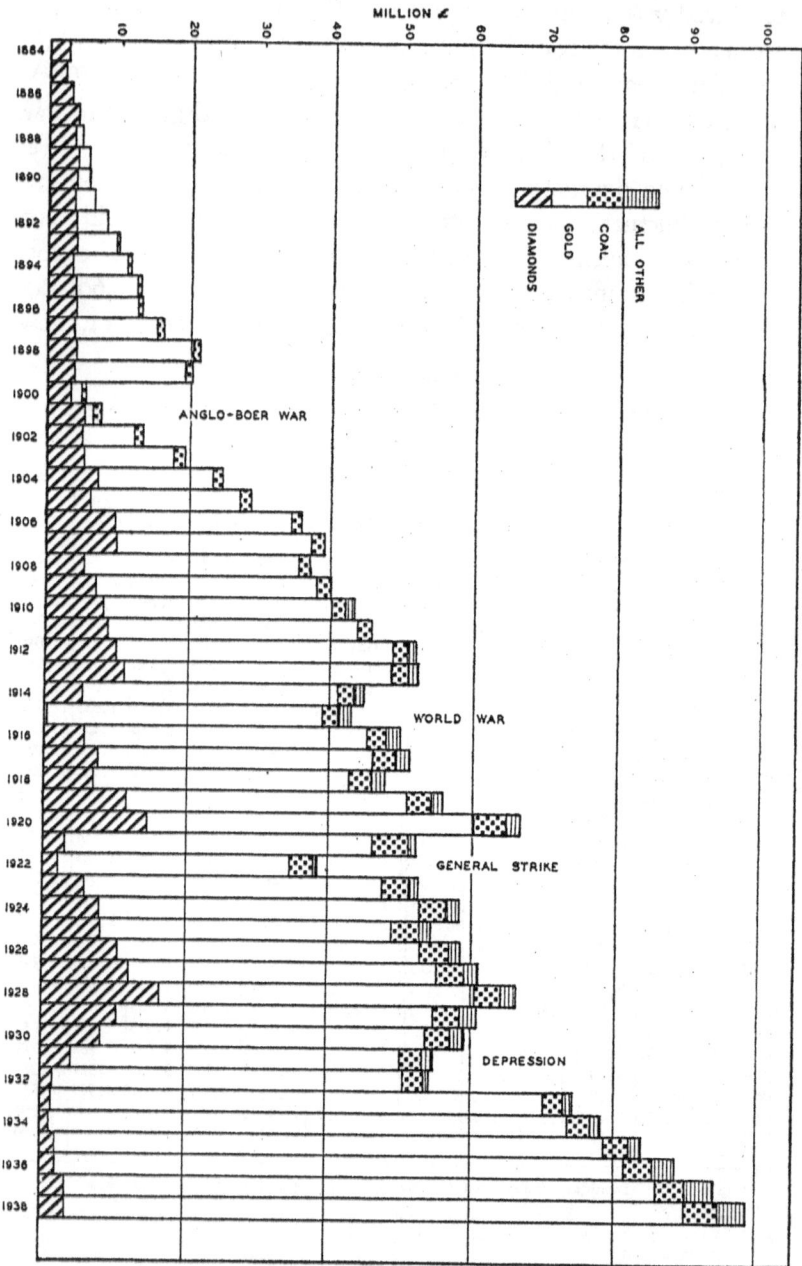

FIGURE 11. Value of output of minerals. Data are from above table XVIII except for insertions, "Anglo-Boer War," "World War," etc.

ever, the value of output declined by over 50 per cent to £5,487,000 and in 1915 to a mere £400,000. During the next few years, however, output again expanded rapidly so that by 1920 the value had increased to nearly £14,800,000. This was followed by another severe slump in the post-war depression years, the value of output in 1922 being £2,270,000. There was, however, another rapid expansion until 1928 when the value of output reached the all-time high of nearly £16,700,000. Another violent contraction took place during the depression years, the output of 1934 being only £1,400,000. Some recovery has since taken place, but in 1938 the value of output was still under £3,500,000. Since 1931 most of the diamond mines around Kimberley and the Premier Mine, which are under the control of the De Beers Corporation, have been closed down or are working on much reduced schedules. A considerable proportion of the output within recent years has been from individually-owned alluvial diamond diggings.

The existence of gold in South Africa was mentioned as early as 1868. Further discoveries were made in 1870, 1873, and 1882. It was not, however, until 1884 that work was begun on what has since become the world-famous Witwatersrand gold fields. The gold mining industry really dates from 1886, when Johannesburg was founded and extensive mining operations began. Up to 1902 the Witwatersrand area had produced 20,797,000 fine ounces of gold, and other districts in the Transvaal another 1,699,000 out of a total of 22,503,000 for what are now the four provinces. Between 1884 and 1938 South Africa had produced 340,116,000 fine ounces of gold, of which 324,620,000 came from the Witwatersrand area alone. During the period 1920 to 1929, the Union of South Africa accounted for over 50 per cent of the annual output of gold in the world. Since then, although production in that country has continued to expand (from 10,716,000 ounces in 1930 to 12,161,000 in 1938), the rapid expansion of gold mining in the United States of America, in Canada, in the U.S.S.R., and in other countries has reduced South Africa's share of world output to less than 40 per cent.

The value of gold produced in South Africa increased steadily from £10,000 in 1884 to £16,241,000 in 1898 (table XVIII and figure 11). During the Anglo-Boer War (October 11, 1899 to May 31, 1902), however, gold mining operations were practically suspended, the value of gold produced being just over £1,000,000 in 1901. From 1902 till 1912 output of gold expanded steadily, the value in 1912 being £38,686,000. During the World War years (1914-18) output remained fairly steady around £38,000,000 a year. Although volume of output did not expand greatly during the first few years after 1919, the realized value of output increased to £45,600,000 in 1920 and exceeded £40,000,000 each year until 1925, with the exception of the year 1922 when output was greatly curtailed during a prolonged period of labor difficulties. A steady increase in volume and value took place from 1926 to 1932. In December of that year South Africa went off the gold standard and reattached the pound (South Africa) to sterling. As a result the realized value of gold jumped nearly £20,000,000 in one year. Although the volume of gold increased from 11,558,000 ounces in 1932 to 12,191,000 in 1938, the realized value increased during the same period from £49,098,000 (gold at £4.24773 per fine ounce) to £86,670,000.

South Africa also produces a large number of other minerals, most of which are of comparatively minor importance as compared with gold, diamonds, and coal (table XIX). Detailed data are not available in regard to the value and output of most of the other minerals (excluding copper and tin) prior to 1912. In that year the value of other minerals (excluding the value of products manufactured from sand and stone, pottery, tiles, bricks, etc.) was £1,303,000. Between 1912 and 1938 there was an upward trend in the combined value of all other minerals, although violent fluctuations characterized such values during the whole of this period. In 1938 gold alone (at realized value) accounted for 87.8 per cent of the total value of all mineral production in South Africa, coal for 4.8 per cent, diamonds for 3.5 per cent, and all other minerals together for 3.9 per cent. The Transvaal greatly exceeds all other provinces in

TABLE XIX
QUANTITY AND VALUE OF MINERALS PRODUCED: UNION OF SOUTH AFRICA 1938

Classification	Quantity units	Quantity	Value £
Gold	Fine oz.	12,161,392	86,669,623*
Coal	Tons	17,536,230	4,729,423†
Diamonds	Carats	1,238,608	3,496,243
Lime and limestone	Tons	2,157,573	802,663
Manganese ore	"	422,757	560,602
Copper	"	14,683	464,466
Asbestos	"	22,282	424,078
Chrome ore	"	128,899	239,888
Platinum	Oz.	38,862	223,776
Coke	Tons	179,630	201,582
Iron ore	"	557,015	134,551
Silver	Fine oz.	1,135,374	99,674
Tin	Tons	1,156	98,108
Iron Pyrites	"	34,191	39,194
Gypsum	"	42,824	37,024
Osmiridium	Fine oz.	5,884	36,523
Soda	Tons	2,275	29,305
Mineral paints	"	6,002	21,809
Tungsten ores	"	111	16,786
Fluorspar	"	5,207	12,705
Coal tar and by-products	..	.....	14,809
Mineral fertilizers	Tons	15,635	12,462
Corundum	"	1,540	12,454
Miscellaneous minerals‡	..	.....	26,366
Other products (mostly quarry)	..	.....	385,417
Total	..	.....	98,789,531

*Gold at realized value. At standard par, £4.24733 per fine ounce, the value was £51,658,311. *Annual Report of the Government Mining Engineer* for 1938, Sec. III, table 11.
†Includes coke (£201,582), tar (£5,242), and other by-products (£9,567).
‡Includes beryl (emerald crystals) (£8,601), magnesite (£5,449), mica (£2,697), natural gas (CO$_2$) (£2,610), talc (£2,558), and bismuth, graphite, kaolin, kieselguhr, lead, tantalite.
Source of data: *Official Yearbook of the Union of South Africa*, No. 20 (1939), pp. 828-829.

regard to the value of its mineral production. Out of the total of £98,790,000, the Transvaal alone accounted for £91,845,000, the Cape Province for only £4,402,000, Natal for £1,858,000, and the Orange Free State for £684,000.

Employment.—Although the mining industry of South Africa was firmly established by 1910, when the Union of South Africa was created, data on the number of persons engaged in mining are fragmentary prior to that year. In 1910 there were some 296,500 persons employed in all branches of mining and allied activities, of whom 75.7 per cent were engaged in gold mining, 12.9 per cent in diamond mining, 7.8

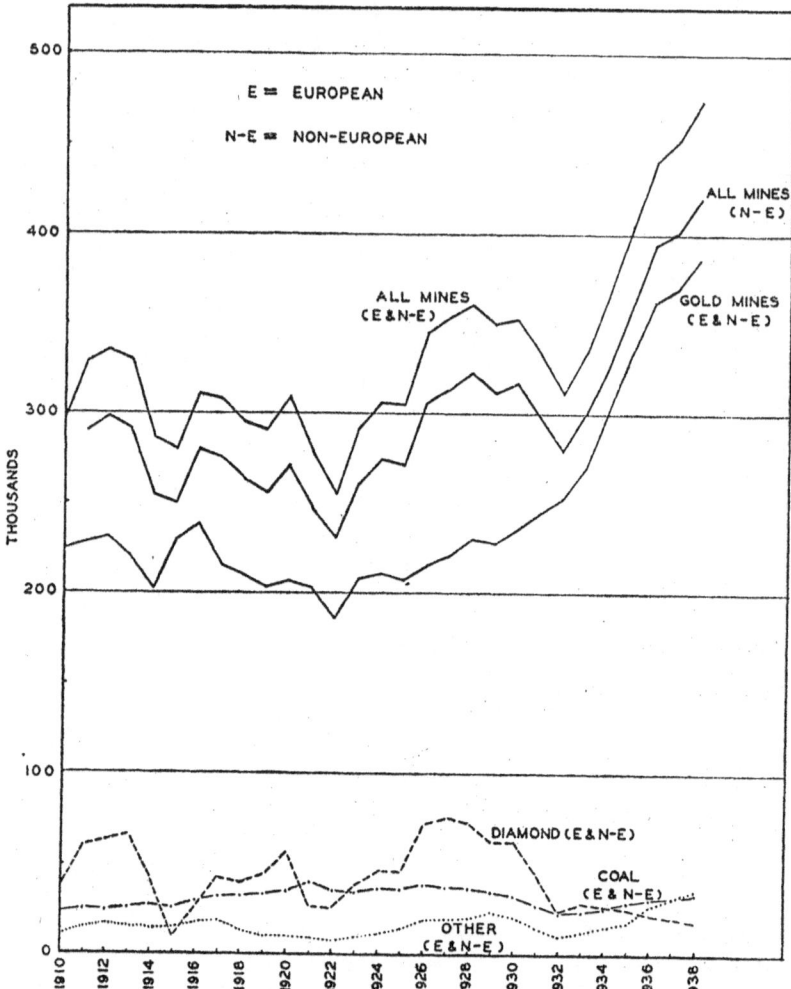

FIGURE 12. Number of persons employed in mining. Data from Appendix, table 7.

per cent in coal mining, and 3.6 per cent in other mining activities (Appendix, table 7, and figure 12). By 1912 the number of employees in mining had increased to 335,000. During the World War the number of employees declined somewhat, the number in 1918 being practically the same as in 1910. In 1922, the year of the general strike, the number declined to

255,700. Thereafter there was a sustained upward trend in employment, which reached a peak of 360,800 in 1928, followed by a downward trend to 311,000 in 1932. From then onwards, however, with the prosperity in the gold mining industry, employment increased rapidly, reaching a new peak of 474,600 in 1938.

TABLE XX

EMPLOYEES IN MINING INDUSTRY OF UNION OF SOUTH AFRICA

Year	Gold	Diamonds	Coal	All other	Total all branches	Europeans	Non-Europeans
1911	228,875	60,476	24,446	14,707	328,504	38,282	290,222
1916	238,054	25,907	29,252	17,467	310,680	31,124	279,556
1921	202,930	27,276	39,911	8,611	278,728	31,624	247,104
1926	215,747	72,041	38,312	18,518	344,618	39,029	305,589
1931	344,987	46,402	27,577	14,174	333,140	34,667	298,473
1936	361,459	22,120	30,925	26,909	441,413	47,090	394,323
1937	369,489	20,370	31,761	31,479	453,099	50,211	402,888
1938	386,607	18,722	33,678	35,581	474,588	53,131	421,457
Per cent of total employed							
1911	69.7	18.4	7.4	4.5	100.0	11.6	88.4
1916	76.6	8.4	9.4	5.6	100.0	10.0	90.0
1921	72.8	9.8	14.3	3.1	100.0	11.3	88.7
1926	62.6	20.9	11.1	5.4	100.0	11.3	88.3
1931	73.5	13.9	8.3	4.3	100.0	10.4	89.6
1936	81.9	5.0	7.0	6.1	100.0	10.7	89.3
1937	81.5	4.5	7.0	7.0	100.0	11.1	88.9
1938	81.5	3.9	7.1	7.5	100.0	11.2	88.9

Source of data: Appendix, table 7.

There were, however, significant differences in the trend of employment in the various mining activities. In gold mining the trend was upward from 1910 to 1912 followed by a decline to 1914, a sharp increase to 1916, and a gradual downward trend till 1922. In that year the gold mining industry employed only 186,300 persons as compared with 224,300 in 1910 and 238,000 in 1916. From 1923 onwards there was a sustained upward trend reaching a peak of 386,600 in 1938, or about 72 per cent in excess of the number employed in 1910. Practically the whole of this increase had taken place since 1929, in which year only 1,500 more persons were employed than in 1910. Although the output of gold had increased by somewhat more than 25 per cent between 1910 and 1929, the number of employees had remained practically stationary, indicating a marked increase in efficiency per employee. The gold mining industry since 1910 has given employment to from 62.6 to 82.4 per cent of all persons engaged in mining activities. It is during periods of war and depression that the percentage of employment in gold mining is highest. This is due to the fact that during such periods the demand for gold remains firm or is increased, whereas the demand for luxury products like diamonds declines. The gold mining industry thus affords more stable employment than most other branches of mining.

In the diamond mining industry employment reached a peak in 1913, when 66,300 persons were employed. This was followed by a violent decline during the first two years of the war to 9,300 in 1915. From 1915 to 1927, although the general trend of employment was again upward, reaching a new peak of 75,600 in the latter year, there were marked fluctuations in the intervening years. From 1927 onwards there was another sharp decline, the number of employees reaching only 18,700 in 1938. As diamonds are a luxury product and thus greatly affected by changes in world-wide business conditions, employment in that industry is of a very unstable character. This industry employed 20.2 per cent of all persons engaged in mining activity in 1913 but only 3.3 per cent in 1915, 9.8 per cent in 1921, 21.4 per cent in 1927, and 3.9 per cent in 1938.

For the coal mining industry the trend of employment was gradually upward from 23,200 in 1910 to 39,900 in 1921. For the next eight years (1922 to 1929), employment in the coal mining industry remained fairly steady, around 36,000 persons. Between 1929 and 1932, however, there was a sharp decline in employment, the number employed in that year being about the same as in 1910. Employment again increased to 33,700 in 1938, which was still somewhat below the level for 1929. The number of persons employed in coal mining in 1938 was about 45 per cent greater than in 1910; output of coal, however, had increased during the same period from 7,112,000 tons to 17,536,000, an increase of 146 per cent, again indicating a great increase in efficiency per laborer. The coal mining industry during the period 1914 to 1929 employed between 9 and 14 per cent of all persons engaged in mining, the average being about 11 per cent. During the past seven years, however, this industry, although prosperous, employed only about 7 per cent of all persons engaged in mining.

The number of persons engaged in other branches of mining (excluding gold, diamonds and coal) increased somewhat irregularly from 10,800 in 1910 to 18,100 in 1917 and thereafter declined to 7,400 in 1922. From then to 1929 there was again a steady increase to 23,500, followed by a rapid decline to 10,100 in 1932, the number being about the same as in 1910. By 1938 the number of persons employed in other branches of mining had increased to an all-time peak of 35,600, an increase of 228 per cent since 1910. These branches of mining in 1938 employed 7.5 per cent of all persons engaged in mining activity.

Throughout the whole of the period 1911 to 1938 the proportion of Europeans to non-Europeans employed in the mining industry has remained remarkably constant. Excluding the unusual year 1922 (general strike) the percentage of Europeans employed has varied from 10.0 per cent in 1916 to 12.5 per cent in 1920. In only two years did the proportion of Europeans exceed 11.6 per cent and in only two years did the proportion decline below 10.4 per cent. Under the circumstances the trends in total number of persons engaged in mining represent closely the trends in numbers of both Europeans and non-Europeans engaged in mining activities. The number of Europeans increased from 37,500 in 1910 to 53,100 in 1938, an increase of nearly 42 per cent. The number of non-Europeans increased during the same period from 291,600 to 421,500, also an increase of nearly 42 per cent.

The ratio of Europeans to non-Europeans, however, varies considerably in the different branches of mining. In 1938 the large gold mines employed 41,739 Europeans out of a total of 370,836, the Europeans thus constituting 11 per cent of the total. In the diamond mines there were 1,429 Europeans out of a total of 6,544, or 21.8 per cent. Of the 33,678 employees in the coal mines only 1,931 or 5.7 per cent were Europeans. Included in the 31,747 non-Europeans employed in coal mining are 634 Asiatics. The proportion of Asiatics employed in coal mining, however, has declined considerably and steadily during the past three decades. In 1911 this industry employed 23,214 non-Europeans of whom 4,466 were Asiatics. Practically all the non-Europeans engaged in other mining activities are Natives. In 1938, excluding the coal mines, only 208 Asiatics were engaged in mining. The number of Colored persons employed is small. In the Transvaal where 384,700 of the 420,600 persons classified as "Natives and others" are employed in mining, the total Colored population (men, women, and children) was only 50,800 in 1936. Probably not more than 10,000 of these would be males, eligible for employment in mining, manufacturing, transportation, and commerce. Although it is dangerous to hazard a guess, it is doubtful whether more than 10,000 Colored persons are engaged in mining in the whole of South Africa.

Wage Trends.—Comparable data on wages paid to Europeans and Asiatics are not readily available prior to 1911. Since that date, however, the Government Mining Engineer has included in his annual report the number of Europeans and non-Europeans employed in each of the main branches of mining and also the total salaries and wages paid such employees. The average annual wage paid to European and non-European employees has been estimated by dividing the total wages paid to each racial group in the large gold mines, in the diamond mines, and in the coal mines by the number of each racial group in these branches of mining. Several significant differences are apparent in the trends of wages and the levels of wages of each racial group and in the different branches of mining.

Wages Paid to Europeans.—In the gold mining industry wages paid to Europeans, which averaged around £330 a year during the years 1911 to 1915, rose rapidly during the World War, reaching an average of £501 a year in 1920, but declined sharply to £372 in 1923 (Appendix, table 8 and figure 13).

From 1924 until 1933 average wages paid to Europeans remained fairly steady around £375 a year, or about 13 per cent above the 1911 level. After 1933 average wages increased steadily to nearly £404 in 1938, or about 21 per cent above the 1911 level. The gold mining industry employed 41,700 Europeans in 1938 as compared with 25,700 in 1911.

In the diamond mining industry average wages paid to Europeans fluctuated violently during the period under review, and at a lower level than in the gold mining industry. Average wages paid to Europeans, which in the diamond mining industry averaged £266 a year in 1911, increased from £262 in 1914 to £412 a year in 1920, declined to £290 a year in 1922, but from then on increased steadily to £347 a year in 1929, or nearly 31 per cent above the 1911 level. During the first three years of the depression, wages declined to £238 a year, or just 90 per cent of the 1911 level. Thereafter wages again increased sharply, reaching £327 a year in 1938 or 23.0 per cent above the 1911 level. In 1938, however, the diamond mining industry employed only 5,115 Europeans as compared with 38,750 in 1911.

European wages in the coal mining industry averaged below that in the gold mining industry until 1922 but since then have been consistently above. In 1911 average European wages in the coal mining industry were about £290 a year. By 1921 they had increased to £466 a year, or nearly 66 per cent above the 1911 level. After declining to £397 a year by 1924, they increased steadily to £419 a year in 1928, or nearly 45 per cent above the 1911 level. By 1932 the level of wages had declined to £394 but thereafter increased steadily to £403.9 in 1938, or over 39 per cent higher than the 1911 level.

Wages Paid to Non-Europeans.—In comparing the trends of wages paid to non-Europeans in the three main branches of mining with those of Europeans, it is necessary to bear in mind that Natives employed in gold mining and in coal mining are provided with food, quarters, and medical attention as well as with a cash wage. In the diamond mining industry Natives are provided with quarters and medical care but have to provide their food out of their cash wage, which averages about £10 above that received by Natives in the gold mining industry. It must also be remembered that in 1911 approximately 20 per cent of the non-Europeans employed in coal mining were Asiatics, who usually receive a wage somewhat above that paid to Natives. The percentage of Asiatics employed in coal mining has, however, gradually declined to just over 2 per cent of non-Europeans in 1938.

The average cash wage received by non-Europeans (almost entirely Natives) in the gold mining industry increased from £28.5 a year in 1911 to £34.1 in 1923, averaging just over £33 a year from 1924 to 1932 (Appendix, table 9 and figure 13). After a slight decline to £32.8 a year by 1934, they again increased slightly to £34.6 in 1938. Average cash wages of Natives did not increase, relatively, to nearly the same extent as average European wages during the World War, being only 15 per cent higher in 1920 than in 1911, whereas average European wages were over 50 per cent higher. On the other hand, average cash wages of Natives continued to increase after the World War and during the period 1921 to 1932 averaged about 17 per cent higher than in 1915. European wages, as was pointed out above, declined rapidly between 1920 and 1922 and from 1923 to 1933 averaged only about 13 per cent higher than in 1911. In 1938 both average cash wages of Natives and average European wages were about 21.3 per cent above the 1911 levels.

Average cash wages of non-Europeans in the coal mining industry increased from £21.0 a year in 1911 to £29.2 a year in 1920, an increase of 39.7 per cent. By 1922 the average cash wage had declined to £27.1, increased slightly in 1923, and from then till 1930 averaged around £28.0 a year. A decline to £26.6 a year in 1933 was followed by a gradual recovery to £28.7, which was 37.3 per cent higher than in 1911. In that year the average cash wage of non-Europeans in the coal mining industry was £7.6 below that of Natives in the gold mining industry. In 1929 the difference was only £3.6 and in 1938 nearly £6.0.

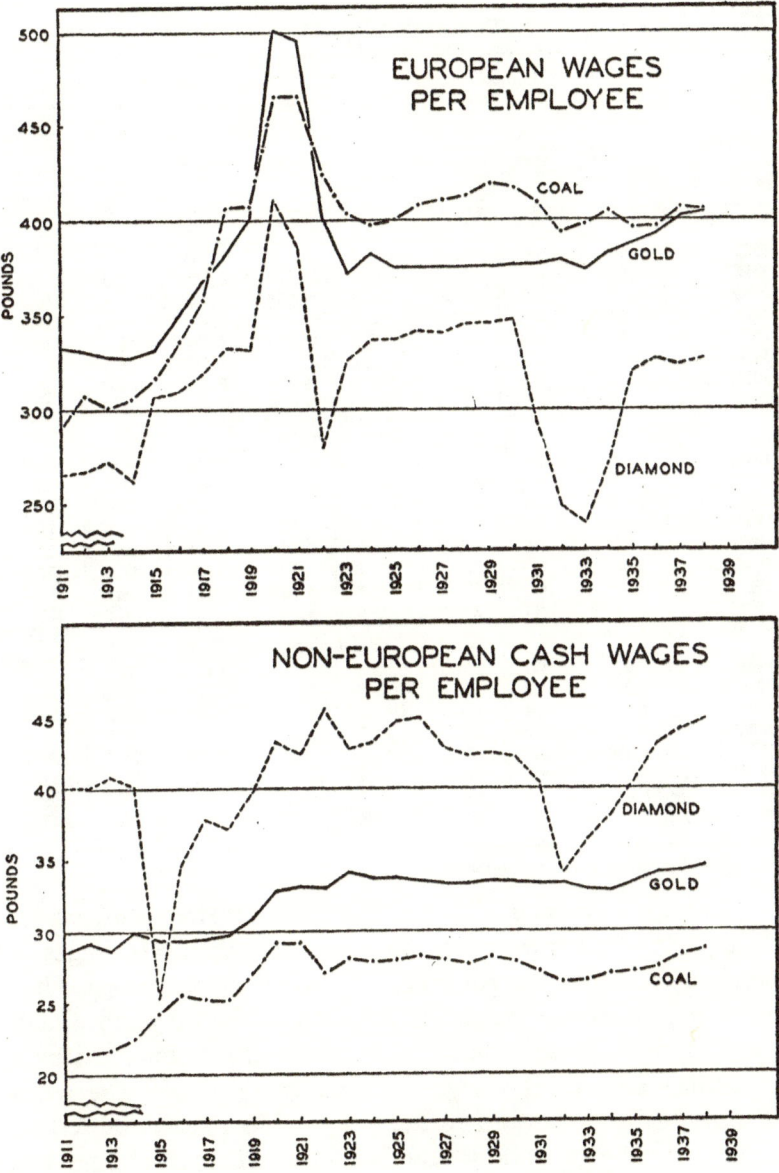

FIGURE 13. Annual wages of Europeans and non-Europeans in mining. Data from Appendix, tables 8 and 9.

TABLE XXI
EUROPEAN AND NON-EUROPEAN WAGES IN THE MINING INDUSTRY

Year	European wages				Non-European wages in cash			
	Number employed	Total wages (£1,000's)	Average annual wages per employee (£'s)	Per cent change in wages per employee 1911=100	Number employed	Total wages (£1,000's)	Average annual wages per employee (£'s)	Per cent change in wages per employee 1911=100
Gold mining								
1911	25,664	8,545	332.9	100.0	201,159	5,743	28.5	100.0
1916	22,922	8,034	350.5	105.3	213,512	6,268	29.4	103.2
1921	21,455	10,641	496.0	149.0	179,987	5,965	33.1	116.1
1926	20,408	7,654	375.0	112.7	192,838	6,461	33.5	117.5
1931	23,159	8,724	376.7	113.2	219,266	7,293	33.3	116.8
1936	36,440	14,330	393.2	118.1	310,073	10,587	34.1	119.6
1937	39,230	15,738	401.2	120.5	314,378	10,753	34.2	120.0
1938	41,739	16,856	403.8	121.3	329,094	11,409	34.6	121.4
Diamond mining								
1911	4,646	1,234	265.6	100.0	38,750	1,556	40.1	100.0
1916	1,973	611	309.7	116.6	11,422	395	34.6	86.3
1921	2,699	1,039	385.0	145.0	7,710	327	42.4	105.7
1926	2,938	1,003	341.4	128.5	17,521	785	44.8	111.7
1931	2,398	697	290.7	109.5	10,032	405	40.4	100.7
1936	1,009	329	326.1	122.8	2,786	120	43.1	107.5
1937	1,374	445	323.9	122.0	5,059	223	44.1	110.0
1938	1,429	467	326.8	123.0	5,115	229	44.8	111.7
Coal mining								
1911	1,232	357	289.8	100.0	23,214	485	20.9	100.0
1916	1,355	455	335.8	115.9	27,897	715	25.6	122.5
1921	2,133	994	466.0	160.8	37,778	1,102	29.2	139.7
1926	1,736	708	407.8	140.7	36,576	1,035	28.3	135.4
1931	1,450	593	409.0	141.1	26,127	710	27.2	130.1
1936	1,770	703	397.2	137.0	29,155	802	27.5	131.6
1937	1,863	757	406.3	140.2	29,898	849	28.4	135.9
1938	1,931	780	403.9	139.4	31,747	911	28.7	137.3

Source of data: Appendix, tables 8 and 9.

Average cash wages of non-Europeans in the diamond industry have fluctuated much more violently than cash wages of non-Europeans in the gold and coal mining industries. They remained relatively steady at £40 a year between 1911 and 1914, declined sharply to £25.3 a year in 1915, followed by a rapid increase to £45.5 a year in 1922. Thereafter the trend was gradually downward to £42.1 a year in 1930, followed by a sharp decline to £34.0 a year in 1932. Thereafter there was another marked recovery to £44.8 a year in 1938, in which year wages were 11.7 per cent above the level for 1911. The relative increase in average cash wages of non-Europeans in the diamond mining industry between 1911 and 1938 was very much less than the increases in similar wages in the gold and coal mining industries.

Native Wages: Cash and In Kind.—In order to compare European and non-European wages, it is necessary to add to the cash allowance of the latter an amount equal to the value of food, quarters, and medical care and to deduct therefrom such expenses as traveling costs from the Native's home to the center where he is employed. Unfortunately, estimates of the value of food and quarters are available only for the large gold mines of the Witwatersrand. The Chamber of Mines estimated that the average cash wage paid to Natives in 1937 was 2s.2d. per shift and that the average cost to the mines of food, quarters, and medical attention was 11d. per shift.[3] In 1938 the corresponding figures were 2s.3d. and 1s.0d. per shift.[4] On the latter basis, the value of food, quarters, and medical care was 12/27 of the cash wages. Thus the annual average total wage in 1938 was £34.6 plus 12/27 of £34.6 or £50.0, assuming, of course, that each Native was employed a full year. Natives are usually recruited to work for 270 shifts a year, which would mean an average total wage of £43.7.6 (3s.3d. x 270). These two figures represent the average cost of wages per Native worker to the mines for a year or 270 shifts as the case may be.

As the individual mines purchase food and supplies in large quantities, the cost to the mines of food and quarters for Natives is much less than if the Natives had to provide themselves with these items. The Chamber of Mines estimates that in 1938 it would have cost Natives at least 1s.6d. per shift to provide themselves with food and quarters. On this basis, the total value of cash and perquisites to Natives would be 3s.9d. a shift or £50.12.6 for 270 shifts. It would probably be more accurate to use the latter figure in comparing the total wages of Natives employed in gold mining with those of Natives working in industries which do not provide food and quarters.

Although no figures are available, it is probable that the

[3] *Forty-ninth Annual Report* (Transvaal Chamber of Mines, 1938), p. 68.
[4] *Report of the Government Mining Engineer* for 1938, p. 24.

cost to the coal mines of food and quarters for Natives is not much different from the cost of these items to the gold mines. On this assumption food and quarters would cost the coal mines £13.5 for 270 shifts or £14.8 for a full year.[5] The full annual average wage (cash and perquisites) of Natives employed in the coal mines in 1938 would thus have been £43.5. The Wage Board of the Department of Labor ordinarily allows 8s.8d.[6] a month or £5.2 a year in computing the value of quarters supplied to Natives in manufacturing establishments. Adding this amount to the annual wage of non-Europeans employed in diamond mining, the total wage cost to the diamond mines in 1938 would have been £50.0 a year or about the same as in the gold mining industry.

Natives, however, have to meet the expense of getting from their homes in Native territories or country districts to the mining centers, an expense not borne by Europeans, who reside permanently where they are employed. The cost to the Native of railroad and other traveling expenses would of course vary in accordance with the distance he has to travel. A very large proportion of the Natives working in the gold mines is drawn from the Transkeian territories in the Cape Province, from which the return railroad fare varies from about £3.4 to £4.5 plus from 5/- to 10/- for food. It is estimated that traveling costs for Natives from the Transkei take from 15 to 20 per cent of their cash wages. Using the lower figure, the net total wage (cash plus perquisites) of Natives employed in the gold mines in 1938 would have been £50 less 15 per cent of £34.6 or about £45. Natives working underground have, in addition, to bear the cost of two pairs of boots a year estimated at 13s.6d. a pair.[7] Natives going to work in the gold mines for the first time usually start on a wage somewhat lower than the average wage. Within a few months, as they become familiar with working

---

[5] Two hundred and seventy shifts would be completed in 11 months. An additional 26 shifts would be required to complete 12 months work. See *Report of the Native Farm Labour Committee*, 1937-1939 (Pretoria, Government Printer, 1939), p. 26.

[6] *Report of the Native Farm Labour Committee*, 1937-1939, p. 23.

[7] *Ibid.*, p. 26.

routine in the mines, their wages are raised. Natives returning for successive periods of work in the mines are usually started on a higher wage than Natives starting in such work. The absolute difference between the highest and lowest wages paid new and returning workers is not great and probably does not exceed 6d. per day.

Comparison of European and Non-European Wages.—Using £45 as the net total annual wage of Natives employed in the gold mining industry in 1938, it is found that this wage is only one ninth of the annual average wage of £404 earned by Europeans in the gold mines in that year. Considering only cash wages, it is found that although the average cash wages of Europeans and Natives in the gold mines increased in about the same relative proportion (21.3 per cent between 1911 and 1938), the absolute difference of wages widened from £304.4 in the former to £369.2 in the latter year. For the coal mining industry the absolute difference between European and non-European cash wages is even greater than in the gold mining industry, namely £375.2 in 1938. The difference in the diamond mining industry, however, is much less (only £282 in 1938) because of the lower level of European wages and because the non-European wages are inclusive of an allowance for food. A consideration of the trends of European and non-European wages in the mining industry to be complete requires that such wages be related to trends in the cost of living. Such a comparison, however, is rendered difficult by the fact that the cost of living index for the Union of South Africa is based upon items entering largely into the European standard of living and also by the fact that Natives are supplied with food and quarters, or quarters only, important items in a cost of living index, while working in the mining industry. Nevertheless, the cost of living index is indicative of the general trend of costs of goods and services which a Native requires for himself and his family.

Retail prices of food only had increased 23.4 per cent between 1911 and 1938; retail prices of food, fuel, light, and rent, 25.3 per cent; retail prices of these items plus sundries (clothing, shoes, vegetables, etc.), 34.2 per cent. Nominal wages (all occupations) had increased 41.2 per cent. There was thus an increase in real wages, whether measured on the standard basis (food, fuel, light, and rent) or on a complete basis (these items plus sundries). In the case of Europeans employed in the gold mining industry, average wages increased only 21.3 per cent between 1911 and 1938. Assuming a level of wages in 1910 approximately that of 1911, the real wage of European employees in the mining industry, whether measured on the standard or complete basis, declined slightly between 1911 and

TABLE XXII

INDEX NUMBER OF RETAIL PRICES AND OF WAGES (1910-38)

1910 = 100

Year	Retail prices			Wages		
	Food	Food, fuel, light and rent	Food, fuel, light, rent and sundries	Nominal	Real wages*	
					Standard basis	Complete basis
1910	100.0	100.0	100.0	100.0	100.0	100.0
1915	122.8	112.6	114.8	104.8	96.2	94.3
1920	204.8	169.8	195.7	171.7	104.8	90.7
1925	137.8	134.0	144.8	137.8	106.4	98.3
1930	126.4	130.0	139.7	140.0	108.8	100.9
1931	120.5	126.8	134.5	135.3	107.9	101.4
1932	109.9	121.1	128.5	130.6	109.2	102.5
1933	113.1	118.0	125.1	132.0	113.0	106.3
1934	119.0	119.7	126.8	131.9	111.2	104.8
1935	116.9	118.5	126.1	137.2	116.9	109.5
1936	116.3	118.9	126.6	139.5	118.3	110.9
1937	117.7	121.1	129.5	140.0	116.4	108.7
1938	123.4	125.3	134.2	141.2	113.4	105.7

*Standard basis = index of nominal wages divided by index of food, fuel, light, and rent. Complete basis = index of nominal wages divided by index of food, fuel, light, rent, and sundries.
Source of data: *Official Yearbook of the Union of South Africa*, No. 20 (1939), p. 321.

1918, and the same would be true of average cash wages of Natives in the gold mining industry. The same would also be true of real wages of Europeans in the diamond mining industry; there was a more marked decline in the real wages of non-Europeans in this industry. In the coal mining industry real wages of both Europeans and non-Europeans would have increased somewhat.

In regard to real wages of Natives, the above statements

overlook one important factor, namely, that the horizon of demand (or the desire to purchase commodities previously unknown) of Natives has increased far more rapidly than that of Europeans. In his primitive state the Native was satisfied with simple foods, simple clothing, and simple furnishings for his home. As contact with European civilization has increased, the Native has developed a desire for, and purchases whenever possible, certain types of food, clothing, and other commodities which did not figure in his primitive existence. There is thus a growing tendency for Natives to spend a larger proportion of their cash income on items other than essential foods and at the expense of such foods—a situation which, with their low cash income, may result in severe malnutrition for themselves and members of their families. This aspect of the problem will be referred to more fully in a later chapter.

Location of Mining Activity.—The location of mines actively producing in 1938 is shown in table XXIII. Of the 253 mining concerns producing gold in 1938, 131 are in the Central Highveld, 113 in the Lowveld, and 7 in the other two regions of the Transvaal. There was only one producing concern in Natal and only one in the Orange Free State. If consideration is given to the number of employees and output of gold, rather than to the number of concerns, it is found that the gold mines of the Witwatersrand in the Central Transvaal Region had 88 per cent of all persons employed in gold mining and about 92 per cent of all gold produced. Of the 14 active diamond mining concerns, 7 were in the Griqualand and 3 in the Northwest Regions of the Cape Province, 1 in the Transvaal, and 3 in the Orange Free State. Of the 79 coal mining concerns, 47 were in the East Highveld and 8 in the Central Highveld of the Transvaal, 18 in the Highveld Region of Natal, 4 in the Cape Province, and 2 in the Orange Free State. The coal mines of the Transvaal, however, alone produced 64 per cent of all coal produced in South Africa, and those in Natal another 28 per cent.

Of the 187 concerns producing other minerals 61 were located in the Central Highveld, 60 in the Lowveld, and 16 in

TABLE XXIII
LOCATION OF MINING CONCERNS IN UNION OF SOUTH AFRICA, 1938*

Region	Gold	Diamonds	Coal	Other minerals
Cape Province				
Southwest	0	0	0	4
Northwest	0	3	0	19
Bechuanaland	0	0	0	8
Griqualand West	0	7	0	14
Northeast	0	0	4	0
Total Cape	0	10	4	45
Natal				
Highveld	0	0	18	3
Middleveld	1	0	0	2
Total Natal	1	0	18	5
Transvaal				
East Highveld	3	0	47	5
Central Highveld	131	1	8	61
West Highveld	4	0	0	11
Lowveld	113	0	0	60
Total Transvaal	251	1	55	137
Orange Free State				
Northeast	0	0	2	0
Northwest	1	0	0	0
Southwest	0	3	0	0
Total Orange Free State	1	3	2	0
Total Union	253	14	79	187

*Includes only mines actually producing in 1938.
Source of data: *Annual Report of the Government Mining Engineer* for 1938, Department of Mines, table 28.

the other two Regions of the Transvaal; 19 were located in the Northwest, 14 in the Griqualand West, 8 in Bechuanaland, and 4 in the Southwest Regions of the Cape Province; only 5 were located in Natal and none in the Orange Free State. Here again the Transvaal has over 66 per cent of other mining concerns, the Central Highveld Region alone having about 33 per cent.

CHAPTER 9

THE MANUFACTURING INDUSTRY

THE MANUFACTURING industry, domestic service, transportation, government departments and commerce provide employment annually for many thousands of Natives and other non-Europeans. The demand of these undertakings for Native labor has increased considerably in the last decade or two.

History.—Data on the early development of the manufacturing industry in South Africa are meager. A census of industries was taken in the Cape of Good Hope in 1891 and another simultaneously in the four colonies in 1904. A third census of industries was taken as part of the general census in 1911, the first year after Union. Among other things, the Statistics Act of 1914 required the Office of Census and Statistics to make an annual census of manufacturing establishments. This first industrial census was taken in 1915-16 and has been continued annually since, with the exception of the years 1930-31 and 1931-32, when, for reasons of economy, it was temporarily discontinued. The last industrial census available in published form is for the year 1936-37.

Unfortunately, because of changes in the definition of a factory, the information contained in the censuses prior to 1911 is not strictly comparable with the data in the 1915-16 and subsequent censuses. Even after 1915-16 certain changes were introduced which undoubtedly modify to some extent the comparability of the data.[1] For example, in 1916-17 the definition of a factory was changed to include establishments employing

[1] *Census of Industrial Establishments,* 1936-1937 (Pretoria, Office of Census and Statistics, Government Printer, 1939), Introductory Note, p. vii.

three hands instead of four as in 1915-16. In 1919-20 (and subsequently) establishments engaged in the construction of roads, waterways, and irrigation works were included for the first time. In 1921-22 laundries were included for the first time, and since 1925-26 certain industries have been omitted from the census while certain other industries were regrouped. In spite of these defects, however, the data collected in the various industrial censuses from 1915-16 onwards do afford a reasonably accurate picture of the general trend in industrial development.

In 1915-16 there were in South Africa some 4,000 industrial establishments employing just over 100,000 persons (Europeans and non-Europeans) and having a gross value of output of £40,400,000 (table XXIV and figure 14). By 1920-21 the number of establishments had increased to just over 7,000, the number of persons employed to 180,000, and the gross value of output to £98,300,000. This remarkable expansion was due to two factors: First, to the change in definition of a "factory" (three instead of four hands), which greatly increased the number of establishments which could qualify as a factory.[2] Secondly, South Africa, like most other industrially undeveloped countries, was unable to obtain many types of finished goods from the belligerent nations during the World War. As a result, numerous secondary industries sprang up to supply domestic needs wherever possible. Much of the increase in gross value of output per plant was due to the general rise in prices, the physical volume of output increasing to a much smaller degree than gross value of output.

Between 1920-21 and 1925-26 there was very little increase in the number of establishments, although the number of employees increased by about 7 per cent. The gross value of output in 1925-26 was actually lower than in 1920-21. The decline in gross value of output after 1920-21 was due in large measure to the general post-war decline in prices, the lack of growth of

---

[2] The effect of this change in definition is seen by the increase in number of factories from 3,998 in 1915-16 to 5,305 in 1916-17 and in the decline in gross value of output per establishment from £1,011 to £933 and in employees per establishment from 25.3 to 23.3.

The Manufacturing Industry

TABLE XXIV

MANUFACTURING PRODUCTION IN UNION OF SOUTH AFRICA, 1904-1936-37

Year	Number of establishments	Gross value of output Total (in £1,000,000's)	Gross value of output Per establishment (£)	Index of* Gross value of output	Index of* Volume of output (excluding repair work)	Number of employees Total	Number of employees Per establishment
	1	2	3	4	5	6	7
1904	4,841	20.6	.....	.....	.....	86,364	....
1911	2,473	17.2	.....	.....	.....	65,916	....
1915-16	3,998	40.4	1,011	.....	.....	101,178	25.3
1916-17	5,305	49.5	933	376	306	123,842	23.3
1917-18	5,918	60.1	1,016	457	374	134,211	22.7
1918-19	5,968	70.9	1,188	539	425	143,088	24.0
1919-20	6,890	92.9	1,348	706	465	175,520	25.5
1920-21	7,005	98.3	1,403	747	437	179,819	25.7
1921-22	7,055	79.4	1,125	604	429	170,951	24.2
1922-23	7,029	74.5	1,060	566	435	172,047	24.5
1923-24	7,112	79.8	1,122	606	469	182,877	25.7
1924-25	7,206	84.2	1,168	640	502	191,598	26.6
1925-26	7,085	91.5	1,292	696	565	193,422	27.3
1926-27	7,170	97.9	1,382	744	587	202,664	28.3
1927-28	7,338	106.8	1,455	811	645	207,588	28.3
1928-29	7,433	113.2	1,520	860	694	217,486	29.3
1929-30	7,695	111.8	1,453	850	745	218,298	28.4
1930-31†	.....	.....	.....	.....	.....	....	....
1931-32†	.....	.....	.....	.....	.....	....	....
1932-33	7,669	90.9	1,186	691	696	192,483	25.1
1933-34	8,530	111.4	1,306	846	860	229,502	26.9
1934-35	9,042	131.6	1,455	1,000	1,000	265,848	29.4
1935-36	9,655	150.3	1,557	1,142	1,156	303,557	31.4
1936-37	9,987	175.8	1,760	1,336	1,322	332,768	33.3

*Year 1934-35 = 1,000.
†No census taken.
Source of data: *Census of Industrial Establishments*, 1936-1937 (Pretoria, Office of Census and Statistics, Government Printer, 1939), p. xiv and p. 1.
Col. 3: Figures in col. 2 divided by corresponding figures in col. 1.
Col. 7: Figures in col. 6 divided by corresponding figures in col. 1.

manufacturing establishments, and the severe competition which the newly established industries were meeting from foreign countries seeking to regain their previous trade outlets. Insistent demands for increased tariff protection were granted in 1925. During the next four years up to 1929-30 there was a steady growth in number of establishments, in gross value of output, and in number of employees.

During the first three years of the depression, however, the manufacturing industry of South Africa, unlike the mining in-

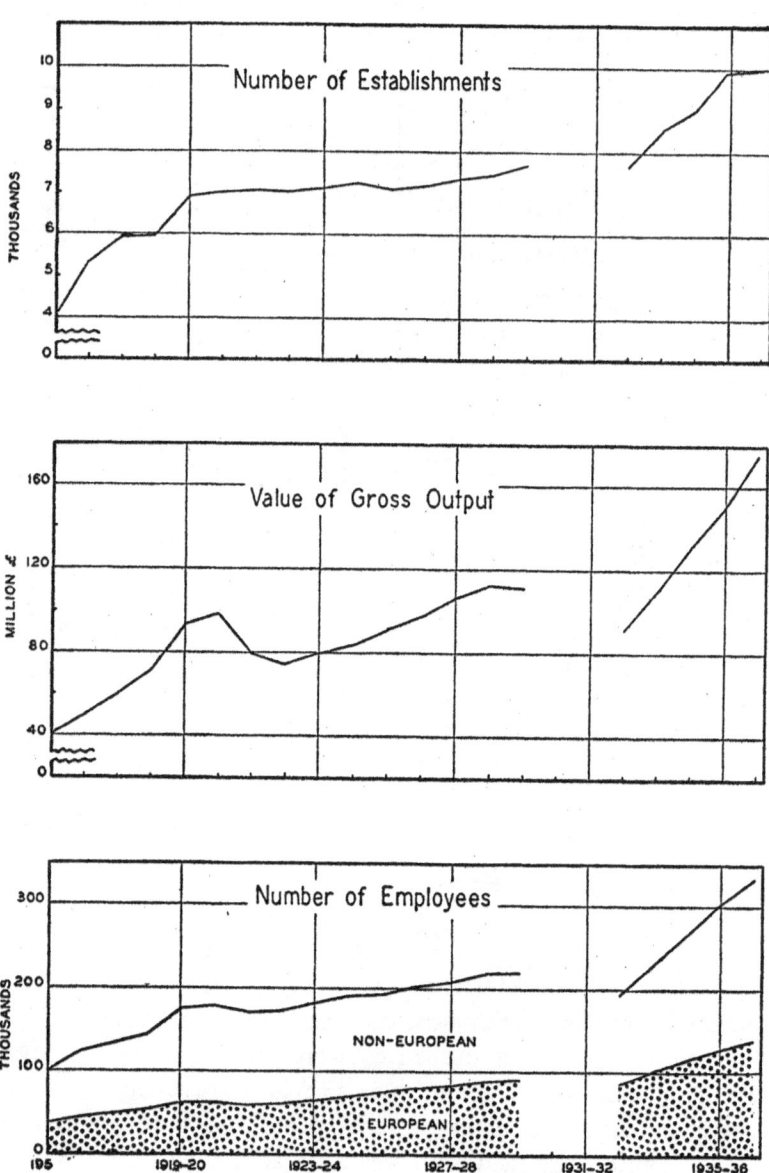

FIGURE 14. Number of manufacturing establishments. Data from table XXIV.

dustry, received a severe but temporary setback. The number of establishments declined only slightly, but gross value of output fell from £111,800,000 in 1929-30 to £90,900,000 in 1932-33, and the number of employees from 218,300 to 192,500. By 1933-34, however, the prosperity spreading from the gold mining industry to the rest of the country began to be felt in the manufacturing industry, so much so that the next four years showed the most phenomenal growth of manufacturing in the history of South Africa. The number of establishments increased from 7,669 in 1932-33 to 9,987 in 1936-37, the gross value of output from £90,900,000 to £175,800,000 and the number of employees from 192,500 to 332,800.

During the period of 22 years (1915-16 to 1936-37) the gross value of output per establishment increased about 76 per cent (from £1,011 to £1,760) and the number of employees per establishment about 32 per cent (from 25.3 to 33.3). Even in 1936-37, however, the value of gross output per establishment and the number of employees per establishment were very small as compared with similar data in countries like England, Germany, and the United States.

There have been considerable fluctuations in prices since 1915-16 so that value of gross output is not a very good measure of growth of manufacturing in South Africa. A more reliable measure is afforded by an index of volume output. During the years 1916-17 to 1920-21 the relative value of gross output (1934-35=1000) increased from 376 to 747, an increase of approximately 100 per cent. The relative volume of output, on the other hand, increased from 306 to 437, an increase of only 43 per cent. Between 1920-21 and 1929-30 the value of gross output increased only 14 per cent (from a relative of 747 to 850), whereas the volume of output increased by about 70 per cent (relatives 437 to 745). During the five years 1932-33 to 1936-37 the value of gross output increased somewhat more rapidly than did the volume of output. Taking the whole of the period under review, 1916-17 to 1936-37, the volume of output by manufacturing establishments showed a slightly more than fourfold increase, nearly half of which occurred during the last five years.

Although the manufacturing industry of South Africa has expanded considerably during the past quarter of a century, that country cannot be regarded as an important manufacturing country in the generally accepted sense of the word. The value of manufactured goods exported, other than processed agricultural and pastoral products, is an insignificant part of the total annual exports, and the annual value of machinery, textiles, chemicals, etc., manufactured in South Africa is small in comparison with the value of such articles imported. A large proportion of the gross value of output of all manufacturing establishments is contributed by industries (1) providing services such as heat, light, and power, and building and contracting; (2) processing and handling perishable or bulky raw products; or (3) finishing partly fabricated materials such as clothing, leather, etc., which are usually regarded as purely domestic industries. Thus private and government-owned industries handling raw materials, stone and clay, etc., wood, food and drink, etc., providing heat, light and power, and undertaking building and contracting, account for £84,000,000 or nearly 48 per cent of the gross value of output of all manufacturing establishments (table XXV). If a breakdown were made of the industries falling in the other classes, it would undoubtedly be found that a considerably larger part of the gross value of output was furnished by industries falling in the above three categories. For example, in the seventh class (table XXV) are included newspapers, in the eighth class garages, in the eleventh class explosives and so on. Government undertakings including railway workshops account for just over 11 per cent of the gross value of output of all manufacturing establishments.

Employment.—The expansion of manufacturing in South Africa has meant a considerable increase in the numbers of both Europeans and non-Europeans employed. In 1915-16 only 39,524 Europeans and 61,654 non-Europeans were employed in this form of activity; by 1929-30 the numbers had increased to 90,858 and 127,440 respectively and by 1936-37 to 140,203

The Manufacturing Industry

TABLE XXV

ESTABLISHMENTS BY CLASSES OF INDUSTRY, 1936-37

Class No.	Class of industry*	Number of establishments	Number of employees	Gross value of output (in £1,000's)	Per cent of total gross value of output
	Privately owned factories				
I	Raw materials	82	1,949	1,561	0.89
II	Stone, clay, etc.	547	29,699	6,921	3.93
III	Wood	362	9,654	4,238	2.41
IV	Metals, engineering	1,116	62,226	27,983	15.92
V	Food, drink, etc.	2,147	44,792	41,145	23.41
VI	Clothing, textiles, etc.	1,060	29,846	10,240	5.83
VII	Books, printing, etc.	467	12,194	7,414	4.22
VIII	Vehicles, etc.	1,714	17,564	9,870	5.62
IX	Ship building, etc.	8	243	73	0.04
X	Furniture, etc.	369	8,063	3,658	2.08
XI	Chemicals, etc.	199	11,630	10,335	5.88
XII	Surgical instruments, etc.	30	176	73	0.04
XIII	Jewelry, etc.	71	730	1,272	0.72
XIV	Heat, light, and power	127	8,749	8,572	4.88
XV	Leather and leatherware	273	13,376	5,396	3.07
XVI	Building and contracting	962	39,380	15,194	8.65
XVII	Miscellaneous	75	3,384	2,217	1.26
	Total privately owned	9,609	293,655	156,762	88.85
	Government and local government undertakings and railway workshops				
IV	Metals, engineering	87	19,712	11,682	6.64
XIV	Heat, light, and power	151	6,244	4,196	2.39
XVI	Building and contracting	34	9,648	2,183	1.24
	All other classes	106	3,509	1,542	0.88
	Total government undertakings	378	39,113	19,603	11.15
	Total private and government	9,987	332,768	175,765	100.00

*For fuller details of classes of industry see Appendix, table 10.
Source of data: *Census of Industrial Establishments*, 1936-1937, tables 5 and 6, pp. 16-21.

and 192,565 respectively (table XXVI). This represents an increase since 1915-16 of 255 per cent in the case of Europeans and 212 per cent in the case of non-Europeans. Perhaps of even more significance is the very rapid expansion (about 82 per cent) in the employment of non-Europeans in manufacturing since 1932-33, at a time when a very rapid expansion of employment of non-Europeans was also taking place in the mining industry.

TABLE XXVI
NUMBER OF EMPLOYEES AND WAGES PAID IN MANUFACTURING 1915-16 TO 1936-37

Year	Number employed		Wages paid		Average salary or wage	
	Europeans	Non-Europeans	Europeans	Non-Europeans*	Europeans	Non-Europeans*
			£1,000	£1,000	£	£
1915-16..	39,524	61,654	6,740	2,173	170.5	35.2
1916-17..	46,100	77,742	7,761	2,676	168.4	34.4
1917-18..	49,918	84,293	9,022	3,206	180.7	38.0
1918-19..	53,598	89,490	10,712	3,763	199.9	42.0
1919-20..	62,483	113,037	13,922	5,197	222.8	46.0
1920-21..	62,962	116,857	16,083	5,824	255.4	49.8
1921-22..	59,995	110,956	14,777	5,353	246.3	48.2
1922-23..	61,296	110,751	13,904	5,282	226.8	47.7
1923-24..	66,189	116,688	14,929	5,577	225.5	47.8
1924-25..	71,004	120,594	15,661	5,844	220.6	48.5
1925-26..	75,987	117,435	16,766	5,933	220.6	50.5
1926-27..	80,745	121,919	17,850	6,281	221.1	51.5
1927-28..	84,898	122,690	18,758	6,512	220.9	53.1
1928-29..	89,141	128,345	19,606	6,914	219.9	53.9
1929-30..	90,858	127,440	20,507	7,019	225.7	55.1
1930-31†.	......	......	......	.....	.....	....
1931-32†.	......	......	......	.....	.....	....
1932-33..	87,173	105,310	16,823	5,052	193.0	48.0
1933-34..	102,232	127,270	20,298	6,102	198.5	47.9
1934-35..	115,971	149,877	24,350	7,325	209.9	48.9
1935-36..	128,995	174,562	28,145	8,691	218.2	49.8
1936-37..	140,203	192,565	31,489	10,042	224.2	52.1

*The non-European wage includes an allowance for food and quarters, where these are supplied.
†No census taken.
Source of data: *Census of Industrial Establishments*, 1936-1937, p. 1.

Wages.—Average wages of Europeans employed in the manufacturing industry increased rapidly from £170.5 a year in 1915-16 to £255.4 a year in 1929-30. With the post-war deflation, European wages declined rapidly to around £220 a year in 1924-25, remaining at around that figure till 1928-29. A small increase in the average level of European wages in 1929-30 was followed by a decline to £193 a year in 1932-33. Thereafter the trend was again upwards so that by 1936-37 the level was within ½ per cent of that of 1929-30. Average wages paid to non-Europeans, which include an allowance for food and quarters where such are supplied,[3] showed a trend somewhat different from that for European wages. The average non-European wage increased from £35.2 a year in 1915-16 to

[3] *Report of the Native Farm Labour Committee*, 1937-1939, p. 23.

£49.8 a year in 1920-21. After declining to £47.7 a year by 1923-24, the trend was again upward, the average wage reaching £55.1 a year in 1929-30. By 1932-33 the average had declined to £48.0 and although from then onward there was a gradual rise, the average non-European wage in 1936-37 was still about 6 per cent below the level of 1929-30.

The average non-European wage of £52.1 a year (1936-37) in the manufacturing industry was considerably higher than the average wage (cash plus perquisites) paid to non-Europeans in the mining industry. This is due in large measure to the fact that whereas the non-European employees in the mining industry are almost entirely Natives, there are relatively large numbers of Asiatics and Colored persons employed in the manufacturing industry. In 1936-37 of the 192,565 non-Europeans employed in manufacturing, 12,413 or 6.4 per cent were Asiatics and 34,367 or 17.9 per cent were Colored, leaving 144,854 or 75.4 per cent as Native employees (table XXVII). The

TABLE XXVII

CLASSIFICATION OF EMPLOYEES IN INDUSTRIAL ESTABLISHMENTS, 1936-37

Province	European		Native		Asiatic		Colored	
	Male	Female	Male	Female	Male	Female	Male	Female
Cape	37,101	11,903	20,623	477	196	20	22,240	8,188
Natal	14,465	2,756	24,277	165	10,951	429	1,009	550
Transvaal	55,396	12,391	94,327	223	750	48	1,733	556
Orange Free State	5,550	641	5,627	66	19	0	87	4
Union	112,512	27,691	144,854	931	11,916	497	25,069	9,298
Females as per cent of total	....	19.7	....	0.6	....	4.0	....	27.1

Source of data: *Census of Industrial Establishments*, 1936-1937, pp. 24-27.

average level of wages of Asiatics and Colored persons is much higher than for Natives. In 1936-37 the average wage of Natives in the manufacturing industry was £44 a year, as compared with £64 a year for Asiatics and £83 a year for Colored persons (table XXVIII). The average wage (cash plus al-

TABLE XXVIII
AVERAGE SALARIES AND WAGES PAID IN PRIVATE MANUFACTURING ESTABLISHMENTS, 1936-37

Area	Europeans	Natives	Asiatics	Other Colored	Total
By provinces					
	£	£	£	£	£
Cape Province	178	50	104	80	117
Natal	259	39	62	108	106
Transvaal	267	45	83	92	130
Orange Free State	185	36	22	59	96
Union	234	44	64	83	121
By classes of industry					
I Raw materials	247	33	48	57	59
II Stone, clay, etc.	288	37	56	63	64
III Wood	279	39	44	75	119
IV Metals, engineering	309	47	54	102	146
V Food, drink, etc.	199	39	49	60	90
VI Clothing, textiles, etc.	119	62	76	75	98
VII Books, printing, etc.	287	59	105	111	221
VIII Vehicles, etc.	195	47	92	82	139
IX Ship building, etc.	215	56	70	126	140
X Furniture, etc.	212	58	134	146	155
XI Chemicals, etc.	254	43	52	75	112
XII Surgical instruments, etc. / XIII Jewelry, etc.	294	66	*	87	217
XIV Heat, light, power	349	44	54	89	140
XV Leather and leatherware	127	56	75	79	104
XVI Building and contracting	284	50	50	107	135
XVII Miscellaneous	255	43	76	82	133
Average all classes	234	44	64	83	121

*Less than 10 employees.
Source of data: *Census of Industrial Establishments*, 1936-1937, pp. 34-35.

lowances) paid to Natives in the manufacturing industry was thus somewhat lower than that paid to Natives in the mining industry.

Actually the disparity between wages paid to Natives, Asiatics, and Colored persons is much greater than is indicated in table XXVIII because of differences in the proportions of females in each racial group. Less than 1 per cent of the Native employees were females as compared with 4 per cent of the Asiatics and 27 per cent of the Colored persons. As females are usually paid a somewhat lower wage than males, the average wage received by both male Asiatics and male Colored persons would be well in excess of £64 and £83 a year respectively.

There are also marked variations in the levels of average wages paid to non-European employees in the different provinces and in different industries. These are due in large measure to three factors: (1) the location of industry in relation to centers of concentration of the various racial groups, (2) the proportion of females employed in the various industries and areas, and (3) the type of industry. In the case of Natives the location factor is shown by the fact that average wages are highest in the Cape Province, where there is a small Native population, and second highest in the Transvaal, which has a Native population inadequate to supply all its needs of Native labor. Wages of Asiatics are highest in the Cape Province (Natal has the densest Asiatic population), followed by the Transvaal; wages of Colored persons are highest in Natal (the Cape Province has the densest Colored population) followed by the Transvaal. Wage levels in the Orange Free State appear not to conform to this pattern, but the explanation is that this province has few industries, employs few Asiatics and Colored persons, and most of this employment is in industries which do not require a high degree of technical skill. In the Cape Province about 37 per cent of the Colored persons employed are females, in Natal about 55 per cent, in the Transvaal about 32 per cent, and in the Orange Free State about 5 per cent.

Native wages vary from £33 a year in the raw material establishments to £62 a year in the clothing and textile industries and £66 a year in the surgical instruments and jewelry industries. The three industries having the highest level of Native wages, however, employ only 4,011 out of the 144,854 Natives employed by all industries. The stone and clay establishments employing 24,300 Natives have a Native wage of £37 a year; the metals and engineering industry with 35,700 Natives, a wage of £47 a year; the food and drink industry with almost 18,000 Natives, a wage of £39 a year; and the building and contracting industry with 21,400 Natives, a wage of £50 a year. Wages of Asiatics vary from £44 a year in the industries working in wood to £105 in the paper and printing industry and £134 in the furniture industry. About 4,400 Asiatics are employed in the food and drink industries at an average wage of £49 a year, and 2,300 in the clothing and textile industry at an average wage of £76 a year. In the case of Colored persons wages vary from £57 a year in the raw materials industry to £146 a year in the furniture industry. About 4,700 Colored persons are employed in the food and drink industries at an average wage of £60 a year, another 2,500 in the leather and leatherware industries at £79 a year, and 3,600 in the building and contracting industry at £107 a year.

Turning attention to European wages in private manufacturing industries, it is found that in 1936-37 these averaged £234 a year in contrast with an average wage of around £400 a year in the gold mining industry. This difference in the average levels of European wages in the two industries is also due in large measure to the fact that a large proportion (almost 20 per cent) of the Europeans employed in manufacturing is females, whereas the proportion in the gold mining industry is insignificant. But even if a comparison were made for males employed in the two industries on work requiring equal skills, it would still be found that wage levels in the manufacturing industry were below those in the gold mining industry. The reasons are not far to seek. First, a large part of the manufacturing industry of South Africa is located in the coastal areas, and there living costs are generally regarded as being lower than in the Transvaal, where the gold mining industry is concentrated. Second, a greater element of risk attaches to mining activities. Third, and perhaps most important of all, is the fact that employees in the gold mining industry are able to share in the prosperity of that key industry, from which the manufacturing industries, as well as other branches of economic activity, derive their prosperity. Thus wages in the manufacturing industry tend to follow those in the mining industry but with a lag of several years and at a somewhat lower level. This is borne out by the fact that during the depression years (1930-1933) wages in the mining industry did not decline and, after 1933, increased steadily to well above the 1929 level. In contrast, European wages in the manufacturing industry declined considerably between 1930 and 1933, and, although they have since recovered somewhat, they had not quite reached the 1929 level by 1936-37.

There is considerable variation in the levels of wages received by Europeans engaged in manufacturing in the different provinces, from £178 a year in the Cape Province to £267 a year in the Transvaal Province. These variations too can be traced to differences in the proportion of females employed in the different provinces and to the predominant types of industry in the several provinces. In the Cape Province about 32 per cent of the European employees were females, as compared with 19 per cent in Natal, 22 per cent in the Transvaal, and 11 per cent in the Orange Free State. The average level of European wages varied from £119 a year in the clothing and textile establishments to £349 in the heat, light, and power plants. The latter industry and the metals and engineering industries had wages averaging over £300 a year. These two enterprises are highly concentrated in the Transvaal, which has about 82 per cent of all Europeans employed in metal and engineering establishments in South Africa and about 70 per cent of those engaged in heat, light, and power establishments. Also both these industries employ very few females. On the other hand, the Cape Province has over one third of the Europeans engaged in the manufacture of clothing and textiles and about 74 per cent of the Europeans engaged in making leather and leatherware. Both these industries employ large numbers of females and have the lowest levels of European wages.

Another interesting point of contrast between the manufacturing and mining industries is the fact that the ratio of Europeans to non-Europeans is much smaller in the former than in the latter. In 1936-37 the ratio of Europeans to non-Europeans in the manufacturing industry was 1:1.37 as compared with 1:8 in the mining industry. In manufacturing generally more emphasis is placed on the skill of individual employees, a condition favorable to the employment of Europeans. In gold mining, on the contrary, outside of a relatively small number of skilled officials and supervisors of Native labor, emphasis is placed upon the strength and endurance of the individual employee, a condition favoring the employment of Native labor.

Location of Industries.—The Cape Province and the Transvaal are nearly equal in regard to the total number of privately owned factories, and together have 7,550 or 78 per cent of all factories in the Union, followed by Natal with 1,333, and the Orange Free State with 726 (table XXIX). The Cape Western area, including Capetown and adjacent cities, and Port

TABLE XXIX
LOCATION OF PRIVATELY OWNED FACTORIES AND NUMBER OF EMPLOYEES, 1936-37

Class of industry and race of employee	Provinces					Industrial areas			
	Cape	Natal	Transvaal	Orange Free State	Union	Cape Western	Port Elizabeth	Durban and Pinetown	Southern Transvaal
	Number of factories								
1. Raw materials	38	20	21	3	82	20	2	13	16
2. Stone, clay, etc.	176	51	288	36	547	82	28	28	235
3. Wood	122	88	143	9	362	61	16	34	114
4. Metal, engineering	315	156	618	27	1,116	203	36	122	539
5. Food and drink	996	255	630	266	2,147	236	36	81	289
6. Clothing, textiles	390	163	467	40	1,060	234	34	141	439
7. Books and printing	209	65	168	25	467	107	18	48	150
8. Vehicles	704	227	540	243	1,714	186	24	106	304
9. Boat and ship building	4	4			8	4		4	
10. Furniture	126	57	173	13	369	68	16	47	161
11. Drugs, chemicals	80	57	61	1	199	48	12	50	61
12. Surgical instruments	13	4	13		30	10	2	4	13
13. Jewelry	28	7	36		71	18	3	6	36
14. Heat, light, and power	18	40	64	5	127	4	3	5	21
15. Leather and leatherware	154	36	73	10	273	54	31	23	64
16. Building and contracting	351	90	477	44	962	163	19	55	423
17. Other	29	13	29	4	75	15	3	8	27
Total	3,749	1,333	3,801	726	9,609	1,513	283	775	2,892
	Number of employees								
European	49,004	17,221	67,787	6,191	140,203	24,174	9,781	12,106	62,815
Natives	21,100	24,442	94,550	5,693	145,785	7,005	3,775	13,711	86,003
Asiatics		216	11,380	798	19	12,413	85	80	6,784	678
Colored	30,428	1,559	2,289	91	34,367	22,317	2,836	1,123	2,189
Total	100,748	54,602	165,424	11,994	332,768	53,581	16,472	33,724	151,685

Source of data: *Census of Industrial Establishments,* 1936-1937, pp. 8-15, 24-27.

Elizabeth, together have 1,796 of the 3,749 privately owned factories in the Cape Province. Durban and Pinetown have over half of all factories in Natal, and the Southern Transvaal area (which includes Johannesburg and adjacent cities), over three fourths of all those in the Transvaal. As is to be expected, some classes of industry are much more highly concentrated than others. For example, 50 out of the 57 chemical factories in Natal are in the Durban and Pinetown area, and all 61 chemical factories in the Transvaal are in the Southern Transvaal. An even greater degree of concentration is exhibited in the shipbuilding, jewelry, surgical instrument, clothing and textiles, and furniture industries. On the other hand, the four main industrial areas have much smaller proportions of the food and drink, vehicles (including garages), heat, light and power, and building and contracting industries.

On the basis of size of plants and number of employees the concentration of industry is much greater than is indicated by the figures on location of plants because the larger factories are usually located in the more important cities. Although the Cape Western and Port Elizabeth areas have less than half of all factories in the Cape Province, these two centers have nearly 70 per cent of all employees. Similarly, the Southern Transvaal area has 76 per cent of all factories in the Transvaal but nearly 92 per cent of all employees. It is interesting to note that nearly 65 per cent of all natives engaged in manufacturing in the Union are employed in the Transvaal. On the other hand, about 91 per cent of the Asiatics are employed in Natal and about 88 per cent of the Colored in the Cape Province.

CHAPTER 10

TRANSPORTATION, COMMERCE, GOVERNMENT, AND DOMESTIC SERVICE

Transportation.[1]—Prior to 1875 the development of the railway system of South Africa was slow and halting. About 1859 construction of a short railway between Capetown and Wellington was begun by a private company, and in the following year another private company started work on a short line at Durban, Natal. By 1874 only 63 miles of railway had been built in what is now the Union of South Africa. In 1872 the parliament of the Cape of Good Hope concluded that, in the interest of economy and the opening up of the country, the government should take over the existing small railway from the private company and itself undertake the building of railways. Similar action was taken in Natal in 1876. After the discovery of diamonds at Kimberley in 1875, the building of the railway from Capetown was pushed ahead rapidly so that by 1880, 906 miles of railway had been constructed in the Cape of Good Hope. In Natal 100 miles of railway had been built. By 1885, the year before the establishment of Johannesburg, the Cape had nearly 1,600 miles of railway, and Natal 176 miles.

Thereafter, construction of the railroad system proceeded more rapidly so that by 1890 there were 2,238 miles of railway in what is now the Union of South Africa, by 1895 over 3,200 miles, and by 1900 nearly 4,000. The Cape of Good Hope had constructed the lines through the Orange Free State, whereas

[1] The information in this section was obtained from the *Official Yearbooks of the Union of South Africa*, No. 1 (1917), pp. 774-802; No. 20 (1939), pp. 491-538.

a private company was organized to build the lines in the Transvaal. By 1900 all the important mining and seaport centers had been linked up. Small portions of the railway system had been built by private companies, practically all of which have since been acquired by the government. By 1910 there were 7,000-odd miles of railway in the Union, by 1920 some 9,500, and by 1938 just over 13,600, of which only 407 were operated by privately owned companies. About 12,520 miles are of 3′6″ gauge, 109 miles of 2′6″ gauge, and 987 miles of 2′0″ gauge.

In 1938 the government-owned railway system, known as the South African Railways, was capitalized at £156,698,000. Except during a few years in business depressions, the South African Railways has operated at a profit. All payments of interest on capital invested have been met promptly, and there has never been any default on capital invested in the system— a very enviable record. The administration of the railways, ports, and harbors is entrusted to the Governor-General-in-Council, operating through the Minister of Railways and Harbours. The Minister of Railways and Harbours is advised by a board of three commissioners. The management and working of the system are carried out by a general manager, who is governed by such regulations as the Minister, after consultation with the Board, shall from time to time promulgate.

Although the railway system of South Africa has contributed greatly to the development of that country, its development has been criticized on two general grounds.[2] The first is that, since Union, many of the branch lines have been constructed for political rather than for economic reasons. As a result, these lines have been unable to meet operating expenses, the deficit in their operation being met out of profits from the system as a whole. The second is that the rate structure of the country has been such as to favor agriculture at the expense of mining and other industries, and as a consequence has greatly influenced the pattern of agricultural development. Many

[2] For a more detailed discussion of this aspect of the problem see: S. H. Frankel, *Capital investment in Africa*, pp. 380-387.

economists believe that the development of the maize industry of the Transvaal and Orange Free State as an export industry rather than as a supplement to the livestock industry is in large measure due to the railway rate structure of the country.

During recent years a more rational policy has been followed in regard to the provision of transportation facilities for outlying districts. The South African Railways operates a road transport service for passengers and freight as a feeder to the railway system. In 1938 the road motor service operated over 13,400 miles of road, a distance almost exactly equal to that covered by the railway system. As a result, many thinly populated agricultural areas are now provided with an adequate and frequent service at very low cost.

The South African Railways also operates an air passenger and goods service, known as the South African Airways. This system links up the main population centers of the Union of South Africa and is coordinated with Imperial Airways.

In addition to the railway system of the Union of South Africa, there are electric tram or motor bus services in nearly all the larger cities. Of the fourteen metropolitan transportation services, only three are operated by private companies, the remainder being owned and operated by municipalities.

Information is not readily available regarding the number of persons employed in the transportation system of South Africa prior to 1917-18. In that year the South African Railways employed 34,371 Europeans and 35,846 non-Europeans (table XXX). By 1929 the number of European employees had increased to 56,900 and the non-Europeans to 38,581. Although there was a sharp decline in the number of employees between 1929 and 1933, there has been a marked expansion of employment since 1934. In that year there were 64,259 European and 53,745 non-European employees. As in the case of manufacturing industries, this expansion in employment in the South African Railways is a reflection of the general prosperity which spread, after 1933, from the gold mining industry to all phases of the domestic economy of South Africa.

Some significant changes have taken place since 1919-20 in

Transportation, Commerce, and Government

TABLE XXX

NUMBER OF EMPLOYEES ON SOUTH AFRICAN RAILWAYS, 1917-18 TO 1937-38

Year	Regular staff				Casual staff		Grand total
	European			Colored non-European	European	Colored non-European	
	Salaried	Other	Total				
1917-18	7,305	26,938	34,243	32,544	128	3,302	70,217
1918-19	7,916	27,367	35,283	34,962	130	2,953	73,328
1919-20	8,501	31,138	39,639	38,190	121	3,013	80,962
1928-29	9,365	43,516	52,881	33,615	4,026	4,966	95,488
1929-30	9,535	43,898	53,433	30,314	3,179	8,864	95,790
1930-31	9,372	42,515	51,887	28,698	1,736	8,135	90,456
1931-32	8,944	39,855	48,799	20,977	2,523	9,778	82,077
1932-33	8,452	38,222	46,674	19,731	2,991	7,493	76,889
1933-34	8,315	38,021	46,336	18,767	2,506	9,506	77,115
1934-35	8,816	40,040	48,856	19,923	3,255	13,055	85,089
1935-36	9,349	42,734	52,083	20,773	4,140	20,698	97,693
1936-37	10,023	44,694	54,177	21,528	5,014	26,884	108,143
1937-38	10,704	47,853	58,557	23,236	5,702	30,409	117,904

Source of data: *Official Yearbooks of the Union of South Africa*, Vol. 4 (1910-1920), p. 772; Vol. 15 (1932-1933), p. 683; Vol. 20 (1939), p. 497.

the type of employment afforded by the railway system. In that year practically all Europeans were on the regular staff, only 0.3 per cent being employed on the casual staff. Of the 41,203 non-Europeans, nearly 93 per cent were on the regular staff and 7 per cent on the casual staff. In 1937-38 about 9 per cent of the Europeans and nearly 57 per cent of the non-Europeans were on the casual staff. Between 1919 and 1937-38 the number of Europeans employed on the regular and casual staffs increased from 39,760 to 64,259 or about 61 per cent, whereas the number of non-Europeans on the regular and casual staffs increased from 41,203 to 53,645 or only 30 per cent. This appears to be in line with the country's "Civilized Labor Policy," which involved the employment, wherever possible, of Europeans in the place of Natives.

The number of employees on urban tramway and bus systems in South Africa increased from 2,013 in 1916 to 2,837 in 1919-20 and to 5,009 in 1937-38 (table XXXI). The number of Europeans increased from 1,432 in 1916 to 3,914 in 1937-38 or about 173 per cent; the number of non-European from 581 to 1,095 or only 88 per cent.

TABLE XXXI

EMPLOYEES ON URBAN TRAMWAY AND BUS SYSTEMS OF THE UNION OF SOUTH AFRICA, 1916 TO 1937-38

Year	Number of Europeans	Number of non-Europeans	Total
1916	1,432	581	2,013
1919-20*	1,945	892	2,837
1937-38†	3,914	1,095	5,009

*Includes cities of Capetown, East London, Kimberley, Port Elizabeth, Durban, Pietermaritzburg, Johannesburg, Pretoria, Boksburg, and Bloemfontein.
†Includes cities of Capetown, East London, Kimberley, Port Elizabeth, Durban, Pietermaritzburg, Bloemfontein, Benoni, Boksburg, Brakpan, Germiston, Johannesburg, Pretoria, and Springs.
Sources of data: *Official Yearbooks of the Union of South Africa*, No. 1 (1910-1916), p. 591; No. 4 (1910-1920), p. 793; No. 20 (1939), p. 523.

Data are unfortunately not readily available on the number of Natives, Asiatics, and Colored persons composing the non-European employees. The South African Railways employs a considerable number of Colored persons as coach (sleeping car) attendants and as porters at railway stations. Natives are employed in construction gangs and to a lesser extent in workshops. From a statement appearing in the Official Yearbook for South Africa (1939) it would appear that average weekly non-European wages in the South African Railways and Harbours increased from 11s. 10d. in 1912-13 to 19s. 0d. in 1920-21, declined to 17s. 0d. in 1929-30, to 15s. 5d. in 1934-35, but had again increased to 17s. 2d. by 1938-39. This would mean an average monthly wage in 1938-39 of about 70s. 0d. The wages of Natives only, however, would be much lower and would probably not exceed those in the gold mining industry.

Commerce.—Satisfactory data do not appear to be available on the number of Europeans, Asiatics, Natives, and Colored persons employed in commercial activities in the various provinces. In the Southwest Region of the Cape Province considerable numbers of Colored persons are engaged in trade either as owners of stores or as employees. In the Transvaal and Natal large numbers of Asiatics living in urban areas are also engaged in trade. It is probable, however, that the number of Natives engaged in trade is relatively small. Outside of stores located in Native urban and rural areas and catering to Native trade, positions as clerks and shop assistants are filled largely by Europeans, males and females. Natives, however, are engaged for heavy work, such as receiving and delivering merchandise and the cleaning of establishments. The Native Farm Labour Committee, on the basis of information supplied by the Director of Census and Statistics, estimated that there were 25,000 Natives engaged in trade in the Union of South Africa.[3]

Other Occupations.—Large numbers of Natives (males) are employed as domestic servants and as waiters and cooks in hotels and restaurants in the Transvaal, Orange Free State, and the eastern part of the Cape Province. In most of the latter province, however, Colored women form the most important source of the domestic labor supply. The Native Farm Labour Committee estimated that there are some 275,000 Natives in domestic employment.[4] This, however, seems to be a rather wild guess based upon the assumption of one Native for each European family in the Transvaal and Natal, where the practice of employing Native males as domestic servants is more common than in the rest of the country. The actual number of Native males engaged in domestic service may be considerably above or below this figure. The Native Farm Labour Committee also estimated that government departments employed about 15,000 Natives in 1938 and that the Provincial Administrations employed another 40,000 on road construction.[5] It is unlikely that the number of Natives employed in government departments will be greatly expanded in the near future. On the other hand, the country has recently embarked upon an extensive program of road building (partly for relief purposes), and it is likely that this activity will continue to utilize considerable numbers of Natives for several years to come—unless, of course, the program is curtailed during the war, a not unlikely contingency.

There is no agency in South Africa which regularly receives and publishes information relative to Native wages in com-

[3] *Native Farm Labour Committee*, 1937-1939, p. 8.
[4] *Ibid.*
[5] *Op. cit.*

merce, domestic service, and government departments. Native wages vary somewhat in different parts of the country. In Johannesburg shopboys and packers in stores get from 15s. to 25s. a week (usually without food and quarters).[6] This would mean an annual wage ranging from £39 to £65, presuming that the Native employee works a full 52 weeks a year.

From information supplied to the writer by several persons in Johannesburg, it would be reasonable to suppose that the majority of Natives employed on delivery and packing in commercial establishments receive a wage ranging between £45 and £50 a year. Such Natives may receive quarters but must provide their own food. In Johannesburg young Natives (under 20 years of age) receive from 20s. to 40s. a month[7] or from £12 to £24 a year plus food and quarters, the wage varying with the age and appearance of the Native. Older and more experienced Natives get from 45s. to 70s. a month or from £27 to £42 a year plus food and quarters. Very experienced Native cooks and waiters get from £48 to £54 a year plus food and quarters. The value of food and quarters is usually estimated at from £1 to £1.10s. a month. Thus the maximum total wage for the most experienced cook or waiter would be £54 + £18 or £72 a year. This again is based on the assumption that the Native domestic servant is employed for 12 months in the year. Many Natives work for much shorter periods and are frequently without work. It is safe to say that the great bulk of mature Natives (males) who work as domestic servants do not receive a wage (including food and quarters) in excess of £45 a year.

Information is not available relative to wages paid to Natives in all government departments. The Native Affairs Department, which employs some 1,600 Natives in regular positions and considerable numbers of casual laborers on soil erosion work, was kind enough to supply the writer with particulars of wages paid to Natives in that department (table

---

[6] Information supplied to the writer by Mr. A. L. H. Muloahy of the Native Affairs Department, Johannesburg, in a letter dated December 4, 1939.
[7] Op. cit.

Transportation, Commerce, and Government 143

XXXII). Because of the nature of its work, this department employs some of the best educated and most capable Natives in South Africa, many of whom have made work with the department their lifework. One Native receives a salary going up to £450 a year; twenty-two, salaries which go up to £225 or £240 a year. The great majority, however, receive salaries which do not exceed £100 a year. Very few of the other

TABLE XXXII
NATIVE AFFAIRS DEPARTMENT: WAGES OF REGULARLY EMPLOYED NATIVES—1939-40

Classification	Salary scale pounds per annum	Number on salary scale
1. Translator	370 x 20 – 450	1
2. Interpreter clerks, grade I	165 x 15 – 225	13
3. Interpreter clerks, grade II and assistant	108 x 12 – 156	84
4. Interpreter clerks, grade III; interpreter messengers, grade II; handyman; boarding house master	96 x 12 – 132	25
5. Clerk; instructor, grade I	120 x 12 – 180 x 15 – 240	9
6. Instructor, grade II; office assistants; agricultural demonstrators	72 x 6 – 120	211
7. Boarding house mistress; rangers; overseers; field assistants; messengers	36 x 3 – 60	214
8. Workmen	60 x 6 – 120	40
9. Lorry drivers; storemen; field assistants; messengers; depot attendants; constables	60 x 3 – 84	911
10. Matron	60	1
11. Matron	24	3
12. Cleaners	42 – 48	6
13. Female depot attendant	18 or 36	2
14. Caretaker	12	1
15. Record-taker	84 x 6 – 96	46
16. Police sergeant	110 x 5 – 125	7
17. Colored police constable	72 x 6 – 100	1
18. Police corporals	88 x 3 – 103	50
19. Police constable (Caprivi)	50 x 5 – 75	1
20. Constable laborers	local rates	7
21. Herd boy	local rates	1
22. Welfare officers (temporary)	150	1
		1,635
23. Unskilled laborers	local rates up to 2s. per day worked	number varies
24. Tractor drivers	local rates up to £6 per month	

Source of data: Summarized from information supplied to writer by the Native Affairs Department, Union of South Africa.

government departments have positions which justify the employment of highly educated and responsible Natives. It is probable that the average wage paid in most government departments to full-time Native employees, all of whom have had some education, will not exceed £75 a year. Unskilled laborers employed on soil erosion and other types of work are paid local rates up to 2s. a day.

CHAPTER 11

WORKING CONDITIONS FOR NATIVE LABOR

IN THE PRECEDING chapters, data were presented to show the development of demand for Native labor in the various fields of employment in South Africa, and also on the trend and level of Native wages in relation to those received by Europeans. This chapter will be concerned with a less tangible, but nevertheless important, aspect of the problem, namely, working conditions for Native labor.

Non-Wage Considerations.—As a general rule, in countries like the United States, the term "working conditions" is regarded as being confined to such matters as hours worked daily and weekly, risk and disutility of particular occupations, relations between employer and employee, compensation for accidents, and so on. In the Union of South Africa, however, the term, when applied to Native labor, must be used in a somewhat wider sense to include, in addition to the above factors, amount and quality of food and quarters provided, freedom of movement after working hours, opportunities for social contacts, and educational facilities. The Native laborer in South Africa, unlike the worker in America, is not free to come and go as he pleases after working hours; his opportunities for social and educational contacts are restricted, although conditions vary greatly from industry to industry and from area to area.

Although the great bulk of Natives in South Africa has now become accustomed to working for wages,[1] it is safe to say

---
[1] The ignorance of Natives in the early days in regard to the value of coinage and the ease with which they could be defrauded is well illustrated by the following story:
In Natal a large part of the railway system was constructed by Scottish

that large numbers of them, especially those who have previously lived only in rural areas, still do not appreciate the significance of money and how to get the most for what they spend. Their purchases are usually in small amounts; they are greatly attracted by color and gaudiness and so are often persuaded to purchase at relatively high prices goods of little value, measured by European standards. Thus the cash wages of Natives usually purchase fewer goods and services than a similar amount spent by Europeans. This situation is one of the main reasons why Natives tend to place so high an appreciation on the quality and amount of food and quarters and on other factors making up working conditions. Natives will frequently work for an employer who treats them fairly and considerately, although other employment at higher wages may be available. Furthermore, Natives show a preference for work in areas where social contacts are available. When such contacts are lacking or denied them, the Natives tend to become restive and dissatisfied, even if wage and other conditions are satisfactory. Natives, especially those who have become urbanized, are also keenly interested in educational facilities for their children and seek to locate their families in areas where such facilities are available. This often necessitates their living at considerable distances from their place of employment.

Restrictions of Freedom.—Natives working and living in urban areas, especially in the Transvaal and Orange Free State, are subjected to numerous restrictions, which have a considerable influence upon their willingness to work in such areas and which also affect their efficiency as workers. Violation of these restrictions is regarded as a crime, punishable by imprisonment and fine. In addition, many acts which are regarded as civil offenses for Europeans constitute criminal offenses for the

---

engineering firms. Paymasters soon found that Natives did not know the difference between half-crowns (eight to the pound) and two-shilling pieces (ten to the pound). The practice soon developed of paying Natives eight two-shilling pieces for each pound of wages due instead of eight half-crowns. It was some time before Natives discovered the difference in the buying power of these two coins. Although Natives are now fully aware of the relative importance of the different coins, they still call a two-shilling piece a "Scotsman."

Native. The situation of Natives on the Witwatersrand (similar conditions prevail elsewhere in the Transvaal and Orange Free State) is stated forcefully as follows:

> Crime for Africans on the Witwatersrand is not the same as crime for the European. A criminal act for the European is the same for an African. But there are many acts which are criminal offences for the African which are not such for the European; for example, offences against Pass laws, the Liquor Acts, the Natives (Urban Areas) Act, and the Native Labour Regulation Act. These are criminal offences for the Natives, as are also the breaking of contracts of service and the non-payment of taxes. A Native is subject to criminal prosecution for carrying sticks larger than specified in urban areas; knives longer than specified; for non-payment of rent; for making and selling his tribal drink, and for being idle in a Native location. . . .[2]

In addition, most towns and cities have curfew laws requiring Natives absent from their place of residence after a certain hour in the evening to be in possession of special passes from their employers. Phillips states:

> A large number of the 32,438 offenders on the Reef under Pass laws, in 1936, were guilty of being abroad after curfew hours without a special Night Pass. This special Night Pass may be signed by any employer; hence it can easily be forged by an African who writes English or Afrikaans. As has been pointed out, a clever criminal will assuredly see that his Night Pass is in order before travelling abroad by night. So the bulk of those caught by the Curfew regulations are new-comers, the forgetful, and those who linger too long away from home without a watch or clock. The blind faith of certain Europeans that the curfew is in some magical sense a protection against crime is pathetic.[3]

In the enforcement of these regulations, Natives are subject to constant surveillance and interference by the police. A

---

[2] Ray E. Phillips, *The Bantu in the city* (South Africa, The Loveday Press, 1938), p. 176.

[3] *Ibid.*, pp. 227-228.

Native may be stopped at any time, day or night, for the inspection of his identification pass, and night pass if after curfew hours. Should a Native inadvertently be without his passes, he is taken to a police station or charge office where he may be detained for several hours before he can establish the fact that he has a pass. It is no uncommon thing for a household to arise in the morning only to discover the absence of the Native domestic servant, who had been detained overnight because he was out after curfew hours. The police may raid a Native home or place of residence at any time, day or night, in search of liquor or unauthorized occupants. Although conditions have improved considerably within recent years, Natives are often subjected to abusive and inconsiderate treatment at the hands of police officers, whether or not they have been guilty of some infringement or other.

These numerous laws and restrictions were introduced ostensibly to: (1) protect Natives from country districts who were unfamiliar with urban conditions; (2) discourage idleness and encourage Natives to work for wages; (3) promote sanitary and more healthful living conditions in urban areas; and (4) check and discourage serious crime among Natives away from customary tribal control. Although it is possible that serious crime has been checked, it is undoubtedly true that petty crime has been greatly increased. In fact, it is almost impossible for Natives living in pass areas to avoid involuntary violation of some regulation or other. Natives thus tend to become petty law breakers and after a while to lose their respect for law. It is a moot question whether the remedy has not been worse than the disease and whether the same objectives could not have been attained by less objectionable means.

Whatever the arguments may be in favor of or against the condition of affairs that has developed in parts of South Africa, there can be little doubt but that the subjection of Natives to numerous restrictions on freedom of movement is bound to have an adverse effect upon their efficiency as workers. Educated Natives who have become permanently urbanized and who may be doing work of some responsibility resent the necessity of carrying passes. They regard this requirement as an effort on the part of the Europeans to keep them permanently in a position of inferiority. Natives from areas where they are not required to carry passes (Cape Province and Natal) find it difficult to understand why they should do so in the "pass areas" of the Transvaal and Orange Free State. Only dire economic necessity (the need to earn money to supplement family income and to pay their taxes) induces Natives to seek work in urban areas and to subject themselves to the many indignities this involves.

In the aggregate, many thousands of hours of work are lost each year by the forceful detention of Natives guilty of some minor infringement, owing largely to ignorance or negligence. This involves serious losses to both employers and employees. Because of the necessity of obtaining passes and fulfilling contracts of service (violation being a criminal offense), Natives are less free than European workers to change occupations. Native employees often have to stand considerable abuse from their employers, although cases of physical violence are rare. It is only in rare instances that a Native can appeal to a labor union for its assistance in attempting to redress real or fancied wrongs at the hands of his employer. Appeal to the police or courts is usually equally futile, unless physical violence or maltreatment can be proved. In any case, there is a tendency on the part of European officials and European juries to favor the white employer in any dispute with his Native worker.

These general conditions surrounding the employment of Native labor have an important and unfortunate bearing upon the morale of a Native and his attitude towards work. Although under tribal conditions the Native is a happy-go-lucky, carefree individual, capable of great endurance and strict adherence to tribal laws and customs, he has tended to become sullen, resentful, and suspicious—a frame of mind hardly conducive to good and continuous work. The well-nigh hopeless situation a Native faces in trying to improve the social, economic, and educational status of himself and his family and the vast chasm between European and Native standards of living cannot but help to have a depressing effect on his psychology, cannot but help to give him a chronic inferiority complex and feeling of frustration. It is not improbable that these conditions, allied with undernourishment and unfamiliarity with a machine economy, are responsible for a considerable amount of the alleged stupidity and lack of resourcefulness shown by Native workers.

The author, in discussing the problem with prominent Europeans familiar with Native problems and with Native leaders, found opinion to be almost unanimous that Natives would become much more efficient and reliable workers if general living conditions were made more attractive, or perhaps it would be better to say, less unattractive and onerous.

So much for the general conditions under which a Native must seek and perform work. Attention will now be directed more specifically to a consideration of factors, such as housing, food, hours of labor, and employer-employee relations which constitute working conditions in individual industries. It is important to realize in this connection that such conditions vary considerably between establishments in the same industry, from industry to industry, and from area to area.

The Importance of Housing.—Occupations for Natives may be divided into two broad categories: (a) those in which Natives are provided with quarters, and (b) those in which they are not.

The gold, coal, and diamond mining companies usually house their Native workers, other than those employed in offices or semi-responsible positions, in enclosed compounds from which unauthorized persons are excluded.[4] The great bulk of the accommodation so provided is for male Natives, although a few mines provide quarters for a limited number of married employees. The housing quarters in the compounds resemble military barracks. As a general rule, the buildings are well constructed with plenty of air. Care is taken to prevent overcrowding and to promote sanitary conditions. Adequate bathing facilities are provided. In nearly all compounds space is set aside for recreation, and organized sports are arranged. In

[4] The supervision of housing in labor areas is under the purview of the Director of Native Labour, operating in terms of the Native Labour Regulation Act of 1911.

the diamond mining industry, Natives are confined to the compounds during their period of employment (in order to avoid pilfering), but in the gold and coal mining industries, employees are permitted to leave the compounds at stated intervals for the purpose of visiting or other reasons. With few exceptions, the accommodations provided by mining concerns for their Native employees are superior to those provided by other industries.

The great majority of Natives employed as domestic servants are provided with a room, usually an outbuilding detached from the main living quarters of the European family. Toilet facilities are provided, but here, too, adequate bathing facilities are lacking, use being made of a faucet or bucket. There is considerable variation in the quality and size of the living quarters provided for Native servants. Buildings may be constructed of wood, brick, stone, or galvanized iron. Some quarters may be well furnished; in others, the skimpiest of furnishings is provided. Although practice varies greatly, many householders do not give much attention to the cleanliness and sanitation of the quarters occupied by their Native servant or servants.

Many Natives employed in commerce and in industry are provided with quarters on the business premises. As a general rule, the number so accommodated is small and confined largely to employees whose presence on the business premises (as watchmen, stable hands, etc.) is absolutely necessary. The standard of such accommodations varies widely, the quarters usually consisting of an outbuilding attached to or above a stable or warehouse. Toilet facilities are provided, but bathing facilities are usually nonexistent, the Native using a faucet or container, such as a bucket, for his ablutions. Often little attention is given by the employer to sanitary conditions.

The South African Railways, as a general rule, does not provide its Native employees with quarters. In some of the larger cities, however, houses are provided for a small number of families at low rentals.

The Natives (Urban Areas) Act, No. 21 of 1925 was

passed with two main objectives: (a) to eliminate existing slums and to prevent the formation of future Native slums, and (b) to ensure the residential segregation of Natives.[5] This Act requires that local authorities provide adequate housing facilities for Natives ordinarily employed within the jurisdiction of such local authorities. The customary method of attack on this problem is to set aside areas to be known as Native locations. Many towns and cities had such locations long before the passage of the Act. Since 1925 new and additional locations have been established around the larger cities and the facilities and conditions in old locations improved.

Policies regarding the provision of living quarters vary considerably in the different cities. In some instances, lots are purchased by permanently urbanized Natives and small houses constructed thereon. In other instances, Natives lease land and erect their own houses. The more common practice, however, is for the local authority to erect houses to rent to Native families. As a general rule, recreational, social, and shopping facilities are provided in the locations. Strict attention is given to the maintenance of sanitary conditions. In most locations, medical officers are in attendance and clinics operated for the benefit of the inhabitants. In spite of efforts to the contrary, overcrowding of Native houses (usually consisting of one to three rooms) is not uncommon.

The expansion of the location system has aided materially in the improvement of slum conditions in the larger cities, although the problem is far from being solved. The main criticism of the system from the workers' standpoint is that considerable time is required for Natives to get from the locations, often situated miles from business and industrial districts, to their places of work. Transportation facilities are frequently inadequate, and the expense is a sizable drain on the slender cash income of Native workers. Equally, if not more, onerous is the rent which Natives are required to pay for their homes. Municipalities have attempted to make the Native locations self-supporting—in other words, to extract from Natives rents suffi-

[5] *Report of Native Economic Commission*, 1930-1932.

cient to meet interest on investment and the cost of supervision and management. This policy is criticized by economists and others on the grounds (1) that the European and not the Native population wanted segregation, which in effect meant moving Natives to considerable distances from their place of work; (2) that Natives generally constitute the poorest members of the urban population and yet receive only a small part of the direct benefits from municipal taxation; and (3) that, because of their generally low income, some form of subsidization by the financially able elements of the population is equitable. Randall of the University of Witwatersrand summarized the situation as follows:

> ... The fundamental fact remains that the wages of Urban Natives in locations are not sufficient to enable them to maintain the standard of living necessary for health. They must, therefore, be subsidized by the richer citizens. Any municipal Native policy which ignores this fundamental fact and insists that the Natives shall pay in full for all services supplied to them, no matter how such payment is extracted, is unjust, and still more unjust is any policy which forces Natives to pay not only in full for all services supplied but to provide a yearly surplus as a contribution to capital expenditures made on their behalf.[6]

In addition to the accommodation of Natives in locations, there exist in nearly all the larger cities hostels for the accommodation of single Native males or single Native females. These hostels, operated by municipalities or private agencies such as churches, accommodate many thousands of Natives in cities such as Johannesburg, Durban, and Pretoria. The rentals, although low, are subject to much the same criticisms as those directed at rentals in the locations. As a general rule, however, the hostels are more conveniently located in relation to commercial and industrial centers.

Housing in Rural Areas.—The housing problem of Natives employed in country areas is even more unsatisfactory from the

[6] R. J. Randall, "Some reflections on the financial policy of certain municipalities towards the natives within their boundaries," *The South African Journal of Economics*, Vol. VII (June, 1939), No. 2.

standpoint of the quality of living quarters. Natives employed on alluvial diamond diggings and small mines usually erect their own huts, often out of the flimsiest materials available—corrugated iron, flattened-out gasoline tins, bags, canvas, and wood. Sometimes a fortunate Native may secure a tent or more substantial wooden hut. The more temporary the mining venture, the poorer the accommodations are likely to be. The only extenuating factor is that in temporary mining ventures, the accommodations of the owner or operator are likely to be little superior to those of his employees. In the more permanent mining activities, even if they are small, it is customary for the owner or operator to provide more substantial and weatherproof living quarters for his Native employees.

On European farms, it is usual for farmers to allot to a newly appointed Native farm worker a site on which to erect a hut or other family building and to allow the Native and his family a certain amount of time to build their dwellings before going to work for the farmer. Not infrequently the farmer supplies part or all of the materials used in building. The type of huts erected by Natives varies in different parts of the country, grass huts placed over interlaced poles being most popular in the eastern sections, and wattle and daub, or sod and green brick in other parts. In the Cape Province stone, brick, and corrugated huts are not uncommon.

Although many Natives occupy well-made dwellings, the great majority of Native huts on farms are poorly made and after a while become ramshackle, providing poor protection against the elements. Native farm workers maintain that it does not pay them to erect good huts because they cannot be sure how long they will work on the farm. Many of them complain, too, that they are not given sufficient time to erect substantial huts. Regardless of whether or not huts are well made, there is a general tendency toward overcrowding. Sanitary arrangements and bathing facilities usually are entirely lacking or inadequate.

In a few instances, farmers have erected substantial living quarters for their farm employees. This practice is more common in parts of the Cape Province, where Colored laborers are employed. In Natal and the Transvaal, producers of sugar cane and wattle trees and a few large maize producers who employ large numbers of Natives erect barracks of corrugated iron, green bricks, et cetera, for their employees. Such quarters, however, are often poorly constructed, allowed to deteriorate through neglect, and are badly infested with vermin.

There is pretty general complaint among farm employees about living quarters on farms, and it would seem essential that if farmers are to compete with industries in urban areas, greater attention should be given to providing Native families and other farm workers with more substantial and satisfactory quarters. The problem is complicated by the fact that in some parts of the country, Natives are averse to living in a hut in which someone has died. Well-built and usable huts are thus often abandoned. The solution may be found in the development of standardized, movable dwellings, which may be taken down and moved from one site to another. As it is now, many Native dwellings are of a very unsubstantial character, but the nature of construction and the type of materials used are such that they cannot be moved.

The housing problem for Native employees in all occupations is still far from having been solved. In urban locations the rent charges are too high in relation to the low cash income of Native families, and overcrowding is all too prevalent. On the farms, although no rent is charged, Natives are put to considerable expense or time in constructing their homes. Sanitary arrangements are largely lacking, and overcrowding is the rule rather than the exception. Natives tend to build homes in accordance with tribal practice. Considerable educational work is necessary to induce them to build and to live in homes in which adequate ventilation and living space are provided. Help and guidance by the farmer will probably pay dividends in the long run by ensuring a more permanent and contented labor force.

Adequacy of Rations.—One of the most important considerations influencing a Native in his selection of work is whether or not he will be supplied with food as part of his wages in kind and what the quality and amount of such food may be. Generally, Natives who are permanently urbanized occupy positions in which food is not supplied, a higher cash wage being paid instead. Natives from rural areas, who have gone to the city in search of work or who are recruited to work in the mines or in industries, prefer to be supplied with food.

As a general but not invariable rule, a Native who is supplied with quarters is also supplied with food. This holds true for Natives who work in the gold and coal mines and in industries where Natives live in compounds, and also for Natives engaged in domestic service. It does not hold true, however, for Natives working in the diamond mines, who, although supplied with quarters, provide their own food. On the other hand, many Natives in domestic service are provided with food but live in Native locations. The situation on European farms will be dealt with at a later stage.

In regard to quality and type of food, a distinction can be drawn between occupations in which large numbers of Natives are housed together and occupations in which only one or a few Natives work in one establishment. The gold mining corporations early discovered the advantages to themselves of providing their Native employees with an abundant and adequate diet; sickness was reduced, and the Natives performed better work and were more contented. After years of research, the gold mining corporations have evolved a simple but adequate diet (containing protective foods). It is claimed by Dr. Orenstein, Chief Medical Officer, Rand Mines, that Natives are usually in better physical condition at the end of their period of service with the mines than when they entered it.[7] Other mining groups and certain industries are following the lead set by the gold mines, and it is probable that if competition for Native labor continues, further improvement in quality and variety of diet provided for Natives will be shown in the future.

There is considerable range in the type and adequacy of

[7] A. J. Orenstein, "Diet of Natives on the Witwatersrand gold mines," *Race Relations*, Vol. VI (First Quarter, 1939), No. 1.

food supplied to Natives who are employed singly or in relatively small numbers, as for example, in domestic service. The two most common practices are (1) for the employee or employees to be supplied with mealie meal (corn meal), meat, vegetables, and such other foods as may be deemed necessary and to let him or them do their own cooking, and (2) to supply the Native with food from the table of the European family. The first practice is common where Natives have not yet acquired a liking for European foods or where several employees have to be fed. The second practice is more common where only one Native is employed, especially if he shows a preference for European foods.

The adequacy of the food supplied to Native domestic servants depends partly upon the financial standing of the European family and partly upon their attitude towards their servant or servants and their knowledge of the health values of food. Poor families are likely to have a diet high in carbohydrates and proteins but low in protective foods, such as milk, fruit, and vegetables. The diet of their servants will show a similar, but perhaps more marked, deficiency. Families with higher incomes are likely to consume a wider variety of foods of better quality, and the diet of Native servants is likely to be more adequate, unless, of course, Natives are supplied with food to cook themselves. Even in the more well-to-do families, the Native employee may receive only the staple foods—bread, meat, cereal, coffee, and some vegetables—but may not be supplied with much in the way of dairy products and fruit. The diet of Native servants thus tends to be deficient or low in the protective foods.

From the standpoint of the Native worker, there are several advantages in receiving food as wages in kind. First, European employers usually purchase more economically than do Natives. This is particularly true of the mining and other corporations which have special purchasing departments and buy in bulk. A given amount expended by Europeans will therefore buy more food than if the purchase were made by Natives. Second, Europeans generally know more about the health values of different foods (especially European foods) than do Natives, particularly if the employer can employ or have access to expert medical advice. Third, Natives are likely to eat more regularly because their meal times tend to coincide with or follow those of their employers. Fourth, Natives are saved some time in not having to go to stores (often located at considerable distances from their place of employment) to make their purchases; also, they are saved the losses due to wastage and breakage. On the other hand, there are several disadvantages. First, the Native may not like the kind of food with which he is supplied; many Natives, especially young Natives who have left their kraals for the first time, still prefer the simple, monotonous, Native foods and cooking to the more varied foods of the European. Second, the European employer may, and often does, skimp on the quality and amount of food issued to his employee or employees. This applies particularly to the protective foods.

Everything taken into consideration, however, and in spite of occasional abuses, it is probable that Natives are relatively better off by being provided with food as part of wages in kind. Competition for Native labor tends to force improvement in the way of better food.

Rations on European Farms.—The conditions described above apply mainly to employment in urban areas. The food problem in regard to Natives employed on European farms is at once more acute and more varied. The variety of food supplied is dependent to some extent upon the predominant type of agriculture in the various areas and on different farms. In dairy areas, or on farms on which dairying is important, whole or skim milk may be supplied as a regular part of the daily rations. Similarly, in areas like Natal, where fruit and vegetables are regularly produced, these may be supplied. These conditions, however, represent the exception rather than the rule. Over most of the country the Native employees are not so fortunate.

Natives employed on farms may be divided into three classes: (a) domestic servants, (b) those employed on a full-

Working Conditions for Native Labor 159

time wage basis, and (c) labor-tenants, who work for the farmer for only part of each year.

In regard to domestic servants, the food supplied is on much the same scale as for domestic servants employed in cities. Food is usually supplied from the table of the European household and is generally adequate in all respects, except perhaps dairy products.

Full-time Native employees (often a Native with a family) are usually supplied with rations. The same privilege is extended to such other members of the Native family as are employed, but on a less generous basis than that of the family head. The most common food (and frequently the only food) issued to Native employees is mealie meal (corn meal), although maize and "boer" meal (coarse flour) may be substituted. In the Cape Province it is more usual to issue "boer" meal, especially to Colored employees. The customary ration of mealie meal is 3 pounds a day to the head of the family and somewhat smaller issues to other members. Custom varies greatly in respect to meat. In some areas of the Cape Province, most farmers supply their farm hands with meat at regular intervals. In the rest of the country, however, less than 20 per cent of the farmers include meat as a regular part of the rations.[8] The situation with regard to milk, fresh vegetables, and fruit is even worse. Over most of the country milk (whole or skim) is seldom or never issued to Native employees, although some farmers issue milk to families which have small children.

The case of labor-tenants is somewhat different. A labor-tenant, as was previously stated, is the head of a Native family residing on a European farm and, with certain members of his family, works for the farmer for a stipulated period each year

[8] The *Report of the Native Farm Labour Committee*, 1937-1939, states on page 44 that: "Meat is not generally treated as part of the Native diet on farms. In the three northern provinces, the number of employers who give it to their employees with any degree of regularity is probably less than 20 per cent. In the Cape, it would seem in places to be as high as 60 per cent. Nevertheless, it is the exception and not the rule to include meat in the ration as a weekly, or bi-weekly, item. Even in the Cape, the usual practice is to give it not more frequently than once a month; it is usually on the hoof and is supplemented by fallen animals which the workers are permitted to eat."

for the privilege of running a limited number of cattle and of cultivating a certain area of land. The labor-tenant and the members of his family involved in such a transaction may or may not receive cash wages during their active period of employment. It is more usual, however, for European farmers to supply rations but not cash to the Native tenant and the working members of his family during their actual period of service with the farmer. During the rest of the year, the labor-tenant and his family have to fend for themselves. Where rations are supplied during the period of service, the type and amount of food issued is similar to that given to full-time workers.

It may be assumed that the labor-tenant owning cattle and cultivating land has an advantage over the full-time worker in that his herd can provide his family with meat and milk, and his cultivated lands can produce needed vegetables and fruit. Actually, however, the variety of foods available to the family of the labor-tenant from the family's farming operations on its own behalf is strictly limited. The tendency has been for European farmers to restrict the number of cattle which a labor-tenant is permitted to run. Such cattle are badly needed by the labor-tenant for draft purposes and are not used for meat purposes until they become too old to work. The quality of most of the few cows owned by Natives is so poor that yield of milk is very low and, as a rule, totally insufficient to supply family needs for more than a few months each year. Because of ignorance, laziness, lack of time, or unsuitableness of climatic and soil conditions, the labor-tenant tends to devote most of the area allocated to him for cultivation to the production of cereals. Some pumpkins and beans may also be produced. Very little green and root vegetables and practically no fruits are produced. In reality, therefore, the range of foods available to the labor-tenant and his family is not much greater than that supplied to the full-time Native worker.

It would thus appear that the food supplied or available to Native farm workers is very restricted in range and, in the vast majority of cases, woefully deficient in protective foods. The Native family can, of course, purchase some protective foods out of cash wages or earnings of the family. Cash farm wages, however, are very low, seldom exceeding £1 10s. a month for an adult worker. Furthermore, most farms are located at considerable distances from trading centers. Country stores often do not carry a wide range of fruits, vegetables, or dairy products, and the prices are frequently considerably higher than in the large cities, especially for commodities not produced locally.

In some parts of the country, particularly in the sugar cane area in Natal, the wattle-growing areas of Natal and the Transvaal, and on a few large maize farms where large numbers of Natives are employed and housed in compounds or barracks, the conditions as to food are somewhat similar to those of Natives employed in the gold mining industry. It is probable, however, that Natives employed under compound conditions in farming areas are not as well fed, from the standpoint of a balanced diet, as in the mining industry.

In fairness to large numbers of European farmers, it must be stated that the diet of many European farm families is also deficient in some of the essential protective foods. This may be due to ignorance of the health values of different foods, to poverty of the farm family, or more often to the fact that the protective foods are not readily available in certain areas during most of the year. For example, in many parts of the Cape Province, Transvaal, and Orange Free State, soil, climatic, and water conditions do not permit the raising of fruits and vegetables. In some parts, where conditions are not suitable for dairying, farmers keep only a few cows whose milk is barely sufficient to supply the needs of the European family. Under such conditions, the European family itself is put to considerable expense to secure its own requirements of the protective foods. On the other hand, the great majority of farms in South Africa are able to raise some vegetables and to produce dairy products and meat animals. There appears to be no adequate reason why, where conditions are suitable, Native farm laborers should not receive a better-balanced diet.

The inadequacy and unattractiveness of rations supplied to Native farm laborers constitute one of the important reasons (along with low cash wages and absence of social and educational amenities) why farmers are experiencing increasing difficulty in obtaining and keeping efficient farm laborers. The two following quotations from the *Report of the Native Farm Labour Committee* (1937-39) bear pointedly upon this aspect of the problem:

> There seems no reason to doubt that in general the great bulk of the farmers consider that they have fulfilled their obligations in the way of feeding by supplying their Native servants with a liberal quantity of mealie meal. Many of them assert that the practice conforms to the habits of the Natives in their kraals. Even if this were so, it should be remembered that one of the objects of an employer should be to attract labour by his conditions of employment, and ensure efficiency and contentment in his service. . . .
>
> While it is recognised that the farmer cannot compete with mines and industries in the cash wages offered to the workers, they are, except in certain areas, in a much more favourable position in regard to the provision of food. In this feature, they should be able to reach standards, little if at all, less attractive than those industries which are at present battening on their labour supplies. The farmers, by adequate and constant attention to the sufficiency and appropriateness of the food given to Natives on farms, could go far toward ensuring a satisfactory position, with the happiest results.[9]

Hours of Labor.—Comprehensive and accurate data are not available on the number of hours worked per day and per week by Natives in the different industries. The great bulk of industries in South Africa, in which organized European labor unions are recognized, adhere to the 48-hour week. This may be regarded as the maximum number of hours worked by European workers, although a few industries and commercial undertakings may have a slightly longer work week. On the other hand, some industries may have a work week of somewhat shorter duration.

In industries where European laborers are organized in

[9] *Report of the Native Farm Labour Committee,* 1937-1939. p. 46.

labor unions, or which have come under the adjudication of the Wage Board of the Department of Labour and in which Natives are employed along with Europeans, the hours of labor of Natives tend to conform to those worked by European laborers. This is generally true in the mining industry (other than alluvial and small mining operations), in the manufacturing industries, in transportation, and in commerce. In small mining operations, especially those of the alluvial type, hours of labor of both Europeans and Natives are likely to exceed 48 hours a week. Work may often be carried on from sunup to sundown, with breaks for meals and short periods of rest. Frequently, however, mining operations have been suspended completely for several hours during the heat of day in the summer months. Quite generally, the Native laborer tends to work the same number of hours as, and along with, his European employer.

Hours of labor of domestic servants are subject to still greater variation. It is usual for the Native domestic servant to be up before 6 A. M. to prepare the fire and the early morning coffee or tea[10] served around 7 A. M. The servant would then set about preparing breakfast. For the rest of the morning, he would be cleaning the house and preparing the midday meal served around 1 P.M. From about 2:30 P.M. till about 5 P. M., the Native usually has no duties. He may visit his friends or occupy his time as he sees fit. In some households, however, he may be required to work in the family flower or vegetable garden. Returning at 5 or 5:30 P. M., the Native would be busy until 7:30 or 8 P. M. preparing, serving, and cleaning up after the evening meal. The total workday would thus be about 13 or 14 hours, with perhaps 2 to 3 hours off in the afternoon. Most European families allow their Native servants from one to three afternoons and evenings off a week, say Wednesday and Sunday. The Native would leave around 2:30 P. M. and return to his quarters at curfew time (10 or 11 P. M.), unless he has a late pass permitting him to return still

---

[10] It is the custom in most homes in South Africa for the members of the family to be served with a cup of coffee or tea before they rise in the morning.

later. The work week of most domestic servants thus varies from about 60 to 70 hours. In households in which there are two or more servants, the work week may be somewhat shorter. It must be stated, however, that during much of the workday, the Native domestic servant does little hard work, but he has to be on duty.

On European farms, the work week of the Native farm hand is likely to be even longer. The day would begin even earlier, around 4 or 5 A. M. in the summer, if animals are kept. It is usually reckoned that the workday on the farm lasts from sunup (or even earlier) to sunset, with time off for meals and perhaps two or three hours off during the day, especially during the summer. Afternoons off or days off are rare. It is probable that the work week of Native farm hands will vary from 60 to 80 hours. During much of each day the Native may have to do strenuous work, unlike the domestic servant who has little hard work.

In regard to hours of labor, the Native farm hand is worse off than Natives who seek work in cities. This factor undoubtedly influences young unmarried Natives to prefer work in cities. Married Natives, however, are willing to put up with the long hours of work on farms in order to be with their families.

Compensation for Injury or Illness.—Act No. 59 of 1934, the Workmen's Compensation Act, amended by Act No. 38 of 1936, consolidated, clarified, and expanded all existing laws in regard to compensation payable to workers or their dependents for injury or illness incurred while engaged as an employee. The law sets up scales of compensation for temporary, permanent, or fatal injury and for certain types of industrial diseases, and requires employers to carry compensation insurance or make such other provisions to guarantee payment of compensation as may be deemed necessary. By definition of employment, persons engaged in domestic service (other than hotels or restaurants) and in agriculture (except where the employee operates a power-driven machine) are exempt from the provisions of the law. Employees not covered under the Act (farm workers and domestic servants) have the right of civil action against their employers for damages.

Payment of medical and hospital expenses is limited in the case of Europeans to one year and to £100; for Natives the maximum amount payable is £25. Compensation for injury or illness is based upon wages received. As a result, the compensation for Natives is on a much lower scale than for Europeans.

In addition to the Workmen's Compensation Act, employees contracting phthisis as a result of their work in mining receive hospitalization, medical care, and compensation under the Miners' Phthisis Act of 1925 as amended. Pensions are paid to afflicted workers and to their dependents; also, to dependents of workers who have succumbed to the disease. The law applies to both Europeans and to Natives, but here, too, compensation and pensions for Natives are on a much less liberal scale than for Europeans.

Although farmers are exempt from the provisions of the Workmen's Compensation Act and from the necessity of paying compensation except in so far as damages may be assessed as a result of civil action on the part of an injured farm hand, a large number of farmers tend to treat Native employees who may be injured in a fairly liberal way. The farmer may pay, and frequently does pay, for all medical and hospital care and may allow the family of the injured Native to continue to reside on the farm. Not infrequently a farmer will pension off a Native who has been in his employ for years and who becomes too old to work. The Native so retired and his family are allowed to occupy a hut on the farm and are supplied with food and sometimes with some cash. In spite of many instances of generosity, however, it must be realized that a farmer is under no legal obligation to compensate an injured Native worker. In this respect, Native farm workers are in a definitely less satisfactory position than Natives employed in urban occupations, other than domestic service. It is important to realize that a Native is a manual worker, often with little or no education. If he is incapacitated for manual work, he, unlike most Europeans, cannot undertake some form of office or other work not requiring the use of legs or arms.

Employer-Employee Relations.—The attitude of an employer to his employee is partly reflected in the wages he may pay, the food and quarters he may provide, and the hours of labor required. For Natives employed in industries in which organized labor unions exist or which are subject to adjudication by the Wages Board, the interests of the employee may be protected and advanced as a result of the good offices of these agencies. Many aspects of employer-employee relations are of a more intangible nature. An employer may be exacting in his requirements; he may adopt an offensive or supercilious attitude towards individual or all employees; or he may show a friendly interest in their welfare and in that of their families. On the other hand, an employee may habitually loaf on his job; adopt an attitude of "ca canny"; or he may be insolent and offensive.

In large commercial and industrial organizations, the relations between employer and employees becomes largely impersonal. The employee may come into contact only with a foreman or paymaster and never see his actual employer. In smaller establishments, there is room for close personal contacts.

These personal relations are of considerable importance to the Native, especially as he is not as free to move from one occupation or one place to another as is a European worker. Natives may and often are subjected to a great deal of personal abuse, although acts of physical violence against Native employees are rare. Natives do select types of employment and employers from whom they are sure of considerate treatment. They also show a preference for occupations in which they come into personal contact with their employers.

In this respect, Natives employed as domestic servants and as farm laborers are in a more satisfactory position than Natives working in large groups or gangs under a foreman or supervisor. As a general rule, farmers who treat their Native workers kindly and considerately have little difficulty in obtaining and keeping Native workers. On the other hand, a farmer who abuses and maltreats his employees may cause dissatisfaction on adjacent farms where Natives are treated with more consideration. Maltreatment is often regarded as a community or communal affair; as a matter affecting relations between European employers as a class and Native employees as a class.

The peculiar delicacy of the employer-employee problem is illustrated by the following occurrence which, the writer was informed, was by no means uncommon. A farmer, who had employed a Native for some years, decided that he would show his appreciation of the Native's good work by raising his wages. Soon thereafter, the Native informed the farmer that he wanted to leave, and it became apparent that he was dissatisfied with his work. Upon enquiry, the farmer ascertained that the Native had come to the conclusion that he had been cheated for a number of years. His reasoning was that if he was entitled to the higher wage now, he was certainly entitled to the same wage during earlier years when he was doing the same type of work.

Another illustration of the same problem arises on farms where a farmer employs a Native and several of his dependents. Native custom presents supreme authority in the head of the family. He allocates work to the members of his family, many of whom may be adults. Many farmers, recognizing this custom, give all orders for work through the head of the family and make all criticisms of work done by individual members to the family head. Most farmers, however, prefer to deal directly with each employee as an individual. This tendency of farmers to deal directly with individual workers is resented by the family, since it is regarded as operating to undermine parental authority and the solidarity of the family unit.

These facts are mentioned to indicate just how delicate and important employer-employee relations may be in a country where a wage economy has been superimposed upon tribal economy in which there was no distinguishable class of workers.

Social and Educational Opportunities.—The Natives of South Africa are becoming more and more aware of the advantages of receiving an education. Native leaders realize that the capacity of Natives, both in industry and in agriculture, to perform a higher grade of work is dependent upon at least a rudimentary education, which will enable them to show an intelligent and reasoning interest in what they are doing. Under present conditions, a Native all too frequently does a piece of work because he is told to, without any clear perception of what the job really is or for what purpose it is done. In industry, this may not be such a serious handicap because he is kept under constant supervision. In farming, it is a serious drawback because the Native is called upon to work without constant supervision, and farm work cannot readily be adapted to routine. Even more important is the problem which arises when the Native has to plan his own farming operations on the land allotted to him on a European farm or in a Native area. It can be expected confidently that with the passage of time, Natives will show a continually growing interest in acquiring for themselves greater educational opportunities. Increasingly large numbers of Natives, in selecting occupations and places to work, give consideration to the availability of school facilities for themselves and their children.

In cities, urbanized Native families who live in locations usually have access to schools provided by the state or religious institutions. Unfortunately, however, although great improvement has taken place in recent years, the school facilities for children, and more especially for adults, are woefully inadequate and fall far short of meeting even the most elementary needs. Because of lack of proper financial support in relation to the number of persons needing education, classrooms are crowded, the subjects taught are few, and large numbers of the teachers employed are unqualified and poorly equipped for their very important task. Some of the Native labor unions attempt to provide some educational facilities for their members. Although it is possible for Natives employed as domestic servants to obtain some schooling in certain areas (at night school), facilities are usually lacking. Furthermore, an attitude of ridicule or of outright opposition on the part of European employers tends to discourage their domestic servants from taking advantage of what educational facilities may be available.

There is need for a vast expansion of educational facilities in urban areas, both for Native adults and children. A very fertile ground for expansion would appear to be among the Natives living in mining compounds.

In the Native areas, educational facilities are available on a more liberal scale than in urban areas. Such facilities again are provided by both the government and missionary bodies. However, education in Native areas has only an indirect relation to the labor problem. It may affect the capability of Natives from these areas who seek work in cities, but it does not have a very direct influence in determining the type of work that Natives will do.

In rural (non-Native) areas, educational facilities for Natives are almost entirely lacking and even if schools were established, Native children would have difficulty in getting to and from school, unless transportation were provided. One of the biggest grievances of the Native farm worker is that, because of the nature of his occupation, he or his family is virtually precluded from any opportunity of obtaining even a semblance of an education.

It can be stated without fear of contradiction that one of the most serious aspects of the Native problem in South Africa is the lack of educational facilities. Greatly expanded facilities and an improvement in the quality of teachers are badly needed in both urban and rural areas.[11] Such expanded facilities cannot be provided by increased taxation of Natives, which is already of a very regressive character.

Social intercourse is possible on a much greater scale in urban than in rural areas. Domestic servants, Native workers in industry and commerce, and Natives living in urban locations have both time and opportunities to visit friends. In the mining compounds, opportunity to make social contacts outside of the compound is somewhat more restricted but is unlimited within

---

[11] See also *Report of the Native Economic Commission*, 1930-1932, pp. 85-97. Ray E. Phillips, *The Bantu in the city*, pp. 146-173.

the compound itself. In the compounds and in nearly all the cities, recreational facilities are being made available to Natives on a continually growing scale. These include organized sports, such as football and tennis, club rooms, and pictures. In contrast, social contacts of the farm Natives are restricted largely to other Native families living on the farm or on adjacent farms. Trips to visit friends on distant farms are few and far between. Recreational facilities are nonexistent.

In conclusion, it may be stated that employment as farm laborers has tended to become less attractive within recent years because conditions of labor, including housing, food, hours of labor, and social and educational facilities are definitely inferior on the majority of European farms to what they are in urban occupations. To some extent, the remedy for this state of affairs appears to be in the hands of the farming community itself. Farmers can do much to improve their chances of competing successfully for Native labor by providing better housing and food for their employees. This alone would do much to overcome the handicap of longer hours and absence of social contacts and recreational facilities.

CHAPTER 12

TOTAL DEMAND FOR NATIVE LABOR

THE ANALYSIS in the preceding chapters makes possible an estimate of average wages paid to Native labor in South Africa, an estimate of the combined needs of all industries in 1938 for unskilled Native labor, and an estimate of possible future trends in the demand for such labor.

In the mining industry average cash wages increased from £27 a year in 1911 to £33.4 a year in 1938, an absolute increase of about £6 in 28 years. The full wage, including the cost to mining companies of food, quarters, and medical attendance amounted to £50 for a full year, or £43 for 270 shifts. It can be said that the maximum annual average wage paid to Natives in the mines for a full year's work is £50. In the manufacturing industry the wages of non-European labor have shown much the same over-all trend as wages in the mining industry, the full wage (cash and allowances) in 1936-37 being £44, or not greatly different from that in the mining industry. Data are not available relative to wages paid to Natives in the transportation industry, but these are probably not greatly different from those paid in the mining and manufacturing industries. Wages paid to Natives in trade also approximate closely those in the above-mentioned industries, and the same is true for wages of Natives in domestic employment. Educated Natives in responsible positions in government departments get wages which, in a few instances, exceed £100 a year, but the great majority receive wages below that figure. Unskilled Natives receive wages which do not greatly differ from those in other industries. It is safe to conclude that the great bulk of Natives employed in all nonagricultural occupations receive wages (including allowances) which do not exceed £50 a year; higher wages are paid to a relatively small number who have exceptional education or exceptional qualifications.

According to the data presented in this and the two preceding chapters, the gold mining industry employed 420,000 Natives in 1937, the manufacturing industry 146,000, commerce about 25,000, transportation 50,000, government (central and provincial) 55,000, and domestic service 275,000, or a combined total of 971,000. Some of these data are obtained from the *Yearbook* and other official publications; others are taken from the report of the Native Farm Labour Committee.

This Committee on page 8 of its report estimates that the total number of Natives engaged in non-agricultural work is 1,145,000, or 170,000 in excess of the above estimate. The main discrepancy between the two estimates appears to be in the number of Natives employed on the mines. The figure given in the report of the Native Farm Labour Committee is 550,000, which coincides with the number shown on page 471 of the *Official Yearbook of the Union of South Africa*, No. 20 (1939), as employed in labor districts. The number of Natives employed in labor districts includes those employed in other occupations as well as in mining. The same page of the *Yearbook* indicates that only 326,000 of the Natives in labor districts are employed in mining. The Committee's report also shows 190,000 Natives as employed in manufacturing establishments. This figure in turn coincides with the figure for all non-Europeans employed in manufacturing as shown in the *Census of Industrial Establishments* for 1936-37. The *Census* figure, however, includes 12,000 Asiatics and 34,000 Colored persons. At best some of these figures are very rough approximations, subject to a considerable margin of error. In view of this fact, a rough estimate of around 1,000,000 Natives employed in nonagricultural pursuits will probably not be far off the mark.

The *Native Farm Labour Committee* report, 1937-1939, on pages 7 and 8, estimates that there are some 1,764,000 Native males of 16 years and over available for work in the various industries in the Union (page 42). Of these, according to their estimates, some 1,145,000 are employed in the various non-agricultural industries, leaving some 619,000 apparently available for agricultural labor. From this number, however, should be deducted the number of Natives employed on sugar and wattle plantations, Native squatters, farmers, and peasants, and the wealthy and mainly idle Natives. Their final estimate of available farm labor is around 320,000, but a considerable part of this consists of labor-tenants in the Transvaal and Natal and certain areas in the Orange Free State. Labor-tenants work on farms usually from three to nine months a year, depending upon the customary practice in different localities. Their final estimate is some 200,000 full-time agricultural labor units. The difficulty of assessing agricultural labor needs is accentuated by the fact that seasonal peaks occur as well as marked fluctuations in output from year to year. Much of agricultural labor is immobile (especially the labor-tenant) and cannot readily be moved from area to area as occasion demands.

The Committee (page 9 of their report) concludes "that the present demand for Native labor in the Union substantially exceeds the developed supply."

Future Needs for Unskilled Labor.—Hazardous as it is to estimate the existing demand for Native labor, the problem becomes even more complicated if an attempt is made to estimate the future needs for such labor. In view of the present conditions in the world, any prognostications as to the future of the economic development of South Africa are extremely dangerous. If a large number of countries abandon gold permanently as a basis for their currencies, the whole domestic economy of South Africa will undergo cataclysmic changes. Similar and even more radical changes will occur if South Africa comes under the domination of the Axis powers, or if its economy is severed from that of the British Commonwealth of Nations. Leaving these eventualities out of consideration and assuming that economic development in South Africa will continue in about the same general direction as during the past quarter-century, certain rough forecasts as to future supply and demand conditions for Native labor are possible. Unfortunately these will have to be confined to those industries for which data are available over a fairly large period of time; namely, mining, manufacturing, and transportation. These three industries, however, employ about 60 per cent of all Natives engaged in nonagricultural pursuits, and as all economic activity in South Africa is so greatly influenced by conditions in the gold mining industry, it is not unreasonable to suppose that the trend of employment will be in the same direction, if not to the same extent, as for the three industries. Between 1911 and 1920 the Native male population of South Africa increased 17.7 per cent, whereas the number of Natives employed in the mining, manufacturing, and transportation industries increased 25.7 per cent, indicating a more rapid increase in the demand for, than in the supply of, Native labor (table XXXIII). By 1930 the number of Native males was 44.8 per cent greater than in 1911, whereas the number of Natives employed in the three industries was only

TABLE XXXIII

POPULATION AND EMPLOYMENT IN SELECTED INDUSTRIES, 1911-38

Year	Native male population	Number of Natives* employed in				Per cent increase in (1911 or 1912 = 100)		Per cent of total Native male population			
		Mining	Manufacturing	Transportation	All three industries	Male population	Number employed in three industries	Mining	Manufacturing	Transportation	All three industries
	1	2	3	4	5	6	7	8	9	10	11
1911† (1912)	2,023,000	298,000	45,000	35,000‡	378,000	....	....	14.8	2.2	1.7	18.7
1921† (1920)	2,382,000	321,000	113,000	41,000	475,000	17.7	25.7	13.5	4.7	1.7	19.9
1930..	2,929,000	316,000	127,000	39,000	482,000	44.8	27.5	10.8	4.4	1.3	16.5
1936†.	3,313,000	394,000	175,000	41,000	610,000	63.8	61.4	11.9	5.3	1.2	18.4
1937..	3,372,000	403,000	193,000	48,000	644,000	66.7	70.4	12.0	5.7	1.4	19.1
1938..	3,435,000	421,000	......	54,000	......	69.8	....	12.3	...	1.6	...

*Natives – predominantly male. In the case of the manufacturing industry, Asiatics and Colored persons are included as the data at the disposal of the writer did not permit exclusion of these groups for earlier years.
†Census years; other 3 years obtained by taking one half of the estimated mean Native population for those years.
‡Estimate by the author.
Sources of data: *Official Yearbook of the Union of South Africa*, No. 20 (1939), Col. 1· pp. 1034 and 1035. Col. 2: p. 833. Col. 3: p. 901. Col. 4: p. 497 and No. 4, p. 772.

27.5 per cent greater than in 1911. In 1930, because of the decline in business activity since 1928 and 1929, there was a relatively plentiful supply of Native labor. In 1937 the number of Native males was 66.7 per cent greater than in 1911 and the number of Natives employed in the three industries about 70.4 per cent higher, indicating again a growing shortage of labor. The position in 1938 was even more acute. The number of Native males in South Africa increased by 63,000 between 1937 and 1938, or less than 2 per cent. The number of Natives employed in mining increased over 4 per cent, and in transportation by over 12 per cent. Although data are not available for the manufacturing industry in 1938, competent authorities were agreed that the manufacturing industry had expanded greatly between 1937 and 1938.

Several important changes have taken place since 1911 in the relative importance of the three industries in regard to number of Natives employed. Although the total number of Natives employed in mining had increased by nearly 100,000 between 1911 and 1937, the proportion of the male Native population employed in mining had declined from 14.8 to 12.0 per cent. The proportion of Natives in transportation likewise had declined from 1.7 per cent in 1911 to 1.4 per cent in 1936. On the other hand, the manufacturing industry employed only 2.2 per cent of the male Native population in 1911 as compared with 5.7 per cent in 1938, indicating a more rapid rise in relative importance of the manufacturing industry as a source of employment.

Sketchy as these data are, they indicate that there is no reason to expect that over a period of time the supply of Native labor will increase at the same rate as demand. On the contrary, in times of boom there may be serious shortages in the total supply of labor, more especially if the boom conditions, starting usually in the gold mining industry, continue for a sufficient length of time to be communicated to other branches of economic activity. In 1938 the competition for labor was considerably more acute than in 1936. During such periods there is pressure upon the Government to encourage the importation of Native labor from adjacent countries such as Rhodesia and Mozambique and to use more female and juvenile Natives. Wages tend to rise somewhat but the absolute increase is small. The general economic policies of the country, as well as the attitude of all European employers, tend to keep the absolute levels of Native wages from rising rapidly. The existence of a large "poor white" population also operates to prevent Native wages from rising.

Hence, considering the position of agricultural labor, it is logical to expect, quite apart from other reasons, that whenever there are boom conditions in South Africa, farmers will experience considerable difficulty in obtaining and holding an adequate supply of farm labor. If in addition to this, conditions of employment on farms are less attractive than in urban areas, there will be a long-time drift of labor away from farms, which will tend to make the farm labor shortage still more acute during boom periods. There is distinct evidence that work on farms has become less attractive to Natives.

Part IV

South Africa's Economic Policies

CHAPTER 13

WAGE POLICIES

THERE IS ALWAYS some danger in attempting to evaluate a country's economic policies, especially if such evaluation must cover a considerable period of time. Economic policies are often implicit rather than explicit. They are often not clearly defined, even by agencies initiating or carrying out the policies. Too frequently they are discoverable merely as an underlying attitude of mind among the people of a country and are reflected in certain definite reactions to economic problems that arise over a period of years. At certain points of time and under certain circumstances, these policies may become clearly defined in legislation and in action programs.

It is not proposed in this section to attempt an analysis of all the economic policies of the Union of South Africa, explicit or implicit, but rather to confine attention to certain aspects of such policies as have a clear bearing upon the unskilled labor problem. These policies will be dealt with under four different headings: wages, taxation, manufacturing, and agriculture. There is a considerable degree of interrelationship between these four policies, for they form an integral part of the whole economic structure of South Africa.

Origin of Present Wage Policy.—This is at the same time one of the oldest and one of the least well defined policies. In some ways it can be regarded as an integral part of a still broader policy of perpetuating the superior economic position of the white man in a country in which Europeans constitute only a small part of the total population. It is thus a part of a policy which unfriendly critics may define as race discrimination.

The wage policy perhaps goes back even beyond 1870, when the rudiments of a wage-earning class were first established with the opening of the diamond mines. The early Boer settlers of the interior of the country regarded themselves in much the same light as the children of Israel entering the Promised Land. The hostile Native tribes of the interior were broken up or confined to areas where they would be less of a menace to the settlers. Native families which were permitted to settle on European farms on the whole received humanitarian treatment but were nevertheless regarded as being inferior human beings. A sort of feudal serfdom existed on individual farms. This philosophy or attitude of mind relative to the superiority of the white population has continued to the present time and is accepted more or less as a matter of course by the vast majority of both the Afrikaans-speaking and English-speaking groups of the European population.

When the diamond mines and later the gold mines were established, it was found that South Africa had no large group of skilled artisans who could be attracted into these industries. It became necessary to offer very high wages to attract skilled artisans and miners from overseas. At the same time considerable difficulty was experienced in obtaining unskilled laborers, although the country had a relatively large supply in its Native population. A laboring class and people working for wages, however, had no place in the primitive tribal economy. The various colonies and republics resorted to taxation in order to force Natives to leave their reserves and locations to undertake work for wages. Gradually, too, pressure of population upon resources forced more and more Natives to go out and supplement their family incomes by working for wages. The great majority of Natives in South Africa have now become accustomed to the wage system and are willing to enter service in mining, manufacturing, or other industries in order to supplement their income from the family farming operations.

It was found that when once the lack of interest in working for wages had been overcome, the Natives were perfectly willing to accept very low wages in comparison with those paid to Europeans. For a number of reasons, the mining companies found it more satisfactory to house their Native laborers in compounds and to provide them with food in addition to the payment of a cash wage. The provision of food and quarters was important to the Native, for this had been for years his prime interest in life. Also, Natives so housed and fed were less subject to exploitation in urban areas where life was entirely strange to them. The cash wage enabled the Native to purchase such comforts or goods as he desired and also to have some money to take back to his family at the end of his period of service. The same practice of supplying food and quarters in addition to a cash wage was adopted for Natives engaged as domestic servants, and later also by municipalities, government undertakings (such as the railways), and manufacturing industries employing relatively large groups of Natives. Manufacturing and commercial establishments which employ merely a few Natives may provide quarters alone if such are available on the premises or may pay a cash wage only, the latter being high enough to include, in addition to the prevailing cash wage, the value of food and quarters.

A labor situation characterized by a relative scarcity of skilled white labor and a relative abundance of unskilled non-European (mainly Native) labor continued for many years after the opening up of the Witwatersrand gold mines. After a while it became customary for employer and employee groups to regard a high European wage and a low Native wage as an established institution. This attitude still prevails in spite of the fact that, since the turn of the century, the labor situation has undergone a radical change. The labor unions and labor laws appear to have as one of their fundamental objectives the protection of the high discriminatory level of wages paid to Europeans.

Development of Trade Unionism.—Prior to Union (1910), trade unionism had made little progress in South Africa and was confined largely to unions of carpenters, engineers, printers, and mine workers. The earliest known union, the Amalgamated Society of Carpenters and Joiners, was established in

1881, followed by the Iron Moulders Society in 1896, the South African Typographical Union, and the Engine Drivers' and Firemens' Association in 1898. For some years prior to Union, organized workers on the Witwatersrand were represented by the Witwatersrand Trades and Labour Council, which was superseded in 1911 by the Transvaal Federation of Trades, which still later became the South African Industrial Federation, an organization representing labor throughout the Union. This organization undertook to develop unionization of workers in all parts of South Africa. After the industrial disturbances of 1922, the Chamber of Mines refused to recognize the position of the South African Industrial Federation and modified its recognition of individual unions in the mining industry.[1] The events of 1922 resulted in a severe setback for trade unionism, but with the passage of the Industrial Conciliation Act of 1924, a new impetus was given to the movement so that by the late 1930's, labor unions had been established in most of the important industries. Working conditions of unorganized industries are regulated under the Wage Act of 1937.

Statistics on the membership of trade unions prior to Union are unreliable. In 1910 the combined membership of the known unions was 9,178.[2] During the war years, membership expanded rapidly so that by 1920 it had reached 135,140, but during the post-war depression and labor disturbances, membership declined rapidly to 81,861 in 1922, then gradually increased to 213,620 in 1927. In 1928, however, membership again declined drastically to 114,516 and continued to decline gradually to 101,888 in 1931. Another rapid increase in membership began in 1934 so that by 1938 trade unions had an all-time peak membership of 253,651. There is some duplication in these figures, as it is not uncommon for craftsmen to be members of more than one union.

On September 30, 1938, there were 166 employees' unions in South Africa, only 17 of which had been in existence prior to 1910; 29 were established between 1925 and 1929; 23 be-

[1] *Official Yearbook of the Union of South Africa*, No. 5 (1920-21), pp. 305-306.
[2] *Official Yearbook of the Union of South Africa*, No. 20 (1939), p. 261.

tween 1930 and 1934; and 57 between 1935 and 1938. Of the 166 unions, 133 with a membership of 216,218 were registered under the Industrial Conciliation Act of 1924, as amended by the Industrial Conciliation Act of 1937. The 33 nonregistered unions or associations had a membership of 37,433.

There is no law against the formation of trade unions by non-Europeans, including Natives. Included in the total membership of nonregistered trade unions are considerable numbers of Natives—the exact number being unknown. A non-European union organized in 1919 had a very chequered career, being torn by internal dissension and difficulties, which led to the formation of subsidiary and rival unions. Another body, known as the Federation of Non-European Trade Unions, was founded in 1928. Under the Industrial Conciliation Act, a trade union must be made up of employees, but pass-bearing Natives are excluded from the definition of employees in the Act. Organizations of pass-bearing Natives may, however, function as nonregistered bodies. Several Colored and Indian trade unions have been formed in different industries.

Although Natives may organize into nonregistered trade unions, these unions have never been powerful numerically or economically and have never been a very potent factor in bettering working conditions and wages of Native workers. The European trade unions, on the other hand, include relatively large proportions of persons engaged in mining, manufacturing, transportation, and government service. Their militant policy, supported by a sympathetic government, has succeeded to a considerable extent in perpetuating and improving, thus far at least, the favorable wage position of the Europeans.

Wage Policies of Trade Unions.—The highest levels of European wages, as was mentioned earlier, have existed in the gold and coal mining industries. Strong labor unions in these industries have in the past been able to share (by means of higher wages) with the mining companies in the occasional periods of boom and have been able to resist to some extent undue declines of wages during periods of depression. These unions, too, have been able to resist with much success the influx of large number of workers from other industries, which might have the effect of undermining the relatively favorable wage levels in the mining industries.

Metaphorically speaking, the level of European wages in the gold mining industry is the star to which is hitched the wage policies of trade unions in other industries. Thus, if the economic position of a particular industry improves as a result of the introduction of more efficient methods of production or as a result of a sustained improvement in demand, the union or unions representing European workers in that industry will strive for an increase in wages and better working conditions. The accumulated effect of such trade union policies applied over a period of time in a number of industries is that a considerable part of the benefits emanating from technological progress is secured by European workers in the form of higher wages. The awards of the Labor Board and the administration of the various acts entrusted to the Department of Labor all tend in the same direction.

In a capitalistic economy, one of the main functions of competition is supposed to be that of distributing widely the benefits of technological progress. This distribution may be effected in one or all of several ways: higher wages, improved working conditions, and lower prices. If technological progress is more or less equal and simultaneous in a large number of industries, benefits in the form of higher wages or improved working conditions will be widely distributed. Such a condition of affairs, however, is seldom encountered in the economic world. Technological progress may be rapid in some industries, slow in others. Thus, if distribution of the benefits of technological progress is made largely in the form of higher wages and better working conditions, the benefits will be confined mainly to workers in the favored industries.

For South Africa, the distribution of benefits of technological efficiency in the form of higher wages to European workers is likely to have a particularly unfavorable effect upon the economy of that country. In the first place, the numerically predominant Native, and to a lesser extent the Colored and Asiatic, populations are excluded from such benefits. In the second place, the relatively large agricultural population is excluded from such benefits. In the third place, it has tended to perpetuate a wage situation that conformed to supply-and-demand conditions in the early days of the development of the mining industry, but is no longer in accord with a condition in which European labor, even skilled labor, is relatively plentiful. In the fourth place, the policy with regard to high European wages has acted and will continue to act as a deterrent to the establishment of new secondary industries and to the expansion of old industries. All forms of government subvention are resorted to in order to aid manufacturing industries to start or to continue in operation. Finally, the exclusion of Natives from participation in the benefits (in the form of higher wages) of technological efficiency has tended to maintain Native labor at a dead level of low efficiency. There is practically no differential wage incentive to encourage Natives to attain higher degrees of manual efficiency.

Changes in the Labor Situation.—The labor situation in South Africa during the past two or three decades is to some extent a reversal of the situation prevailing during the last quarter of the nineteenth century. The supply of European workers in relation to the restricted number of highly paid positions has become abundant, whereas there appears to be an inadequate supply of Natives to fill the large number of unskilled positions. The problem is, of course, complicated by the fact that large numbers of Europeans are by nature, training, or inclination unfit to occupy skilled positions and "white collar" jobs and are fit only to do unskilled work. On the other hand, considerable numbers of Natives and especially Asiatics and Colored persons have gradually acquired special skills for which, however, because of the perpetuation of an outmoded wage situation, they are inadequately recompensed. The situation is well summarized in the following statement:

> The labour supply no longer consists of a small European labour force superimposed upon a mass of non-European unskilled labour with a low standard of living.

Economic forces have now drawn Europeans into the unskilled labour group, while some of the non-Europeans have elevated themselves into the semiskilled and skilled groups. But notwithstanding this radical change in the structure of the labour supply, the South African wage structure has in the meantime remained essentially unaltered.[3]

In order to meet the problem of unemployed Europeans, the country after 1920 embarked on what has come to be known as the "Civilized Labour Policy," which in effect involves the employment, wherever possible, of unskilled or semiskilled Europeans in place of non-Europeans, particularly Natives.[4] The government, labor unions, and various other organizations have brought pressure of one form or another to bear upon firms to employ greater numbers of Europeans. The government, as an example, has gradually placed Europeans in many types of employment formerly occupied by Natives. There has been a tendency to award government contracts and higher tariff protection to firms showing a willingness to conform to the "Civilized Labour Policy."

As Europeans filling unskilled labor positions receive wages several times higher than those paid to Natives doing the same type of work, the Civilized Labour Policy has indirectly served to place a brake on any upward movement of Native wages generally. Europeans tend to be placed in semiskilled positions which might be available to Natives who have acquired a greater degree of manual dexterity and skill. Also, if the unskilled wage bill is increased by the employment of higher-wage European labor, business firms, which are coerced into employing more Europeans, will try to offset this to some extent by employing Natives at the lowest possible wage rates.

Criticism of Labor Policy.—Looked at from a broad economic standpoint, the wage policies that have been maintained in the Union of South Africa must raise grave doubts. These policies have had the effect of artificially perpetuating a labor

[3] *Report of the Industrial Legislation Commission* (Pretoria, Government Printer, 1935), p. 14.
[4] *Official Yearbook of the Union of South Africa,* No. 20 (1939), p. 248.

and wage situation once justified by demand-and-supply conditions for skilled and unskilled labor, but no longer in conformity with present circumstances. A heavy burden of overhead is placed upon all productive industry, not only because of high European wages but also because of the lack of economic incentive towards greater efficiency by Native workers. But the situation is even more involved because, under our economic system, wages constitute one of the chief sources of buying power. In South Africa, however, the wage policies followed so far have tended to place severe limits on the extent to which the combined buying of Natives can expand. Industry is thus burdened by high wage costs and a restricted market.

Economists are generally agreed that high wages are justified only if there is a large output per man-hour. A large output per man-hour in turn is dependent upon an efficient combination of labor, capital, and management. Under modern conditions of industrial development, such combinations depend upon large-scale operation. But in order to have large-scale operation, there must be a large market for the product of manufacturing industries. In other words, mass production industries can continue to operate successfully only if our economic system is so organized as to generate mass buying power.

Unless and until the Natives are supplied with a greatly expanded buying power, the development of efficient manufacturing industries in South Africa will be severely limited. The time for abandonment of the artificial wage policies in South Africa appears to be long overdue.

Abandonment of the wage policies followed heretofore does not necessarily involve a lowering of the level of European wages. It does mean, however, that the differential between Native and European wages must be narrowed. If this change is brought about by the gradual rising of Native wages as a result of development of greater efficiency, the development of secondary manufacturing industries will be stimulated rather than retarded. More attention will have to be given also to the gradual lowering of prices in line with developments in technological efficiency. A general and sustained decline in prices of goods and services, produced primarily for consumption in the country, resulting from more efficient methods of production will in the long run, and in spite of temporary dislocation, benefit all members of the population, for it means an increase in real wages.

On the other hand, if South Africa does not abandon its highly artificial wage policies, it will be necessary for the government to resort to more and more restriction and more and more subvention of agriculture and industry until the whole economy is placed in an economic strait jacket. Eventually, however, its whole economy will collapse if that country continues to pursue policies which appear to be in direct opposition to sound economic principles. Collapse has been prevented so far only because the country has been fortunate enough to have mineral resources for which the demand has been greatly though temporarily stimulated.

CHAPTER 14

TAXATION POLICIES

THE TAXATION POLICIES followed in a country over a period of years may have a very profound effect upon the economic development of that country and upon the trend of employment and wage levels in different industries. This is particularly the case when certain forms of taxation are imposed primarily to induce large groups of the population to offer themselves as laborers. In a country like South Africa, where the state owns and operates the railway system, freight charges may be used as an adjunct to the taxation system in so far as freight rates influence the location and development of industry. Adjustable import duties may also be used to influence the wage and employment policies of groups of employers, as well as their ability to compete with each other and with other industries for the use of land, labor, and capital. Only such aspects of the taxation policies of South Africa as have a direct bearing on the problem under review will be dealt with here.

Government Revenues and Expenditures.—Government expenditures, both those of the Union government and the provincial administrations, have nearly quadrupled since Union (1910). In 1911-12 the net expenditures of the Union government amounted to £10,226,000 and that of the four provincial administrations to £2,884,000, or together to £13,109,000.[1] By 1937-38 the expenditures of the Union government had increased to £32,629,000 and that of the provincial administrations to £17,572,000, or together to £50,201,000. Since 1911-12 there has been an excess of revenue over expenditure in 16

[1] *Official Yearbook of the Union of South Africa*, No. 20 (1939), p. 563.

years and a deficit in 11 years. The total of the surpluses, however, greatly exceeds that of the deficits so that, taking the period as a whole, the financial position of the country's government is very strong.

In 1937-38 the gross revenue of the Union government amounted to £43,611,000, of which 14.48 per cent was expended as subsidies to the provincial administrations, 14.41 per cent expended for law, order, and protection, 10.88 per cent spent for pensions, 12.26 per cent expended on public debt, and 3.69 per cent spent in direct assistance to farmers (table XXXIV).

TABLE XXXIV
REVENUE AND EXPENDITURE: UNION GOVERNMENT—1937-38

REVENUE			EXPENDITURE			
Sources	Amount (in £1,000's)	Per cent of total	Items	Amount (in £1,000's)	Per cent of total	Per cent of total plus surplus
Customs and excise*....	13,577	31.13	Provincial subsidies.....	6,315	16.08	14.48
Posts and telegraphs....	5,540	12.70	Law, order, and protection...............	6,284	16.00	14.41
Native taxation*.......	630	1.40	Post office...........	3,985	10.14	9.14
Mining taxation........	9,607	22.03	Pensions.............	4,743	12.07	10.88
Other direct taxation...	8,856	20.31	Lands and agriculture...	2,294	5.84	5.26
Public estate..........	1,548	3.55	Public health.........	1,313	3.34	3.01
Interest..............	2,458	5.64	Higher education......	1,165	2.97	2.67
Miscellaneous.........	1,394	3.20	Public works..........	1,664	4.24	3.82
			Mines, etc...........	898	2.29	2.06
			Labor and social welfare.	1,273	3.24	2.92
			Native affairs.........	868	2.21	1.99
			General government....	1,522	3.87	3.49
			Public debt...........	5,348	13.61	12.26
			Assistance to farmers...	1,610	4.10	3.69
			Total ordinary expenditure..........	39,284	100.00	90.08
			Surplus..............	4,327	......	9.92
Total..........	43,611	100.00	Total...........	43,611	......	100.00

*Net after deductions.
Source of data: *Official Yearbook of the Union of South Africa*, No. 20 (1939), p. 567.

The surplus amounted to 9.92 per cent of gross revenue so that the operation of all government departments and agencies (other than police, justice, and defense) amounted to 34.36 per cent. Customs and excise provided 31.13 per cent of the total revenue of the Union government, mining taxation (including income taxes and export tax on diamonds) 22.03 per cent, other direct taxation 20.31 per cent, posts and telegraphs 12.70 per cent, and all other 13.79 per cent.

Several of these revenue items represent net revenue, after deduction to loan, trust, or other funds. For example, the total customs collections in 1937-38, after refunds and allowances to other administrations, were £12,291,000, of which £1,613,000, representing 3d. a gallon on all imported gasoline, was credited to the National Roads Fund. Similarly, the gross revenue from mining was £14,579,000, of which £4,390,000 was credited to the Loan Account (table XXXV). Of the gross revenue from mining, £9,845,000 was obtained from taxation and £4,734,000 from lease revenue on state-owned properties and from state mining (diamonds). The gross revenue from taxation of Natives amounted to £2,372,870. Only £630,000 of this was retained by the Union government, the balance being paid over to the South African Native Trust Fund or to provincial administrations.

The gross revenue of the four provincial administrations in 1937-38 amounted to £17,188,000, of which £8,233,000 was collected as taxes, licenses, etc., by the provincial administrations, £6,319,000 was obtained as a subsidy from the Union government, £817,000 as a grant from the South African Native Trust Fund, and £1,809,000 as a grant from the National Road Fund. Of the total expenditures of £17,572,000 by the four administrations, £9,611,000 or nearly 55 per cent was for education, £4,385,000 or about 25 per cent for roads, bridges, and local works, just over 8 per cent for hospitals and charitable institutions, and the balance for administration and other local government activities.[2]

Taxation of the Mining Industry.—Reference has been made previously to the fact that the mining industry, especially gold mining, of South Africa plays a central role in the economy of that country. Not only does it provide a ready market for a considerable part of the products of the manufacturing and agricultural industries of the country, but it also contributes a

[2] *Op. cit.,* pp. 600, 603.

TABLE XXXV
MINING AND TOTAL REVENUE—UNION OF SOUTH AFRICA

Source of revenue	1911-12	1919-20	1929-30	1937-38
	(£)	(£)	(£)	(£)
Gold mines				
Income tax or mining tax	1,003,546	943,296	1,128,460	9,455,880
Excess profits	....	....	....	....
State ownership (lease revenue)*	....	....	1,996,214	4,037,013
Bewaarplaatsen	140,611	205,452	72,409	98,535
Share of profits	....	630,353	....	....
Total	1,144,157	1,779,101	3,197,083	13,591,428
Diamond mines				
Income tax or mining tax	475,445	593,337	409,517	16,402
Export duty	....	1,331,500	783,647	237,863
State ownership (lease revenue)*	333,176	....	170,036	....
State mining	....	....	2,066,571	187,402
Share of profits	....	879,504	....	....
Total	808,621	2,804,341	3,429,771	441,667
Other mines				
Income tax or mining tax	32,627	108,513	95,194	134,939
State ownership (lease revenue)*	16,540	....	5,749	12,250
Share of profits	....	4,567	....	....
Total	49,167	113,080	100,943	147,189
Licenses and "mynpacht" dues	304,651	279,380	313,818	399,056
Total mining revenue	2,306,596	4,975,902	7,041,615	14,579,340
Less amount credited to loan account	....	....	3,177,000	4,389,712
	2,306,596	4,975,902	3,864,615	10,189,628
Other revenue	15,062,434	21,910,055	26,621,843	33,421,113
Total revenue: Union government	17,369,030	26,885,957	30,486,458	43,610,741
Mining revenue as per cent of total revenue	13.3	18.5	12.6	23.3

*Includes revenue credited to loan account.
Source of data: *Official Yearbooks of the Union of South Africa*, No. 1 (1910-1916), pp. 606-607; No. 5 (1910-1921), pp. 817, 819; No. 20 (1937-1938), pp. 570, 571.

large and growing share of the total revenue of the Union government. In 1911-12 the total revenue from mining was £2,307,000; in 1937-38 it was some £14,579,000, a more than sixfold increase since 1911-12 (table XXXV). Of the amount of £14,579,000, some £4,390,000 was credited to the Loan

Account and £10,190,000 to the General Revenue Account. In 1911-12 mining revenue amounted to 13.3 per cent of the total revenue of the Union government; in 1937-38, after deducting the amount credited to the Loan Account, it represented 23.3 per cent.

In 1911-12 the gold mining industry provided just under 50 per cent of the total revenue from mining, the diamond mining industry about 35 per cent, and other branches of mining the balance of 15 per cent. In 1937-38 the gold mining industry provided about 93 per cent of all revenue from mining, and the diamond mining industry only 3 per cent, 4 per cent being from other sources. Of the £14,579,000 total revenue from mining, income tax provided £9,607,000, export duty on diamonds £238,000, licences and "mynpacht" dues £399,000, lease of state properties £4,049,000, and state mining (diamonds) £187,000.

As the mining industry is also one of the most important users of imported products and of locally produced goods on which excise duties are levied, it also contributes a considerable part of the indirect taxes of the country. The rate structure of the railways also tends to place a differential burden on the mining industry, both as regards products used in mining and upon the output of the mines.

The growing tax burden being placed on the mining industry should be a matter of grave concern for two reasons. First, there is serious danger that taxation may appropriate such a large part of the income from mining that the investment of new capital for the expansion of existing facilities or for the development of new sources of supply may be discouraged. Second, experience has shown that the huge accretion of revenue from mining may result in prodigal and unwise expenditures.

Mining is at best a very speculative undertaking, and it is usual for investors to wait years before they can receive any return upon their capital.[3] From a standpoint of good statecraft, there is every justification for the people of South Africa

[3] For an excellent discussion of the economic factors influencing investment in gold mining, see S. H. Frankel, *Capital investment in Africa*, Chapter III.

to share along with investors in the proceeds from the exploitation of scarce and exhaustible natural resources. There appears, however, to be a disposition on the part of the government of South Africa and on the part of large sections of the community to regard the mining industry, especially gold mining, as a cow that can be milked indefinitely without any danger of running dry. There is, therefore, a constant danger that too heavy a tax burden or a tax burden unwisely applied may cause a contraction in an industry upon whose prosperity the well-being of the whole country is based. The danger is especially great because all mining operations are not equally profitable. A heavy tax burden may have little effect upon the operations of a high-grade mine but may cause a low-grade mine to close down or curtail operations.

An examination of the economic structure of South Africa raises grave doubts in the mind of an impartial investigator as to the extent to which the well-being of the people of the country as a whole has been advanced as a result of taxation (direct and indirect) of the gold mining industry. Certainly the increased mining revenue has not been used to decrease the regressive tax burden on the Native population, nor to provide greatly extended governmental services to that numerically important racial group. There has been a vast expanse in government activity, but the benefits of much of this expansion have accrued mainly to certain segments of the European population. There also seems reason to believe that part at least of the increased revenue from mining taxation has been used to bolster up uneconomic secondary industries and inefficient production methods. It is significant that in 1937-38 the Union government expended £1,610,000 in direct assistance to farmers.[4] During the years 1931-32 and 1937-38, over £17,083,000, or an average of £2,440,000 annually, was expended on direct assistance to farmers.

Many competent authorities in South Africa are inclined to believe that, far from advancing general welfare, the diversion

[4] As will be shown later, other and even more material assistance was rendered to agriculture under the various marketing control schemes.

of income by means of taxation or otherwise from mining to other branches of economic activity has tended to reduce the national income below what it might have been without such diversions. This is expressed by Frankel in the following statement:[5]

> If by taxation or other measures, resources are artificially diverted from, say, mining to other activities which are not able to make a net contribution to the national income, or whose net contribution is smaller than that which could have been obtained from existing or expanded mineral or other forms of production, then the diversion is uneconomic. Large uneconomic diversions of this kind have taken place in the Union.

Taxation of Natives.—Attention was drawn in the preceding chapters to the generally low level of wages of Natives. In rare instances only do adult males receive gross wages (cash plus allowances) in excess of £50 per annum, net wages being still lower because Natives are faced with the necessity of paying each year transportation expenses from their homes to the city in which they seek temporary work. In view of the generally low incomes of Natives, especially their cash incomes, it would appear that they are subjected to a very high rate of taxation.

Long before Union, the various governments had passed legislation for the purpose of taxing Natives. Revenue from this source appears to have been only a minor objective; a major objective was pressure upon Natives to seek work in agriculture, mining, or manufacturing. The various Native tax measures of the four colonies, carried over after Union, were unified and consolidated in the Natives Taxation and Development Act, No. 41, of 1925, as subsequently amended. Natives were subject to the following taxes:

(1) A general (or personal) tax of £1 a year, payable by each male Native between 18 and 65 years of age. Indigent Natives not able to earn, Natives whose permanent residence is outside the Union, and Natives attending approved educa-

[5] S. H. Frankel, *Capital investment in Africa*, p. 111.

tional institutions were exempted from this and other Native taxes.

(2) A local tax of 10/- a hut a year with a maximum of £2 a year.

(3) A quit-rent payable in some parts of the Cape Province. Natives paying quit-rent are exempt from the local tax.

(4) Pass fees. Most of these are paid by the European employer at the time of registration of labor contracts.

The total direct taxation of Natives in 1937-38 was £2,373,000.[6] The general tax provided £1,412,000, the local tax £225,000, quit-rent £67,000, pass fees £666,000, and the hut or poll tax £2,000, which amount had accrued prior to 1926 under former laws.

Act No. 41 of 1925, as amended, provides that the proceeds of the local tax and the quit-rent collected in the various areas are to be paid to the Native local councils, if such happen to operate in the areas where the taxes are collected, otherwise to the South African Native Trust Fund. Two fifths of the general tax accrue to the Union government (namely, £567,000), the remaining three fifths going to the South African Native Trust Fund. The revenue so derived is used for educational and other purposes among Natives. Of the amount of £666,000 raised as pass fees, £604,000 was paid to the Transvaal provincial administration, £62,000 accruing to the revenue of the Union government.

Natives, insofar as they are consumers of goods imported and of locally made goods on which an excise duty is levied, also contribute considerable amounts to the customs and excise revenues of the Union government.

Whatever may have been the economic justification for the original imposition of taxes upon Natives, there is serious question as to the equity of this heavy direct and indirect tax burden upon a part of the population whose incomes, especially cash incomes, are on such a low level. The general tax alone probably absorbs at least 2 per cent of the gross income of the great majority of Natives and probably at least 3 per cent of their

[6] *Official Yearbook of the Union of South Africa*, No. 20 (1939), p. 468.

net cash income. It is significant that Europeans whose incomes do not exceed £400 a year are not required to pay income tax. The direct and indirect taxation upon Natives appears to be most regressive, especially in view of the fact that the whole wage policy of the country has been directed toward keeping Native wages and incomes at a low level compared with the levels for Europeans.

A remission of the whole or part of the taxes upon Natives alone would result in a very material increase in their buying power. The argument is raised that such a remission of taxes is impracticable, first, because it would take away the economic incentive for Natives to work for wages, and second, because educational and other services for Natives would have to be curtailed since the bulk of the taxation of Natives is spent on these services.

There may be some merit to the first of these arguments. Natives are notoriously improvident and shortsighted. On the other hand, this characteristic may be due largely to the fact that Natives have been subjected to a form of economic life totally at variance with tribal life. It is possible that now that Natives have become more accustomed to a wage economy and are finding it increasingly difficult to wrest a livelihood from their farming activities in the Native territories, they will continue to seek work in mining and other economic activities.

The second argument, that Natives would be deprived of educational and other services now paid for out of taxes on Natives, appears to be even less valid. Europeans whose incomes do not exceed £400 a year pay very little in the way of taxes, mainly indirect taxes, and yet they are supplied with services infinitely superior to those supplied Natives. Principles of equity would appear to justify the use of a large part of the increased revenue from mining for services among Natives, as the predominant numerical element in the population. The fact that Natives have been taxed indirectly by being forced to accept artificially restricted wages would appear to be another good argument in favor of remission of their very regressive, direct tax burden.

Another important consideration in this connection is the fact that an expansion of Native buying power is of vital necessity if efficient secondary industries are to be developed in South Africa. A remission of direct taxes on Natives would probably increase their buying power immediately from 2 to 4 per cent. If at the same time the existing wage policy, which tends to reduce all Native labor to a dead level of low efficiency, could be replaced by a policy allowing higher wages for greater efficiency, the buying power of Natives, as well as their productive efficiency, would be increased still further.

Finally, it would appear that even selfish considerations for the welfare of the Europeans themselves would indicate the necessity of raising the buying power of Natives, whether by remission of taxes or higher wages. If, as will be shown in a later chapter, the vitality and physique of the Native population is deteriorating, the efficiency of the large Native population will be still further reduced—a very serious prospect for the economy of the country. On the other hand, if the efficiency of the Native workers is to be maintained or increased, the buying power of the Native population must be raised.

CHAPTER 15

PROMOTION OF THE MANUFACTURING INDUSTRY

It is not the writer's purpose to analyze in detail the merits or demerits of South Africa's policy, inaugurated in 1925, of encouraging the development of the manufacturing industry by means of tariffs or other means of subvention, nor of reiterating the well-known arguments for and against a free trade policy. From a broad national viewpoint, however, an analysis of the government's policy for the promotion of manufacturing industries is important because its effect is to direct human and physical resources from some lines of economic activity to others and hence has a direct bearing upon wage levels and trends of employment in different industries.

Up to the time of the World War (1910-14), South Africa's two main branches of economic activity were mining and agriculture. Several important secondary manufacturing industries, such as the explosives, cement, and furniture industries and industries providing various types of services, such as power, repairs, printing, and transportation, had grown up over a period of years with little or no tariff protection or other forms of government support. High transportation costs and the nature of the goods produced or services rendered gave local producers adequate protection (other than high tariffs) against foreign producers of such goods and services.

As was pointed out before (page 122), the conditions arising out of the World War resulted in the establishment of several additional manufacturing industries to produce goods previously supplied by the belligerent countries. Many of these industries experienced great difficulty in meeting the renewed competition from foreign countries after the war and, without tariff protection, would doubtless eventually have gone to the wall. They, however, brought great and growing pressure to bear upon the government for adequate tariff protection.

Policy of Economic Self-Sufficiency.—In 1924, after several years of industrial disturbances arising out of the post-war depression, there was a change in government in South Africa. The new government, a coalition between the Nationalist and Labor parties, frankly and avowedly was interested in a policy which ostensibly would widen the basis of the economy of South Africa and at the same time decrease its dependence upon the economy of the British Empire in general and of the United Kingdom in particular.[1] Three programs to effectuate this policy were adopted. The first aimed at expanding trade with foreign countries; the second, at establishing certain basic manufacturing industries under government sponsorship or supervision; the third, the encouragement of secondary industries and agricultural industries by means of tariff protection or other means of state subvention.

Under the first program, diplomatic and trade representatives were installed in all the more important countries of Europe, Asia, and the Americas. One of the primary functions of these representatives was to develop new outlets for South African products (mainly agricultural) and new sources of supply of manufactured products. This program has been only partially successful in regard to exports but relatively successful in regard to imports. The proportion of all exports to foreign (non-British) countries increased from an annual average of 14.31 per cent for the years 1920-1924 to 21.65 per cent for the years 1925-1929, but declined to 12.92 per cent for the

[1] There was a strong anti-British sentiment in the Nationalist Party, which had as its long-time objective the eventual establishment of a free and independent republic in South Africa. Later, as the political and economic status of the Dominion was more clearly defined in the Statute of Westminster, 1931, and in the various Imperial Conferences, the more moderate elements in the Nationalist Party, led by General Hertzog, abandoned the republican objective, temporarily at least. The agitation for a republic was revived with greater vehemence at the outbreak of the present war (September 3, 1939), when the majority of the members of Parliament decided to sever diplomatic relations with Germany.

Promotion of Manufacturing

years 1930-1934 and to 12.85 per cent in 1938. The proportion of total imports from foreign countries, however, increased from an annual average of 32.25 per cent for the years 1920-1924 to 39.72 per cent for the years 1930-1934 and 46.67 for the year 1938.[2] It is significant in this connection that the Union of South Africa was one of the first of the few members of the British Commonwealth of Nations that developed an extensive barter trade with Germany and the other totalitarian countries.

Industrial Undertakings of the Government.—The second program involved the more rapid expansion of the power industry and the development of the iron and steel industry. The policy of developing electric power was actually embarked upon in 1922. The government that came into power in 1925 merely hastened the expansion of this activity. The Electricity Act, No. 42 of 1922, provided for the establishment of two agencies, the Electricity Control Board and the Electricity Supply Commission. The function of the former was to supervise and coordinate the development of power in South Africa; it was a regulatory, rather than an operating, agency. The function of the latter (the Electricity Supply Commission) was to undertake the erection and operation of plants for the supply of electricity. It, as well as private power companies, is under the general supervision of the Board. The Electricity Supply Commission is a corporate body set up by statute. Although it is relatively free from political control, its members are appointed by the government. In the beginning its capital was supplied by loans from the Union government. These loans have since been repaid, and the Commission is now financed by means of registered stock subscribed to by the investing public. The Commission established generating plants in many parts of the country, the first output of electricity being in 1925. In 1926 approximately 160 million units of electricity were sold; by 1938 the quantity sold had increased to 2,986 million units, and further expansion was under way. As far as could be ascertained, the Electricity Supply Commission is deemed by competent authorities to be operating on a very efficient basis.[3]

[2] *Official Yearbook of the Union of South Africa*, No. 20 (1939), p. 970.
[3] *Op. cit.*, pp. 224-225.

In spite of moderate tariff protection and other forms of encouragement by the government under the Iron and Steel Encouragement Act of 1922, very little progress had been made up to 1930 in developing the iron resources of South Africa. In 1928, however, Parliament passed a new act known as the Iron and Steel Industry Act, which provided for the establishment of a corporation to be known as the South African Iron and Steel Industrial Corporation. This corporation has a total capitalization of £7,500,000 made up of 500,000 Ordinary A shares of £1 each, 5,500,000 Ordinary B shares of £1 each, and £1,500,000 five-per-cent debentures. The Ordinary A shares were subscribed to by the government (nominally Governor-General) from funds appropriated by Parliament for that purpose and may not be transferred, except by act of Parliament. They entitle the government to majority control in the corporation. The greater part of the B shares and of the debentures is also held by the government. The dividends on A shares are limited to 6 per cent per annum, and on B shares to 12½ per cent per annum. Interest on the debentures is guaranteed by the government. The corporation may not be wound up except by act of Parliament. It is managed by a board of seven directors, four of whom are appointed by the government.[4] In 1938 the chairman of the Board of the Steel Corporation was also chairman of the Electricity Supply Commission.

A large plant has been erected at Pretoria, with blast furnaces and heavy and light rolling mills, sheetworks, and by-products departments. In 1939 the corporation's factory had a capacity of 325,000 tons per annum, and further expansion of capacity was under way. The Union Steel Corporation of South Africa, Ltd., established as a private corporation in 1912, is associated with the South African Iron and Steel Industrial Corporation. It has an open-hearth capacity of 60,000 tons per annum. These plants provide much of the bulk iron and steel requirements of the railways and the mining and building industries, and also steel for some of the local metal industries producing simple types of machinery.

[4] *Op. cit.*, pp. 222-225.

The South African Iron and Steel Industrial Corporation has operated successfully as a business corporation in that it has shown a net operating profit. It must be remembered, however, that it operates in a highly protected market and has a virtual monopoly on certain types of iron and steel products. There has been much complaint in South Africa on the score that the corporation practices a discriminatory monopoly, charging to certain industries, such as the mining industry, a price that is considerably higher than the price paid by the South African Railways for the same grade of product.

Tariff Protection to Secondary Industries.—The third program in the industrial policy of South Africa was to encourage the development of secondary manufacturing industries in South Africa behind a screen of high tariff protection. Under the Customs Tariff and Excise Duties Amendment Act. No. 36 of 1925, import duties on all important categories of manufactured goods were increased appreciably. At the same time, provision was made for preferential duties on imports from the United Kingdom, other parts of the British Empire, and such other countries as entered into most-favored-nation treaties with South Africa. This Act has been amended from time to time, mainly to define more clearly the degree of preferential treatment accorded to various countries. In 1939 there was a three-line tariff in effect. The minimum rates are applicable to the United Kingdom or any other part of the British Commonwealth of Nations with which South Africa has concluded an agreement as provided for at the Imperial Conference held in Ottawa in 1932. The intermediate rates which embodied the maximum rates in effect in 1935 were to be extended to foreign countries according to South African most-favored-nation treatment. The maximum rates, which will be put into effect gradually, apply to all other nations and to goods to which no special agreement applies. Provision is also made for suspended duties and for dumping duties to be imposed as the occasion arises.[5]

Under the increased tariff protection introduced in 1925,

---

[5] *Official Yearbook of the Union of South Africa*, No. 20 (1939), pp. 949-955.

the boot and shoe industry has expanded considerably, its gross value of output in 1935-36 being 3.4 million pounds as compared with 1.6 million pounds in 1924-25. Imports of boots and shoes have been reduced considerably. Mr. S. J. Swanepoel (Assistant Secretary of the Board of Trade and Industries), however, considers that the boot and shoe industry is far from efficient and that if the industry could be reorganized into fewer units with a larger output per unit "the industry will, no doubt, be able in the future to compete with foreign producers, not only under the present duty, but also under a reduced duty, and it will be able to reduce footwear prices still further."[6] In regard to manufacture of furniture, he concludes that tariff protection is of little practical value to the industry. The industry was well established prior to 1924 under a moderate protection of only 15 per cent. The bulky nature of the product and high freight rates constitute an effective natural protection even in coastal towns. He arrives at similar conclusions in regard to the cement and explosives industries which were firmly established with a large volume of output prior to 1924. High tariffs, however, have undoubtedly been an important factor in stimulating a large number of secondary industries. Tariff protection is also extended to agriculture.

Secondary Industry as a Stabilizing Factor.—It is undoubtedly true that certain industries or branches of industries in South Africa have at times been subject to somewhat violent fluctuations in output. The diamond industry, particularly, has experienced several periods of severe contraction. As a general rule, however, other branches of mining have expanded at the same time that the diamond industry has contracted so that employment in the mining industry as a whole has maintained a remarkable degree of stability. Somewhat similar conditions obtained in those manufacturing industries that had been established prior to 1925. Certain branches of agriculture and certain agricultural areas have at all times been subject to violent fluctuations in output and employment due to climatic conditions and the prevalence of pests and diseases. However,

[6] S. J. Swanepoel, Government control in industry (unpublished thesis), Part II, Chapter I.

as such fluctuations are usually localized by area and crop, output and employment in agriculture as a whole have been much steadier than in particular branches thereof. The expansibility and contractibility of the newly created industries and their mobility as between areas would have to be great indeed to absorb the occasional surpluses of agricultural labor due to crop or livestock failures. There is nothing to indicate that the government's policy of encouraging secondary industries has contributed to more stable employment conditions in the country as a whole. On the contrary, the newly created industries, as well as the old, all showed a considerable decline in output and employment during the depression years 1930 to 1933.

Nor was there any evidence that there was a surplus or a threatened surplus of labor in 1925 which could be assured employment by the creation of additional manufacturing industries. Ever since the opening up of the diamond and gold mines and the development of other types of mining, the mining industry as a whole has shown a steady growth. The same was true for agriculture and for the manufacturing industry. No doubt, with the passage of time and the development of new techniques of production, more and more manufacturing industries would have been established and the range of economic activity thus widened. There is no evidence that the government's policy merely hastened this development. On the contrary, there is evidence that the high protective policies stimulated the expansion of several industries which were relatively inefficient in the utilization of human and physical resources as, for example, the sugar and wheat industries.

As pointed out before, the mining industry, and especially the gold mining industry, ever since it was first established, has experienced difficulty in securing adequate supplies of unskilled labor. To meet the needs of the mining industry, Native labor has to be imported from all over the southern part of the continent of Africa. The farming community, too, has for years past been complaining about the difficulty of securing farm labor in competition with the mining, manufacturing, and other industries.

It is true that there existed in 1925 a large and growing "poor white" population. The bulk of the able-bodied persons of working age in the "poor white" population are unskilled. Included in this segment of the population are probably large numbers who would be regarded as unemployable—people who are temperamentally or physically unfit for any type of labor. It is extremely doubtful, however, whether the existence of a large "poor white" population is an indication of a super-abundance of labor in South Africa.[7] On the contrary, this phenomenon appears to be the result of a rigid and artificial wage structure, which maintains an extremely high level of wages for skilled Europeans and a very low level of wages for unskilled Natives, both of which appear to be independent of the demand-and-supply situation for skilled and unskilled labor. It is extremely doubtful whether the artificial stimulation of secondary industries in South Africa will accomplish the absorption of a large portion of the "poor white" population under the existing form of economic organization in South Africa.

In the first place, most productive undertakings in South Africa operate on the basis of utilizing a relatively small number of highly paid, skilled Europeans in combination with a relatively large number of low-wage, unskilled or semiskilled non-Europeans. Thus if there is to be an expansion in the number of Europeans employed, there would also probably be some expansion in the number of non-European (mainly Native) workers. But the demand for unskilled Native labor (at existing wage rates) already exceeds the supply. It is possible, of course, that productive enterprises may substitute a certain amount of Native labor by unskilled European labor (receiving a higher level of wages than the Natives), but this would tend to increase unit operating costs unless the greater efficiency of Europeans resulted in a sufficiently larger output per man-hour. If it did not, the enterprises forced to employ

[7] All "poor whites" of working age could readily be absorbed into the mining and manufacturing industries of the country as unskilled laborers, were they willing and able to accept wages more nearly in line with those received by Natives. Such a level of wages would not, however, enable European families to maintain a decent standard of living.

more high-wage European labor would be severely handicapped in their competition for raw materials, supplies, and capital, with industries employing chiefly low-wage Native labor. New industries or enterprises established for the purpose of absorbing more European labor would face the additional difficulty of dealing with less efficiently located resources and with less efficient techniques than industries already well established without special government support.

It is significant that although the government's policy of encouraging the development of secondary industries has been in operation for nearly fifteen years, these have provided additional employment for only a comparatively small number of Europeans and have made no significant dent upon the "poor white" problem. The large increase in employment in South Africa between 1933 and 1938 is almost entirely due to the prosperity flowing to all branches of economic activity from the gold mining industry and cannot by any stretch of the imagination be regarded as a result of governmental aid to secondary industries.

Although the possibility of providing employment for larger numbers of Europeans was undoubtedly an important motive underlying government policy since 1925, considerable emphasis was also placed upon the desirability of developing a wider base for the economy of South Africa. The argument raised was that South Africa was too greatly dependent upon the gold mining industry and that, if new resources could be tapped and new industries created, the basic economic structure of the country would be strengthened. Superficially, there appears to be considerable merit to this argument. Actually, however, accomplishment to date has fallen far short of hopes. The reasons are not far to seek. The mere existence of resources does not mean that they can be efficiently utilized. Mineral resources, for example, iron, may exist in a country, but they may be of very low quality and poorly located. It is often more economical to import such materials or the products manufactured from such materials rather than to divert labor and capital from local industries which are effectively and efficiently utilizing other types of resources. An excellent illustration of this attempt to utilize relatively inferior resources is the expansion of wheat production in South Africa since 1930. In order to make such expansion possible, consumers have at times been required to pay domestic producers a price twice as high as that for which a better quality of wheat could have been imported. Furthermore, in the struggle to produce wheat under unfavorable conditions, much land eminently suitable for production of other crops or products has been ruined, abused, or misused.

Furthermore, it is extremely doubtful whether a wider range of economic activity, in and of itself, will ensure greater economic stability in times of peace as well as in war.[8] Developments during the world-wide depression that started in 1930 would indicate that countries like the United States, with the broadest possible base to its economy, suffered just as severe a recession as countries having a much smaller range of economic activities. Under our modern economy all branches of economic activity within a country, whether they be many or few, are intimately interrelated. A long and severe depression in one industry or group of industries is bound, sooner or later, to be communicated to other branches of economic activity.

In South Africa the advisability of stimulating a rapid development of relatively inefficient manufacturing industries is especially open to question because this has tended to divert capital and labor resources from the two main branches of economic activity, mining and agriculture. Operating costs in both these industries have been increased, or at least held at levels above what they would have been had both these industries had access to world markets for their supplies. It is more than likely that the national income of the country has been decreased as a result of the artificial diversions of economic resources to relatively inefficient manufacturing industries.

It could be argued, of course, that a policy favoring a wider range of economic activity, although it decreases the national

[8] This is quite apart from the broader problem of the extent to which policies aiming at national self-sufficiency contributed to the depression which started in 1930, and to the present war.

income temporarily, is an insurance against possible future collapse of the gold mining industry as a result of the depletion of the gold resources of the country or because of a decline in the value of gold resulting from the abandonment of this metal as a basis of international currencies. Here again the argument is plausible, but the accomplishments are far from convincing. Very few of the newly developed industries cater directly to the wants of the general consumer. As a matter of fact, many of the newer, as well as the older, industries look directly or indirectly to the needs of the mining industry. They supply goods and services needed by the mines or household and other supplies used by people, a large proportion of whom derive their income from the mining industry.

If the gold mining industry fails or declines, large numbers of manufacturing industries, commercial concerns, the transportation industry, and even other branches of mining (for example, coal) which serve mainly the gold mining industry, or persons employed in that industry, would collapse or decline with it. In fact, the whole economic fabric of South Africa as it is now organized would crumble. A long transition period would be necessary before the economy of the country could be organized on a different basis. In any case the other resources of South Africa would not appear, in the light of the present economic development, to be adequate to support a population of its present size without a tremendous reduction in the standards of living of the European, Colored, and Asiatic populations. The standard of living of Natives is already so low that further reduction would mean virtual starvation. In any case, transition to a greatly modified economy in South Africa would be rendered very difficult because of the tremendous institutional rigidities that have grown up in the country.

CHAPTER 16

SUBSIDIZATION OF THE AGRICULTURAL INDUSTRY

THE ATTITUDE of successive governments in South Africa towards agriculture, both before and since Union, has been one of benevolent paternalism. This is based on three factors. First, a great but gradually declining majority of the European population of South Africa is directly or indirectly dependent upon farming or is only a generation or two removed from it. Even at the present time, large numbers of persons prominent in government, in business, or in the professions also own farms or have close relations who are engaged in farming. Second, the philosophy of agricultural fundamentalism has always been very strong in South Africa. The belief is still prevalent that, although the diamond and gold mining industries have contributed much to the wealth and progress of the country, the supplies of these precious minerals would eventually be exhausted. The country would then have to fall back upon agriculture and such manufacturing as had been developed. Third, the farming community and the "poor white" population, largely composed of dispossessed farmers or their descendants, are very powerful political forces in the country. In the past, and probably for many years to come, no political party could long remain in power without the support of at least a part of the farming population. Hence, all governments are only too ready to lend a sympathetic ear to the demands of agriculture or of particular branches of agriculture.

Unfortunately, there has never been in South Africa any powerful nonagricultural group, such as labor, transportation, commerce, or industry, to act as an effective check upon agriculture. Politically, the mining interests have been comparatively weak. The large Native population is almost entirely without political power. Even the powerful labor unions have been mostly neutral on questions involving farm policy, partly because large numbers of laborers are directly related to persons engaged in farming and partly because the unions have been relatively successful in the past in securing better working and wage conditions.

It is not proposed here to analyze in detail all phases of the agricultural policy in South Africa, but rather to present briefly some of the outstanding features of the marketing controls developed since 1920, which have had, and will continue to have, a profound effect on the labor problem and on the whole domestic economy of South Africa. Government assistance to agriculture has in the past taken numerous forms, some of a temporary and local character, some of a national and more or less permanent character.

Railway Rates for Farm Products.—Outstanding among forms of government assistance to agriculture has been the railway rate structure, introduced in the early days when the railways were first developed and continued up to the present time with minor adjustment. Farm products have always been carried on the government railways at rates considerably below those applicable to minerals and manufactured products. The railway rate structure has had considerable influence in determining the location of different types of farming. Significant in this connection is the fact that for many years farm products of foreign origin were carried at higher rates than similar products of South African origin. Thus it was possible for many years to sell Australian sugar (paying a moderate import duty of 3s. a 100 pounds plus 1s. a 100 pounds excise duty) in the coastal areas but not in the interior because the higher freight rates applicable on Australian sugar raised the price above that of domestic sugar. Lower transportation rates on domestic wheat also gave domestic wheat producers an advantage in interior markets. This discrimination in freight rates between domestic and foreign agricultural products was removed in

1920.[1] Since 1930 high import duties have practically excluded foreign sugar and wheat from the South African market.

The government has also undertaken the construction of numerous irrigation projects all over South Africa. Under Act No. 26 of 1912, establishing the Land and Agricultural Bank, loans have been made to farmers to acquire farms and facilities, and to cooperative societies to acquire facilities and to cover working expenses.[2] During periods of drought, flood, or other disaster, the government has borne the cost of transporting seed and livestock, made advances (frequently unpaid) to producers to acquire seed and livestock, and so on. In addition, farmers are given very liberal treatment under the income tax laws of the country. Universities and experiment stations are generously supported out of public funds to conduct research and teaching, and an elaborate and an efficient Department of Agriculture and a Department of Lands have been developed for regulatory and numerous other purposes. In fact, it can be stated without fear of contradiction that no industry or economic group within South Africa has received more sympathetic and liberal treatment at the hands of the government than the agricultural industry.

Marketing Controls in Agriculture.—Except for moderate import duties and differential railway rates on certain farm products, none of the policies followed prior to 1920 aimed directly at raising the prices of farm products in South Africa above world levels. Since 1920, and especially since 1930, numerous schemes have been introduced which aim directly at stabilizing and raising farm prices by various forms of marketing control plus prohibitive tariff protection. The history of government control[3] or government-sponsored control over the marketing of farm products in South Africa can be divided into

[1] W. J. Pretorius, *An economic inquiry of the wheat industry in the Union* (Bulletin No. 141 of the Union of South Africa Dept. of Agriculture, 1935), p. 7.
[2] *Official Yearbook of the Union of South Africa*, No. 20 (1939), p. 642.
[3] The term "government control" is used whether such control is exercised directly by a government department or is delegated by law to some agency, such as a producers' control board, operating under the supervision of a government department.

Subsidization of Agriculture

three phases: first, specialty commodity control initiated during the period 1920-1930 but continued up to the present time; second, basic commodity control, 1930-1938; third, coordinated and expanded control from 1938 onwards.

Specialty commodity control: This was applied to only three products: distilling wine (1924), tobacco (1926), and sugar (1926). The conditions leading to the introduction of controls were different in each case, and different forms of control were introduced.

In the case of wine grapes, producers had experienced difficulties in disposing of their annual production ever since the turn of the century. Various voluntary producers' organizations to control the surplus situation were tried at one time or another with little success. In 1917 the producers organized a centralized cooperative association, known as the Kooperatiewe Wynbouwers Vereeniging, to which some 95 per cent of the grape producers of the country belonged. This association became the sales agency for the products of its members, selling wine, distilling wine, and brandy to the large wine and spirit distributing agencies. For various reasons, however, its control was far from complete, and in 1923 the wine industry of South Africa was in a very precarious position. On appeal to Parliament, the Wine and Spirits Control Act, No. 5 of 1924, was passed, vesting in the Kooperatiewe Wynbouwers Vereeniging full control over the sale of all distilling-wines or spirits, producers maintaining control over good wine. Prices were immediately stabilized on a more remunerative basis. Up to 1927 there seems to have been little increase in acreage, but from then onwards the number of vines in the country increased rapidly so that by 1935 there were 102,244,000 vines as compared with 71,075,000 vines in 1927, an increase of nearly 44 per cent.[4] The number of vines continued to increase after 1935.

The tremendous increase in production since 1924 had by 1939 resulted in a surplus problem even more burdensome than

[4] *Report of the Wine Commission* (published by authority, Pretoria, Government Printer, 1937), pp. 9-11.

in 1924. New legislation was under consideration in the 1940 session of Parliament for the stabilization of the industry.

The tobacco industry has been experiencing very low prices since 1920. In 1925 a new Cooperative Societies Act was passed which, among other things, provided for the centralized sale of products produced in a certain area if 66 per cent of the producers were in favor thereof and if the Minister of Agriculture approved. This provision was applied in 1926 to the marketing of tobacco grown in all the more important tobacco-growing areas of the country. A centralized association, known as the Central Cooperative Tobacco Company of South Africa, Ltd., was formed and became the sole agency through which the large tobacco manufacturing companies could obtain their supplies (except for tobacco grown in areas not included). The Central Cooperative Tobacco Company immediately raised its prices to the manufacturing companies to levels considerably higher than those that had prevailed prior to 1926. Producers of tobacco, anticipating a continuance of very favorable prices, increased their output so that in 1928 over 23 million pounds of tobacco were produced as compared with just under 14 million pounds in 1925. Much of the tobacco was of poor quality and types for which there was little demand. The manufacturing companies, with several years' supply of leaf on hand, purchased only their minimum requirements from the Central Tobacco Cooperative Company, which was soon faced with an enormous accumulated surplus of low-grade tobacco. The chief of the Division of Economics and Markets, Department of Agriculture, was seconded to the Central Cooperative Tobacco Company and was sent overseas to try to dispose of the surplus stocks of tobacco. This was eventually done at prices involving severe losses to producers. As a result of the ensuing low prices, production again declined to just over 13 million pounds in 1929.

Since 1928 the Central Cooperative Tobacco Company and its local affiliates have followed a more reasonable price policy. Prices are determined each year in consultation with the tobacco manufacturing companies. By means of type and grade differentials in price, a moderate increase in production of desirable grades of tobacco has been encouraged, whereas production of undesirable grades has been discouraged. Under the Tobacco Control Amendment Act of 1935, a Tobacco Industry Control Board[5] was established as an additional means of stabilizing the tobacco industry of South Africa. When it is considered that the manufacturing phase of the tobacco industry of South Africa is highly monopolized, the control over marketing established in 1926 and augmented in 1935 has merely had the effect of strengthening the bargaining position of producers. Since 1928 centralized marketing control appears to have been reasonably effective in maintaining prices to producers and in guiding production (through price response) into types of tobacco for which there is a market. There is no evidence to indicate that tobacco control has resulted in the enhancement of prices paid by consumers.

The history of sugar control, on the other hand, presents a less favorable picture. In 1925, as a result of complaints by certain sugar-cane producers as to the working of an agreement between themselves and the sugar mills in Natal, an inquiry into the sugar industry was made by the Board of Trade and Industries. In its report (No. 66), issued on April 14, 1926, this government investigational agency concluded that the sugar-cane industry was far from efficient compared with sugar-cane industries in other countries: farm lands were highly overcapitalized; the predominant variety of sugar-cane, "Uba," was of hard fiber and low sucrose content; a cutting of cane was obtained only in 22 months as compared with 12 months in countries where production conditions were more favorable; labor was costly and not very efficient; and milling facilities (also overcapitalized) were often poorly located in relation to supplies of cane. In spite of these strictures and the fact that there were at the time (and still are) only about 600 European

[5] The members of this and other control boards, with the exception of the Sugar Industry Control Board, are appointed by the Minister of Agriculture from names submitted to him by the various groups interested. One member is usually appointed to represent consumers. The number of farmer members on each of the control boards greatly exceeds the total number of members representing all other interests.

producers, the Board of Trade and Industries recommended that the tariff, plus excise duty, be increased from 4/- to 8/- per 100 pounds. This was done. Producers and the mills also drew up a new agreement with more favorable terms for producers. In order to protect the interests of consumers, legislation was passed placing an upper limit on retail prices of sugar. In 1930 and 1932, following additional investigations by the Board of Trade and Industries, the import duty, plus excise tax, was raised first to 12/- and then to 16/- a 100 pounds, virtually shutting out foreign sugar from the South African market. In 1936 a control board, known as the Sugar Industry Control Board, was established to coordinate and regulate matters of an industrial nature.

Under the stimulus of the more favorable prices prevailing from 1926 onwards, the area under cane increased from 217,000 acres in 1925 to 300,000 in 1929, to 336,000 in 1933, and to 360,000 in 1937. Owing to the introduction of improved varieties of cane and better cultural methods, the volume of cane produced increased from 2,147,000 tons in 1926-27 to 4,659,000 tons in 1938-39, and sugar from 243,000 tons in 1926-27 to 523,000 tons in 1938-39.[6] In 1925-26 imports of sugar amounted to 6,100 tons and exports to 70,600 tons. In 1937-38 imports had declined to 1,400 tons, but exports had increased to 267,000 tons or just over 50 per cent of the total production for that year. Most of the sugar exported went to the United Kingdom, where, after paying all shipping charges, it was sold in 1938 for a price averaging 1d. a pound below that paid by consumers in South Africa.

Thus, sugar control in South Africa resulted in such a favorable level of prices to producers that an expansion of acreage of nearly 70 per cent and of sugar production of over 100 per cent was encouraged in just over ten years. The ten million consumers of the country have been required to pay a price sufficiently high not only to induce 600 producers to increase greatly their acreage and output but also to cover the

[6] *Official Yearbooks of the Union of South Africa*, No. 15 (1932-33), pp. 421-423; No. 20 (1939), pp. 773-777.

annual losses involved in dumping up to half the production on foreign markets at prices considerably below those prevailing in South Africa.

Basic commodity control: Control of basic commodities was initiated in 1930 for wheat and dairy products, in 1931 for maize, and in 1932 for livestock. Here again, the conditions leading to the introduction of control and the form of control adopted varied for each product.

The Union of South Africa is not a good wheat-producing country, owing largely to limited areas of suitable rainfall and poor soil conditions. Pretorius is responsible for the following statements:

> ... It is generally acknowledged that South Africa is not a country that is exceptionally well suited to the production of wheat. So far, she has not been able to produce sufficient for her own needs. From 25 to 40 per cent of her annual wheat production is still imported.
>
> Only a limited area along the southwest coast has a rainfall which enables wheat to be produced fairly successfully. Other parts of the country experience either a heavy summer rainfall which is disastrous for this crop, or a fall that is so variable that only in exceptionally good seasons is it possible to produce a profitable crop.
>
> Wheat is to a certain extent grown under irrigation in the interior, but the quantity thus produced forms only a small proportion of the total production of the Union ...
>
> Even this southwestern corner languishes under serious natural disabilities, and were it not for the bolstering of the industry by means of a protective import duty, it is doubtful whether wheat production would continue much longer in that area.[7]

The soils in the southwestern section were low in phosphates and, owing to poor cultural methods, also low in humus. During the period 1926 to 1928, yields per morgen in South Africa averaged about 5.4 bags as compared with 7.2 bags in

[7] W. J. Pretorius, *An economic enquiry into wheat farming in the Western Cape Province* (Bulletin No. 103 of the Union of South Africa Dept. of Agriculture, 1931), pp. 7-8.

Australia, 8.8 bags in the Argentine, 9.5 bags in the United States, and 13.3 bags in Canada. In addition, wheat lands (cultivated lands only) were capitalized from £10 to £14 a morgen, about $24 to $33 an acre, a very high capitalization for poor wheat lands. Finally, most of the wheat grown in South Africa is composed of the "soft" varieties with poor baking qualities.

Towards the end of 1929, world wheat prices began to decline rapidly. Wheat farmers in South Africa were in a serious plight and appealed to Parliament for aid. In an effort to sustain domestic prices, the tariff on wheat was raised to 5/4 a 200-pound bag early in 1930, and in terms of Act. No. 10 of 1930, wheat and flour could be imported into the Union only under a special permit issued by the Minister of Finance. In 1931 a further act was passed providing for a flexible import duty which, added to the import price of wheat, would result in a minimum landed price of 22/6 a 200-pound bag. Regulation of imports plus a minimum landed price of 22/6 continued in effect until the outbreak of the present war (September, 1939). In 1935 a new law (No. 58 of 1935) provided for the establishment of a Wheat Industry Control Board with very extensive powers. In 1940 this agency established local buying agents; determined the prices to be paid to producers; graded all wheat produced in the country; fixed wholesale prices of wheat and flour (miller's margins) and retail prices of bread (baker's margins); and also was vested with the function of regulating imports of wheat.

With a domestic price that in several years after 1930 was more than double the world price of wheat, domestic production expanded rapidly. In 1931-32 the area harvested in South Africa was 820,000 morgen as compared with 407,000 during the period 1925-26 to 1928-29, a more than twofold increase. Owing to an extension of wheat production to less suitable areas and farm lands, production of wheat increased somewhat less rapidly from 2,244,000 bags (average 1925-26 to 1928-29) to 4,114,000 bags in 1931-32. During the next two years, acreage and production declined somewhat, owing to unfavor-

Subsidization of Agriculture 219

able weather conditions and the abandonment of some areas which were found totally unsuited to wheat production, even under such favorable price conditions. In 1934-35, however, output again increased to 4,912,000 bags and in 1935-36, a year in which production conditions were exceptionally favorable, to 6,901,000 bags, or over three times greater than the output for the period 1925-26 to 1928-29.

In many sections the area under wheat production was increased as much as 300 and 400 per cent after 1930. Much of this acreage has since gone out of wheat production, and some of this soil has had its fertility greatly depleted as a result of trying to force a wheat crop on land totally unsuitable for wheat production. Finally, consumers have been very severely burdened by having to pay a high price for an essential food product.

The world price for maize (corn) also declined very rapidly from the end of 1929, and maize producers were in a very parlous situation. Cooperative marketing of maize had proved far from successful. In 1931, at the urgent request of maize producers in the Transvaal and Orange Free State, Parliament rushed through a law, the Mealie Control Act, No. 39 of 1931, the main features of which were (a) control or regulation by the Minister of Agriculture of imports, (b) the licensing of all dealers, and (c) the determination each year by the Minister of Agriculture of an export quota. Much difficulty was experienced in administering this law which was hastily drawn up, and amending and clarifying legislation had to be introduced in subsequent sessions of Parliament. In 1935 a further law, the Mealie Control Amendment Act, No. 59 of 1935, was passed, providing for the establishment of a Mealie Industry Control Board.

The chief purpose of the maize control legislation has been to maintain for that portion of each year's crop sold in the domestic market a price which is above the world price, the balance being dumped on the world market for whatever price may prevail at the time. For this purpose the Minister of Agriculture would determine at the beginning of each crop year what per cent of the crop not used on the farm was to be exported. Assuming that the estimated crop was 19,000,000 bags and that total domestic consumption would be 13,000,000 bags, of which 7,000,000 were used on the farm, then the quantity marketed would be 12,000,000 bags, of which 6,000,000 had to be exported. The export quota was thus 50 per cent. If the domestic price aimed at was 10s. a bag and the export parity price was 6s., the farmer would receive an average price of 8s. Of each two bags purchased by the local dealer, one would have to be set aside for export.

This plan was not applied each year because in a few years, notably 1932-33 and 1935-36, production was so low owing to crop failures[8] that no export quotas were set up.

Considerable difficulties were and still are encountered in administering maize control. There was a tendency each year to underestimate the crop, necessitating liberal grants in some years from the public treasury to recompense dealers for threatened or alleged losses. Farmers and dealers used every device possible to circumvent the laws and regulations. But perhaps the most serious defect of all was that the law, designed to aid commercial maize producers in the Transvaal and Orange Free State, was applied almost without modification to Natives in Native areas who produced maize for their own requirements. This resulted in considerable hardship to Natives as producers. As their sales were usually in small quantities, dealers paid them a price often much below the blended price received by European farmers. The maize control schemes also involved a severe burden on the low-income Natives, who are the chief consumers of this product. Part of this burden was borne by large employers of Native labor, such as mines and municipalities, which fed and housed their Native labor. Livestock producers also complained bitterly that the maize control scheme raised their operating costs. The maize control scheme has to this extent hampered the expansion of the livestock industry, notwithstanding the fact that agricultural economists and farm

---

[8] It is because of the enormous year-to-year fluctuations in output of cereals that Parliament has frowned on attempted production control.

leaders generally are agreed that, as a sound, long-time policy, South Africa should aim at expanding this industry.[9]

The very considerable year-to-year fluctuations in output of maize make it somewhat difficult to determine to what extent an increase in production has been encouraged under the maize control scheme. The growing of maize has been extended since 1930 to areas which previously had grown little or no maize. Furthermore, the two largest maize crops on record were obtained in 1936-37 and 1938-39.

South Africa has never been an important dairy country. During the World War, dairying was expanded considerably; cheese and butter factories were erected all over the Union. After the end of the War, however, the dairy industry was in continuous difficulties. These difficulties were increased towards the end of 1929, when world prices of manufactured dairy products started to decline. After several years of agitation for relief, Parliament enacted the Dairy Industry Control Act, No. 35 of 1930, which, among other things, provided for the establishment of a Dairy Industry Control Board, for a levy on manufactured dairy products sold in the domestic market, for the determination of an export quota each year, and for the licensing of all butter and cheese factories. The losses on exported butter and cheese were paid out of the levy.

As a result of this control, prices to producers and to consumers did not show nearly the same degree of fluctuation during the period 1930 to 1938 as was the case in other countries. During this period, however, production of butter in South Africa expanded from 29,400,000 pounds to 43,300,000 pounds a year or nearly 47 per cent, and cheese from 7,663,000 pounds to 12,462,000 pounds a year, an increase of about 63 per cent. Production apparently has been expanded in many areas not very well suited to dairying. The number of butter and cheese factories remained substantially the same over the whole period. In spite of the fact that output per factory increased considerably during the years 1930 to 1938, operating margins

---

[9] Hubert D. Leppan, *The organization of agriculture* (Johannesburg, Central News Agency, 1936), p. 52.

of creameries (difference between buying and selling prices) did not decline to any extent. From 5 to 20 per cent of the annual output of butter and cheese is exported.

In 1939 dairy control was extended to milk markets, where the market-agreement type of control has been introduced. These marketing agreements provide for control of producer and retail prices. In 1940 the Dairy Industry Control Board extended the range of its control still further, fixing prices for all dairy products all the way from the producer to the consumer.

The most unfortunate aspect of dairy control in South Africa is the fact that consumption of dairy products is very low, particularly among the "poor white" population and the large non-European populations. Medical men in South Africa are generally agreed that a material increase in consumption is desirable from a general health standpoint. Under its State-Aided Milk and Butter Scheme, the government is providing milk (or cheese) free or at a nominal price to European and Colored school children and is making butter and cheese available to indigent families (excluding Natives) at prices about half the prevailing retail prices for these products. These privileges, however, are not extended to Natives. No effort has been made in South Africa to determine the elasticity of supply of dairy products. It is not inconceivable that a slight decrease in retail prices of dairy products would so expand the total volume consumed that producer prices could be maintained without the necessity of export.

Considerable confusion had existed for many years in the movement of livestock to the two main markets in South Africa, Johannesburg and Capetown. Act No. 29 of 1932 provided for the establishment of a Meat Trade Control Board to advise the Minister of Agriculture on matters pertaining to the livestock industry and also to carry out certain permissive functions in regulating movement of livestock to the two principal markets. This law was superseded two years later by Act No. 49 of 1934 providing for the establishment of a Livestock and Meat Industries Control Board with greatly extended powers.

Up to 1939, this Board had concerned itself mainly with the regulation of the flow of livestock to the two main markets of the country. This is accomplished by means of weekly permits. The Board has also undertaken to subsidize exports during certain periods of forced marketing of sheep and to subsidize exports of quality lamb and cattle with a view to developing an overseas demand for South African meat. In addition, it has subsidized the introduction into South Africa of breed rams and ewes for the purpose of improving the quality of South African lamb and has established a price reporting service.

Coordinated and expanded control: Ever since 1930 Parliament had been devoting a great and growing amount of time to consideration of amendments to existing control legislation or of proposals for new controls. It had become apparent also that many of the control schemes were working at cross purposes. In addition, the general supervision of the various controls was placing a heavy and growing burden upon the Minister of Agriculture. In order to coordinate, facilitate, and improve the whole control mechanism, Parliament passed the Marketing Act No. 26 of 1937. One of the main purposes of this Act was to provide for the establishment of control schemes and to confer upon the Minister of Agriculture general supervisory and regulatory powers over existing and future control schemes. All control schemes in existence at the time the Act was passed, with the exception of the wine and sugar controls,[10] were brought under the purview of the Marketing Act.

One of the most important features of the Act was that providing for the creation of a National Marketing Council to consist of five members[11] (with provision for a sixth) to advise the Minister of Agriculture on all existing and proposed control schemes. Although the Marketing Council is nominally only an advisory body, it actually exercises considerable powers. It

---

[10] Wine control continued to function under the Wine and Spirits Control Act of 1924. The sugar control continued under the general supervision of the Board of Trade and Industries.

[11] The chairman and deputy chairman must be officers of the Department of Agriculture; the other three members are appointed by the Governor-General. In 1939 the Council consisted of the Secretary of Agriculture (chairman), two economists, and two farmers.

investigates all policies and proposals of control boards and reports to the Minister thereon. The latter is to a considerable extent influenced by the recommendations and findings of the Council. Since its passage, control schemes have been investigated and approved for dried fruit, chicory, deciduous fruit, and citrus. The control schemes for fruit products dealt largely with the regulation of export marketing. The only important agricultural products which were not under marketing controls in the beginning of 1940 were eggs and wool. Steps were being taken to draw up draft control schemes for these two products.

The above description of the salient features of the agricultural controls developed in South Africa indicates clearly the dangers and weakness of state efforts to guide and direct economic activity in the interest of militant and articulate producer pressure groups. Controls introduced originally as relief measures have become permanent institutions. If the earlier forms of control failed to secure for producers the advantages sought, further and fuller powers were usually demanded. With the passage of time, more and more producer groups have demanded the right to control schemes in order to improve, if possible, their economic conditions. Eventually every important branch of agriculture must have its control plans. Many of the controls work at cross purposes and serve to limit the advantages sought by other groups of producers from their schemes.

But even more unfortunate from the standpoint of the national economy is the effect of these plans upon the utilization of natural resources and upon the interests of consumers. In practically every instance where a control scheme has been introduced in South Africa, a marked expansion of output has been encouraged, often into areas ill-adapted for particular types of production. In some instances, the price advantages accruing from controls have been capitalized into higher land values; in other instances, inflated land values have been preserved. The rape of much farm land through attempts to force production of crops for which they were not suited has led to the near-destruction of soil fertility.

In many instances, because of poor administration and inability to predict the influence of all the variables, the operation of the control schemes has involved individuals and groups in severe losses which the government has, in many cases, underwritten.[12] In addition to the heavy toll exacted by agricultural producers from consumers and other branches of economic activity in South Africa by means of levies and administered prices, the government has contributed millions of pounds to agriculture. In many instances, these contributions were made to defray losses resulting from or connected with the operation of control schemes.

Perhaps the most undesirable feature of all is that many of the control schemes have been extremely regressive in their tax or toll effects. Sugar, maize, wheat, and dairy products are foods consumed in large quantities by the poor. Maize, especially, is the staple food of Natives, the lowest paid group in South Africa. It is almost incredible that a country could follow policies so detrimental to the interests of such a large and submerged part of its population, more particularly as it appears highly improbable that the control schemes will ensure permanent benefit to even the farm groups, who have had a temporary advantage from their operation.

Criticism of Agricultural Policy.—The conditions sketched all too briefly in the preceding pages would indicate to an impartial analyst that the wage, taxation, manufacturing, and agricultural policies are not separate and distinct phenomena. On

[12] For example, the government paid £250,000 in 1935-36, £51,000 in 1936-37, £200,000 in 1937-38, and £390,000 (estimate) in 1938-39 for the redemption of mealie export quotas; £550,000 in 1933-34 to the maize pool to cover losses on export operations; £120,000 in 1933-34 and £33,000 in 1934-35 for losses on the wheat pool; and £4,000 in 1936-37 and £6,000 in 1937-38 to the Wheat Industry Control Board for storage losses. These were only part of the total of £20,559,000 of assistance granted by the government to agriculture during the eight-year period, 1931-32 to 1938-39. Nearly £18,000,000 are not refundable by farmers. Included in the amount of £20,559,000 were £10,223,000 paid as export subsidies on agricultural products during this period (see Appendix, table 11).

the contrary, they appear to be merely several phases of a more comprehensive policy to advance the well-being of the European part of the South African population. It would perhaps be unfair to say that this wider policy has been followed with the deliberate intention of benefiting Europeans at the expense of other racial groups. Rather, it would appear that there was a naïve belief that if the interests of Europeans were advanced, other groups would benefit as well. This is somewhat analogous to the post-war economic philosophy in the United States, namely, that nothing should be done to curb or restrain the genius of American business and financial executives and entrepeneurs because their efforts were bound to advance the well-being not only of corporate and financial institutions but also that of labor and agriculture and all other groups within our economy.

Events have shown that this philosophy is no more valid in South Africa than in the United States. In South Africa, the artificial development of manufacturing behind high tariff protection and other forms of government subvention has placed a heavy, indirect tax burden on mining and agriculture. On the one hand, the forced development of manufacturing has increased the competition which agriculture has to face in securing an adequate supply of Native labor; on the other hand, the increase in the cost of farming (higher prices for supplies) has decreased the ability of farmers to pay wages to Natives sufficiently high to attract them from competing industries.

It is true that, since 1930, certain branches of agriculture have been themselves more heavily subsidized by levies and direct government grants. This has merely placed other branches of agriculture, such as the deciduous and citrus fruit industries, the poultry industry, and the very important sheep industry, which for one reason or another were not able to secure the privilege of control schemes, at a still greater disadvantage. Finally, it seems inevitable that in so far as South Africa is successful in decreasing its imports of manufactured goods from foreign countries, these countries will decrease their imports of exportable South African agricultural products, either in retaliation or because of a lack of credit. It was indeed fortunate for South Africa that the United Kingdom stood ready during the whole of the period 1930 to 1939 to take all South African agricultural products dumped in the United Kingdom. How long this willingness would have continued, is difficult to say. Records in the Department of Agriculture indicate that Canada resented the virtual exclusion of her wheat from South Africa and was unwilling to open or expand her market for South African citrus and deciduous fruits.

The combined effect of all the direct and indirect taxes upon the domestic economy of South Africa is well summarized by Frankel in the following words:[13]

> The economic policy of successive Governments since Union has rested, and continues to rest mainly on the direct and indirect taxation of the urban communities, in order, in particular, to benefit Europeans engaged in agriculture. A large part of the burden of this taxation, as already mentioned, eventually falls on those export industries which receive no offsetting advantages and cannot pass on the tax. Of the export industries, mining, particularly gold mining, is the most important. Moreover, since 1925 the burden has grown because of the increasing protection granted to manufacturing industry. A part of the cost of this, of course, also falls in the first place on agricultural export industries, but in many cases, these are now so organized that, by discriminating between the prices charged in local markets and those ruling in world markets, they largely succeed in shifting again the whole or part of the burden onto urban communities. As a result of the multiplication of rigid, protected and/or sheltered markets, sectional interests are favoured at the expense of the economy and community as a whole.

In this statement the problem of diversion of resources is stressed from the standpoint of urban population. Elsewhere in his book, Frankel draws attention to the adverse effects of these and other policies upon the Native population, which de-

[13] S. H. Frankel, *Capital investment in Africa*, p. 111.

rives much of its buying power in the form of wages earned in urban occupations. In so far as living costs are increased or prevented from declining as a result of government price-supporting measures, the buying power of the Native, already pitifully low, is prevented from improving.

Part V

Effects and Remedies

CHAPTER 17

HEALTH AND EFFICIENCY OF NATIVE LABOR

Food in Relation to Health.—Closely related to and partly arising out of conditions analyzed in the preceding sections is the problem of health and physical fitness of Natives and other groups within the population of South Africa. Quite apart from any economic considerations, the ruling classes or politically dominant groups within a country have a moral and ethical responsibility for the maintenance of healthful conditions among the subservient or submerged groups within that country. This principle is recognized in the care given in all so-called civilized countries to animals and in the positive sanctions against cruelty and gross maltreatment of animals. Civilized communities, moreover, are only too ready to support generously efforts to prevent mass starvation at home or abroad due to war, pestilence, or famine. It is all the more remarkable, then, that only within recent years there has developed a public awareness of the effects of slow mass starvation due to deficiencies in the diet. This situation was partly due to ignorance, until quite recently, of cause and effect relations in regard to health and food. Extensive medical research has, within the past few decades, demonstrated clearly that many common diseases and defects in stature and vitality are directly connected with deficiencies of certain vital food elements in the diet. It is, however, regrettable that, having come to a realization of the problem, so little progress has been made in most countries in remedying the situation.

This tardiness in the correction of a very serious problem arises out of the fact that malnutrition, although partly due to lack of knowledge on the part of consumers of the health value of various foods, is largely due to poverty. Poverty is a relative concept related not only to monetary income but also to range of wants and desires and the cost of satisfying such wants and desires. This concept is of particular importance when considering the position of primitive peoples, whose quantum of wants and desires expands enormously when first brought into contact with people accustomed to a varied and higher standard of living. The South African Native undoubtedly now spends a considerably larger portion of his monetary income, which has not increased greatly, upon clothing, cigarettes, candy, and knickknacks, and a proportionately smaller amount on food than he did fifty years ago. People with low incomes in terms of wants and cost of goods tend to adopt a monotonous and limited diet composed largely of low-cost bulky and starchy food, high in calorific value but low in protective elements. Nutritional research has shown that the prolonged use of such a diet adversely affects health, physique, and stamina (ability to do continuous hard work and resistance to disease). Although better and more universal education in nutrition will aid in correcting the situation, the real solution lies in the elimination or reduction of poverty, an objective which even progressive countries like the United States have so far been unable to accomplish. On the contrary, many countries, under the euphonious name of "economic planning," appear to have adopted policies which, though ostensibly designed to relieve economic distress among certain groups within such countries, actually have aggravated the nutrition problem among the poorer groups.

From a strict economic standpoint, the ability of a country to reach and maintain a high degree of output per capita is dependent to a considerable extent upon the physical and mental fitness of its people. Nowhere is this more important than in countries like South Africa where, owing to the size of the country, to the poverty of its resources other than precious minerals, and to the backwardness of its agricultural and manufacturing industries, human and animal power have been replaced to only a minor extent by mechanical power. Even in the highly mechanized and progressive mining industry, it is still necessary to use large supplies of skilled and unskilled human labor. In neither agriculture nor manufacturing is there the widespread use of labor-saving devices as is common in Western Europe and the United States of America. Under the circumstances it would seem that the continued economic progress of South Africa (Europeans and non-Europeans alike) is vitally dependent upon the maintenance of the stamina and physical fitness of its large Native population. By the same token any evidence of the progressive deterioration of the health of Natives generally, or the existence of conditions which may lead to such deterioration, should be viewed with grave misgiving. Furthermore, constructive measures to stop such deterioration, if it is taking place, or to prevent the emergence of such conditions, should engage the constant and earnest attention of the government of the country.

Recent Interest in Nutrition.—Although the newspapers of South Africa and various other agencies have given great prominence within recent years to the problem of malnutrition, it appears to be an extremely difficult matter to determine whether, and to what extent, deterioration in physique and physical fitness of the Native population has actually taken place. The medical profession and public and private agencies have undertaken extensive nutritional studies among both Europeans and non-Europeans within the last few years. Interest in the problem was brought to a head at a nation-wide nutrition conference held at Capetown on May 10th and 11th, 1939.[1] At this Conference attended by prominent members of the medical profession, economists, and social welfare workers, papers were read on the economic, medical, and social aspects of the problem. The Conference believed the problem to be of such magnitude that it recommended to the Government the establishment under statutory authority of a permanent National

[1] The proceedings and findings of this Conference were reported in *Race Relations* (Official quarterly Journal of the South African Institute of Race Relations), Vol. VI, No. 1 (First quarter, 1939), and Vol. VI, No. 3 (Third quarter, 1939).

Nutrition Council, to be composed of representatives of the medical profession, economists, social workers, and agriculture. The function of the Nutrition Council would be to serve as a clearinghouse for all nutrition enquiries in South Africa and to advise the Government on matters of food policy. The establishment of such a body was under consideration at the 1940 session of Parliament and there seemed every prospect of adoption.

Unfortunately all current nutritional studies in South Africa, particularly in so far as the Native population is concerned, are handicapped by the fact that there is no previously established base for comparative purposes. Consequently, it is difficult to determine, other than on the basis of general observation, whether there is progressive deterioration in the health and physical fitness of the Native and other population groups. With widespread and coordinated research on this problem in the future, the inability of research to measure quantitatively the dynamic aspects of nutrition and health will no doubt be partially remedied. Meanwhile, conclusions on the extent and seriousness of malnutrition have to be based, first, upon opinions of medical and other competent authorities familiar with conditions of Natives in the territories, on European farms, and in urban areas; and, second, upon an assessment of the ability of Natives to procure out of earnings and agricultural production the range of food necessary to insure a balanced diet.

It has long been a matter of common observation in South Africa that there are marked differences in the physique and muscular development of Natives living in the several parts of the country. This is supported by the experience of the Witwatersrand Gold Mines, which employ more than 200,000 Natives each year, and by the experience of medical men who are familiar with conditions in Native areas.[2] These differences in physique and stamina are due to two general conditions: First, climatic, soil, and other natural conditions which influence not only the health of Natives but which also limit agricultural

---

[2] F. William Fox, "Diet and Health in South Africa: (2) Malnutrition," Reprint from the *South African Medical Journal*, Vol. X (Jan. 11, 1936), pp. 12-16.

possibilities, vary greatly in the several areas occupied by Natives. Second, before the advent of Europeans, the physically and numerically weaker tribes had been driven by the stronger and more warlike tribes into the less healthful and less fertile parts of the country.

Allowing for differences in the capacity of different areas to support a healthful Native population, competent medical opinion seems to be agreed that the primitive Native diet, although monotonous in the extreme measured by European standards, contained all the essential food elements. This diet consisted of milk, meat from cattle and game, millet or kaffir-corn used in various ways, including "kaffir beer," and "infino" or wild spinach made up of various edible plants.[3] Since contact with Europeans this diet has undergone radical change for two reasons. First, Natives show propensity, unfortunate in certain respects, to mimic European food, clothing, and other habits. Thus they have developed a preference for white bread, sifted maize (corn) meal, sugar, and other refined foods. These habits acquired in the cities are carried back to the Native areas and to families living on European farms. It is only fair to state that this mimicry of European food habits has not all been to the disadvantage of the Native diet. Natives are now able to grow and consume many types of vegetables which were unknown before contact with Europeans. Unfortunately, the total quantity of vegetables grown appears to be small and a considerable proportion is sold to Europeans. In addition many areas are unsuited to such production.

Second, conditions under which Natives have come to live have limited their ability to procure the elements of their primitive diet or even to fulfill their European-influenced diet. Overgrazing of land has depleted the countryside of many of the plants which composed "infino" or wild spinach, added to which there is a growing dislike for this unpalatable type of food. The quality of Native cattle is extremely poor, whether from the standpoint of draft animals or of milk and meat supply. Al-

[3] F. William Fox, "Some Nutritional Problems Amongst the Bantu in South Africa," Reprint from the *South African Medical Journal*, Vol. XIII (Feb. 11, 1939), p. 4.

though the number of animals has undoubtedly increased within recent years, the number of animals per family has probably declined. To make matters worse, there appears to be a growing maldistribution of ownership of cattle.[4] Some Native families have comparatively large numbers of cattle, whereas others have none or barely sufficient numbers for draft purposes. Many Native families are unable to procure sufficient milk to meet the bare minimum requirements, and meat is becoming a luxury. Vegetables are available in very small quantities, and at certain times of the year are not obtainable at all. Fruit and berries are almost nonexistent luxuries as far as the family in Native areas is concerned. Sifted maize meal and flour are important and frequently the sole elements in the two or three main meals of the day.

These conditions are true even for Natives living on European farms, although in many parts of the country farmers supply their Native labor with meat, meal, and with skim milk, if such are available.[5] It must be remembered, however, that in many parts of the country European farmers themselves have insufficient milk, green vegetables, and fruit.

It must not be assumed that, even in the areas where the physique of Natives is good, general health conditions are satisfactory. The adult Natives are a highly selected group which has survived the hazards of childhood and adolescence. Statistics on infant mortality among the Natives of South Africa are very unsatisfactory and alarming misstatements are rife.[6] Such information as is available, however, indicates that a large percentage of the children born never reach working age (18 years). Superstition and ignorance are important factors resulting in high infant mortality, as is shown in the following quotation from evidence submitted before the Native Economic Commission in 1930.

[4] Information supplied to the writer by responsible Natives and members of the staff of the Adams Mission Station, Natal, and by various other persons, familiar with conditions in Native areas, who were contacted during the course of this study.

[5] See also *Farm Labour in the Orange Free State*, South African Institute of Race Relations, Monograph Series No. 2 (April, 1939), p. 18.

[6] *Report of Native Economic Commission*, 1930-1932, pp. 115-116.

The Natives (Zulus) lose 50% of all babies before the first year of their life, and the reason for this is that the Native has the most peculiar ideas about the child suckling from the mother. During the first week of its life, the child must not take the mother's milk. They get sour milk instead and the result is that babies get diarrhea and die.[7]

In the course of an investigation in the Transkeian territories, Dr. Fox, who is a biochemist attached to the South African Institute for Medical Research, Johannesburg, analyzed data supplied by several doctors on the child-bearing history of over one thousand Native mothers living in different parts of the Transkei. According to this rather meager and unsatisfactory sample, 15 to 20 per cent of the children died during the first year, 25 to 38 per cent before reaching two years, and from 30 to 60 per cent before reaching eighteen years.[8] The Transkei is one of the best agricultural areas occupied by Natives in South Africa. If these conditions are typical in that area, infant and child mortality is likely to be even worse in some of the less fertile areas of the country.

Extensiveness of Malnutrition.—A survey of the literature in South Africa on the health of Natives in rural areas and even in the cities and knowledge of agricultural and living conditions of Natives in all parts of the country, indicate beyond doubt a most unsatisfactory condition of affairs. Although the absence of basic data does not permit conclusions as to the progress of malnutrition, most medical authorities in Native areas seem to be agreed that there is progressive deterioration. Fox made the following statement about conditions in the Transkeian territories:

> The amount of malnutrition and disease that exists must, however, be appalling, more particularly when it is remembered that so much of it is of a directly preventable type being due to ignorance, superstition, inadequate sup-

[7] F. William Fox, "Diet and Health in South Africa: (2) Malnutrition," p. 20.
[8] F. William Fox, "Some Nutritional Problems Amongst the Bantu in South Africa," p. 14.

plies of suitable food, and dirt. There is fairly general agreement, both amongst Europeans and Natives that the standard of physique is deteriorating; several obvious causes probably account for this and since they are liable to continue to operate with the addition of a progressively inferior diet, it may be presumed that further deterioration is inevitable . . .[9]

Dr. Fox and other persons interviewed by the writer indicated that similar conditions would obtain in most of the other Native areas. Although stress is placed in the above quotation on superstition and ignorance as important factors contributing to the unsatisfactory situation in regard to Native health, the consensus of opinion among competent authorities in South Africa is that the disturbance of customary dietary habits and dire poverty are the outstanding causes in the decline of health and physique of Natives. Contact with European food habits appears to have made changes in the food habits of Natives inevitable. This of itself should be no cause for disquiet. What is to be deprecated is the fact that changes have been along the line of greater emphasis on starchy foods at the expense of protective foods. It will probably be impossible to reverse the tide now. The problem thus resolves itself into a search for ways and means to give Natives access to a wider range of foods embodying all essential nutritional elements.

The analysis of conditions in the Native areas presented in the preceding section indicates that the food situation of Natives, in urban as well as in rural areas, is, in the absence of corrective measures, likely to deteriorate still further rather than to improve. Impoverishment of the soil as a result of primitive cultural practices and overgrazing is likely to decrease still further the capacity of the Native areas to supply sufficient greens from edible, indigenous plants and to supply sufficient milk and meat. An ironical aspect of the problem is that in some areas Natives sell a part of their vegetables, which they so badly need, to Europeans in order to obtain cash for the

---

[9] F. William Fox, "Nutritional Problems Amongst the Rural Bantu," *Race Relations*, Vol. VI (First Quarter, 1939), No. 1.

purchase of maize and other filling foods. In another area a creamery has been erected to which Natives are encouraged to sell their cream, thus still further depleting an already inadequate supply of milk.

Even the foodstuffs available are not consumed in their most beneficial form.[10] The demand is for maize meal and wheat with the germ removed. Natives are inclined to believe that Europeans are trying to "put something over" on them when they are urged to consume the whole cereal. The importance of educational work to overcome ignorance, superstition, and suspicion cannot be overstressed. Educational work must also be directed at changing purchasing habits of Natives. Most purchases are in relatively small amounts and at a much higher cost than if foods were bought in larger quantities. This is largely due to the fact that Natives seldom have sufficient ready cash to buy in bulk. It is also due, however, to the fact that even now Natives have not adapted their thinking to a monetary economy and are to a considerable extent unaware of the economies possible by buying less frequently and in larger amounts.

Although educational work will help, the problem of poverty still remains. The Native may be brought to a realization that he should consume more milk, more meat, and more fruit and vegetables, but he is still faced with the necessity of purchasing them. A more varied diet would require greater

[10] The following quotation taken from a mimeographed paper dated December 6, 1939, by Dr. C. C. P. Anning, Medical Officer of Health for Benoni, Transvaal, and entitled "Studies in the Nutrition of the People of Benoni," illustrates this point:

"Apart from the inadequacies in the diet of both European and non-European families disclosed above, the census (of food habits and expenditures made by the Health Department, Benoni) has shown how much waste of money is permitted in the daily purchase of foods. This is especially true among the ignorant natives who, becoming urbanized, develop a form of snobbishness which is expressed in a demand for 'white' foods. 'White' bread, 'white' mealie meal (corn meal), 'white' rice, etc., have almost completely replaced the unsifted, unrefined coarser foods which retain the essential vitamins and minerals. In the wider diet of the financially fortunate these deficiencies are made up in other foods to a large extent. Not so in the Native diet. Yet the unsifted meals cost no more, frequently less, than the refined foods. Out of every 6 lbs. of sugar bought by Natives, 4 lbs. are of the 'white' type, yet the 'brown Government' sugar contains just as much sugar and is ·1 d a lb. cheaper."

expenditures of money and a great increase in variety and efficiency of production in Native areas.

The problem is involved and difficult, varying in degree, if not in direction, in the several Native areas, on European farms and in urban areas. An improvement in the lot of Natives, vital as it is for the future of Natives and the continued progress of South Africa, must depend in the last analysis upon drastic modification of the economy of South Africa and the part played therein by the Native population. The system must be so modified as to insure Natives of a larger income, in cash or in kind, whether such increased income is derived from greater efficiency in farming practices in Native areas or greater efficiency as laborers. This matter will be referred to in the final chapter.

Nutritional Situation of Other Groups.—This discussion of the nutritional aspect of the labor problem in South Africa would be inadequate and possibly misleading did it not give some attention to the position of the other groups in South Africa. The Report of the Carnegie Commission on the Poor White Problem of South Africa drew attention in no uncertain terms to the dire distress among the "poor white" groups in the country.[11] Recent surveys[12] indicate that there is considerable evidence of malnutrition amongst European children and adults in different parts of the country. Although in some areas this is due to absence in those regions of sufficient, or certain types of, foods, especially milk, fruit, and vegetables, an important factor is ignorance of the nutritional value of foods, as well as poverty, which necessitates restrictions of the amount of money spent on milk, vegetables, and other protective foods. In these respects the nutritional problems of Europeans in South Africa are similar to those found in the United States,

---

[11] Published in 1932 by the Pro Ecclesia Drukkery, Stellenbosch.

[12] Report of the Nutritional Condition of European School Children in the Union of South Africa (mimeo.), Feb., 1940, 19 pp., and Nutrition Survey: Interim Report (mimeo.), April, 1940, 9 pp., both issued by the Department of Public Health.

Annual reports of the Medical Officer of Health, Town and Council of Benoni, Transvaal.

the United Kingdom, and elsewhere. Although the problem for small groups is serious and may become worse, it does not have the universal aspect of malnutrition among the Native population. Local charities also serve to provide food and clothing to European families that are in need. As a general rule, cash incomes of European families, even those employed on unskilled work, are considerably above those earned by Native families, and it is thus possible for Europeans to spend a larger absolute amount on food, even though living in distressed circumstances.

No data are available on nutritional conditions among the Asiatic population of South Africa. Generally, Asiatics are in receipt of higher wages than Natives and many Indian families engaged in trade are wealthy, measured even by European standards. The traditional diet of the Indian, however, is long on rice (starch) and short on protective food values. Undoubtedly, among large numbers of Indian families, poverty has played an important part in still further restricting diet. The Institute of Race Relations makes the statement that such evidence as is available indicates that malnutrition and undernourishment are widely prevalent among Indians.[18] The further statement is made that the Institute expects to make a survey of nutrition among Indians in cooperation with the Agent General for India (in South Africa) and the Natal University College.

In regard to the Colored population, there are also many indications of undernourishment and malnourishment. Colored persons generally, whether employed in urban or rural areas, earn incomes higher than those earned by Natives but usually below those earned by Europeans doing comparable grades of work. Long contact with Europeans has given the Colored population food and living habits that cannot be differentiated from those of Europeans. In their efforts to maintain their position of superiority over the Natives and live more nearly on the European plane, Colored families usually spend a rel-

[18] *Race Relations*, Vol. VI (First Quarter, 1939), No. 1, p. 11.

atively large proportion of their income on home and clothing. Even at that, overcrowding is very prevalent in Colored sections of cities like Capetown and Port Elizabeth.

Dr. J. P. de Villiers in a paper read before the Nutrition Conference held at Capetown in 1939 makes this statement:[14]

> The problem of under-nourishment among large sections of the community, and more especially the Colored section, is fast becoming a vicious circle leading to physical degeneration which must be stopped soon if any good is to be done. . . .

He goes on to state:

> At the root of all this trouble lie two great evils, abject poverty and ignorance; but the greater of the two, by far, is poverty, for man must eat to live and profoundest knowledge of what is required will not satisfy the hunger pains of those who are starving in our midst.

It is evident from this that the nutritional problem is also serious among certain sections of the European, Asiatic, and Indian populations. As regards the Native population, the problem is more universal and at the same time embraces the great majority of the population of South Africa, the part of the population with the lowest incomes and whose former mode of life has undergone the most radical changes.

In this connection it is interesting to note that the State-Aided Milk and Butter Scheme introduced in 1935 provides free milk or cheese for indigent European, Asiatic, and Colored school children and butter at greatly reduced prices to indigent families of the same racial groups. These privileges, however, are not extended to the Native population (largely because of the cost) whose need appears to be equal to, if not greater than, that of other groups.

[14] Dr. J. P. de Villiers, "Malnutrition Amongst the Colored People," *Race Relations*, Vol. VI (First Quarter, 1939), No. 1, p. 10.
Dr. de Villiers is Medical Officer of Health, Divisional Council of the Cape.

CHAPTER 18

WHENCE AND WHITHER?

SINCE THE EARLY colonization of the various parts of the present Union of South Africa, each new development has seen a greater divergence in the degree to which the Native and European populations share in the economic life of the country. This division became particularly pronounced with the opening up of the gold mines, when very high wages had to be offered to attract skilled European labor while the wages of unskilled Native labor were only a fraction of those paid to Europeans. This was the origin of the "Civilized Labour" policy, the object of which was in all things to maintain European labor on a very superior level in comparison with Natives. This policy has been perpetuated not only by successive governments but also by the trade unions, which are almost exclusively European. In recent years the government's policy of control of agricultural commodities has also indirectly strengthened the system of discrimination between Native and white labor, since these controls were regressive in effect, the heaviest burden falling upon those with the smallest incomes, namely, the Natives. As a consequence, there have been very grave indications of deterioration in the health and general well-being of the Natives, even to the point of affecting their usefulness as laborers. It is clear that on humanitarian grounds, as well as on economic grounds, the onus of improving the lot of the Native population clearly rests upon the shoulders of the European population. The Native population has no direct voice in the government of the Union of South Africa. The basis of the Native tribal life and of their tribal economy has been destroyed or greatly undermined. Natives, through their contact with Europeans, have acquired desires which they did not have previously but which they are entirely unable to satisfy out of their meager cash earnings.

The problem of raising the standard of well-being is an intriguing one, the solution of which will take time and some sacrifice on the part of the European population of South Africa. The direction in which the solution must be sought seems clear; ways and means to approach the solution, however, are not so clear. The first and foremost requisite is a change of attitude on the part of the European population towards the Native population. During recent years more and more legislation has been directed towards segregating the Native population from the white population territorially, socially, and economically, at a time when mining, agriculture, and manufacturing have come to rely more and more upon a continued supply of Native labor. None of the present industries in South Africa could long survive without Native labor. On the other hand, the Natives have not participated to any extent in the exploitation of the mineral and other resources of the country. On the contrary, there has been too great a tendency on the part of the white population of the country to regard the Native population itself as a part of the country's natural resources.

There does not appear to be any prospect of turning back the tide—of restoring Natives to conditions more nearly approaching those in existence before the advent of the white settler. The Natives, themselves, are too conscious of the potential benefits of a higher civilization to want to return to the primitive conditions of tribal life. In any case, there is not enough free land available to make this possible.

The only solution appears to be in the direction of greater participation by the Native population in the economic life of the country. Natives must be accorded a greater share of the total national income than they now receive and must be granted greater facilities for advancement. Essential to any long-time program for enlarging the monetary income of the

Native population is an increase in the efficiency of individual workers, both in industry and in agriculture. And this, in turn, can come about only if the real wages of Native workers and the productivity of Native labor are advanced. The gap between the average level of European and Native incomes must be narrowed. This does not mean that European wages and incomes must, as a consequence, be reduced. If the efficiency of Native labor can be increased, wages could be advanced in line with such increased efficiency. But under present conditions in South Africa there is little or no monetary incentive for Natives to acquire greater skill. Some improvement will result from the introduction of differential wage rates, based on varying degrees of ability. But because of the backwardness and ignorance of the great majority of Natives, much educational work will be necessary. An extensive program to provide Natives in urban occupations with manual training at vocational schools would have very desirable results, not only by increasing the efficiency of those who attend, but also by keeping young Natives fully occupied and off the streets.

Even more necessary is educational work among Natives engaged in agriculture. An improvement in cultural practices in Native territories is absolutely essential if further deterioration of these fertile areas is to be prevented and if Natives are to produce for themselves a larger part of their food requirements. The educational work carried on by the agricultural section of the Native Affairs Department is meritorious—but in view of the gravity of the situation and the complexity of the problem the work is woefully inadequate. Such work must overcome a great deal of ignorance, superstition, and suspicion —but it must be done.

One of the most difficult problems will be to modify the "lobola" system by substituting quality for quantity of cattle. There can be little doubt but that Natives could very materially increase their milk and meat supply by running fewer but better grades of cattle. Unfortunately, Natives use their cattle for several purposes—for milk, meat, and draft purposes. If better grades of milk and meat animals could be introduced, a possible solution of the draft or hauling problem would be for such cattle to be owned on a tribal or cooperative basis and for each family to use such cattle in rotation. In some areas it may even be possible to provide tractors on a tribal or cooperative basis. Regardless of the manner in which this problem is finally handled, a reduction in the total number of cattle in Native areas is an inescapable necessity.

Improved cultural practices would enable Natives to produce not only more food for themselves but also some feed for livestock and thus decrease the strain on the natural cover-grasses and bushes.

The real wage of the great mass of Natives could be raised immediately and substantially by a remission or reduction of the direct and indirect taxes payable by them. During the year 1935-36 Natives paid over £1,550,000 in direct taxes (excluding pass fees) as well as numerous indirect taxes, such as excise duty on sugar and import duties. In the light of the very low cash incomes of most Natives, these taxes are extremely regressive in character and relatively far greater than those paid by Europeans. It is true that a large part of these taxes is returned to Native areas for educational and other improvements. On the other hand, Natives derive very little benefit, compared with Europeans, from mining and other forms of taxation.

The argument may be raised that direct taxation of Natives is necessary in order to induce them to work. This was the original purpose of some of the direct taxation and the same conditions may still exist. However, this difficulty could probably be overcome by making remission of taxes conditional upon satisfactory performance of work. If this were not feasible, taxes could still be levied but could be paid back to Natives in the form of direct subsidies on food and clothing.

Natives working in urban areas but living in Native locations usually situated some distance outside of the urban areas are subjected to considerable expense for rent and for getting to and from work. This segregation of Native urban workers has to a considerable extent been accomplished at the request and for the benefit of European urban population. That being the case, it would seem only equitable that the European population bear all or a major proportion of the cost so involved. A substantial reduction of the cost of transportation and rent would result in a material increase in the net cash income of Natives in urban occupations—income that would be available for expenditure on food and clothing.

Between 1933 and 1938 the revenue of the government of the Union of South Africa from direct taxation and other sources increased by over 50 per cent. In spite of a substantial increase in expenditures, very little of which redounded to the direct benefit of the Native population, and substantial payments into capital account, net operating surpluses aggregating several million pounds were forthcoming each year. It is a tragic commentary that the lot of the Native population was not improved during the unparalleled period of prosperity experienced by South Africa from 1933 to 1938.

History affords few, if any, examples of countries which have developed a progressive and lasting economic system, the basis of which was the exploitation of a large submerged population. On the other hand, modern economic history indicates that an advancing standard of living is contingent upon an advancement in technological efficiency (resulting in a greater output per man-hour) and a wide distribution of national income. Under modern methods of standardized production, mass output is necessary for greatest efficiency in operation. But if mass-production industries are to continue to operate successfully, it is necessary that an economy be so organized as to generate mass buying power.

In South Africa the possibility of building up efficient mass-production industries is limited because, under present conditions, the market is restricted largely to the relatively small European population of that and the surrounding countries. With larger effective buying power among the Native populations of the sub-continent, the market would be greatly extended. If the government of the Union of South Africa is to attempt to influence the direction of development of manufacturing industries, it would seem that a primary consideration would be to encourage industries which would provide goods and services for the Native population—the provision of clothing, housing, and food, with perhaps more stress on amusement and recreation.

The development of a wider range of efficient manufacturing industries and the expansion of the buying power of the Native population are closely related and govern and condition each other. The one is not possible without the other. Moreover, in the interrelated process the European population would also benefit from any lowering in the cost of goods and services. The whole economic system of South Africa appears to rest on a very insecure and unsound base. In the first place, every phase of economic activity depends to a greater or lesser degree upon one basic industry—gold mining. This industry is one of the most important single purchasers of farm products—especially of meat, cereals, and vegetables for feeding its large aggregation of Native workers. Its white workers also constitute an important market for farm products. A large part of the coal produced in the country is used directly or indirectly by the gold mining industry. Much of the revenue of the transportation industry (mainly the South African Railways) is derived directly or indirectly from the gold mining industry. Not only are transportation rates on gold very high, but the same is true for transportation rates on manufactured products used in that industry. An important part of the manufacturing industry produces goods and services used by the gold mining industry. Furthermore, nearly one fourth of the revenue of the government of the Union of South Africa is derived from taxation of mining industries.

In the second place, institutional interferences by government, labor unions, and other agencies have tended to distort the pattern of economic development. Undue expansion has been encouraged in certain branches of agriculture. Relatively inefficient branches of agriculture have been bolstered up by means of tariff protection or other forms of government subvention; in other instances, such support from the government has forced production into relatively inefficient areas. Similarly, tariff and other forms of government assistance have served to encourage the establishment of new branches of manufacturing or the expansion of older branches, many of which are relatively inefficient. Such developments have been made possible only by placing a heavier direct and indirect burden upon the mining industry and upon the indigent and politically impotent Native population.

Should the gold mining industry for any reason (and the future of the industry is far from assured) decline, the whole domestic economy of South Africa will collapse like a house of cards. As it is organized, the domestic economy of South Africa is so rigid and artificial that the country will experience extreme difficulty in adjusting itself to future changes in domestic and international economic trade. The only logical alternative to the situation that has arisen, is for the government to encourage in every way possible the development of primary and secondary industries which will aim directly at serving the needs of the people of South Africa. In any such program the needs of the Native population must loom large because of the numerical superiority of this racial group.

This would still involve some interference by the government in economic activity. The economic life of all countries has become so complex that some conscious direction of economic activity by the governments of individual countries appears inevitable. What is important is not that government interference should take place, but that such interference should be in the right direction. In South Africa, as in other countries, the government has interfered to advance the welfare, temporarily at least, of particular groups within its borders—pressure group economics.[1] The aid given to farmers, or particular groups of farmers and to certain manufacturing industries, has been at the expense of the mining industry, other branches of farming, the Native population, and so on. In other words, government interference has tended to advance group welfare at the expense of general welfare.

If the economy of South Africa is to be placed on a sounder

[1] For a discussion of the implications of "pressure group economics," see Henry C. Simons, "The requisites of free competition," *American Economic Review*, Vol. XXVI (Supplement, March, 1936), No. 1, pp. 68-76.

basis, from a long-time standpoint, the primary objective of government policy and action programs should be to promote general welfare. This may be to the temporary disadvantage of certain privileged groups—but unless it is done soon, the ultimate and inevitable reorganization of the domestic economy of South Africa on a sounder basis will be rendered more difficult and will entail greater economic dislocation and suffering.

South Africa has the resources to develop purely domestic industries for the production of goods and services for consumption locally. Industries to more fully meet domestic needs have not been developed because the policies of successive governments, labor unions, and the white population generally have been primarily directed to preserving the economic and social "status quo" of the European, as opposed to the non-European population. A reversal or drastic modification of this attitude of mind is a prerequisite to any reorganization of the South African economy on a sounder basis.

It would indeed be presumptuous to pretend that the suggestions offered above constitute a full and final solution of the Native problem of South Africa. The suggestions cover merely one phase, an important phase, of the place of the Native population in the economic life of that country. Even if a broad policy to raise the standard of well-being of the Native population were adopted in principle and vigorously pushed forward, it would be many years before substantial progress could be made. Programs to increase the skill and efficiency of Natives must be carefully planned so as to avoid undue dislocation in the various industries; they must be flexible; they will encounter opposition and obstacles arising out of the ignorance and suspicion of Natives themselves and out of the biased attitude of important segments of the European population. Furthermore, extreme caution will have to be exercised to ensure that the Natives build up a social and economic culture which, although it may parallel that of the Europeans, will nevertheless include the best and most desirable features of Native tribal customs. Cognizance must be taken of the fact that both Natives and Europeans, but especially the Europeans, would be absolutely opposed to any development that threatened to result in a complete merging of Native and European social and economic life.

But even more vexing is the problem arising out of the fact that the location of supply and the location of demand for Native labor do not coincide. Because of the attachment of Natives to land and because of the desirability of preserving at least the basic structure of tribal life, it does not appear practical, at least at this stage of development, to move large numbers of Natives permanently from the Native territories and reserves to the centers of economic activity. This would involve doubling and trebling the population of the Witwatersrand, where housing difficulties are already acute. Nor can the solution of the problem be found in moving or relocating economic activity. The mining and agricultural centers are fixed by natural conditions. Some manufacturing, but relatively little, could be relocated nearer to centers of Native population. The possibilities of greatly modifying the regional dislocation between the demand for and supply of Native labor, appear to be small —at least in the near future.

Possibly with the passage of time and with the growth in individual efficiency of Native laborers, larger numbers of Native families could be absorbed into urban areas. In order to avoid social difficulties they would have to live in locations, but there is no reason why the locations could not be converted into attractive Native towns with adequate educational and other social facilities. This, however, will be a slow process, partly because Natives are not adapted to urban life and partly because difficulties are bound to arise in mixing Natives of various tribes.

Meanwhile, however, the problems arising out of the prolonged separation of adult males and females will continue and probably become more acute. This has caused and will continue to cause the undermining of Native family life and probably also the increase of prostitution and the spread of venereal diseases. This problem is engaging the attention of responsible groups among Europeans and Natives, but so far no satisfactory answer seems to have been found.

Another aspect of the broader social problem, which has a direct bearing on the Native labor question, needs comment. Natives are hedged in by such a multiplicity of laws, rules and regulations that it becomes almost impossible for them to avoid becoming law-breakers. Many of these regulations have been imposed to restrict Natives as workers or to induce them to work. It would appear, however, that burdensome restrictions are hardly conducive to efficient and conscientious work. Moreover, these restrictions are a great and continuous source of irritation to Native workers, especially to those who have acquired some education and who occupy positions of some responsibility. Native leaders feel that these laws place them in a position of permanent inferiority to the white man. Very serious consideration should be given to gradually, but definitely, decreasing the extent and severity of the restrictions surrounding Natives as laborers. No doubt the necessity for much of this legislation would disappear as Natives acquire greater skill and as they tend to specialize by occupation.

Another question is that connected with the employment of farm labor. There can be little doubt that the institution of labor tenancy is on the way out. It results in the very inefficient use of farm labor and is becoming increasingly unsatisfactory from the standpoint of both farmers and labor-tenants themselves. Farmers will come to rely more and more on the employment of full-time Native laborers. Under existing conditions, however, employment in agriculture is so unattractive farmers are experiencing much difficulty in securing adequate supplies of Native labor. As in other countries, monetary wages of farm laborers will probably continue to lag behind those paid in urban occupations. The only apparent solution of the farmers' problem is to increase the attractiveness of employment in agriculture by providing their workers with better housing and food and above all with better educational facilities and opportunities for social contacts.

An improvement in the lot of the Native population of South Africa is vital not only from the standpoint of the Natives themselves, but also from the standpoint of the future progress and prosperity of the white population. Further serious deterioration in the quality and efficiency of labor and in the agricultural resources of South Africa can be prevented only by eradicating the root cause—exploitation of Native labor. Real wages and the efficiency of Native labor must be advanced—such advancement should become one of the primary policies of the country. The direction in which the necessary changes must take place is clear. The question is whether the white population of the country will have the foresightedness and courage to undertake the slow and involved process of advancing the well-being of the Native population. The Union of South Africa has a unique opportunity for social and economic experimentation, the results of which will be of inestimable value in indicating the solution of similar problems in other parts of the world. The experience of South Africa will indicate whether and to what extent a governing white population can advance the well-being of more backward peoples, without unduly jeopardizing the high standard of living attained by the white population itself.

Appendix

APPENDIX

Table 1
List of Commercially Produced Crops and Pastoral Products with Recent Volume Data

Branch or Product	Number or volume produced	Year	Branch or Product	Number of trees or vines	Year
Livestock			*Fruits and Vineyards* (European only)		
Cattle (includes dairy cattle)...........No.	11,372,000	1938	Apples............trees	2,677,467	1937
Woolled Sheep........No.	32,796,000	1938	Apricots...........trees	1,940,262	1937
Non-woolled Sheep.....No.	6,206,000	1938	Avocados................	....	....
Angora Goats.........No.	632,000	1938	Bananas.................	....	....
Other Goats..........No.	5,494,000	1938	Cape Gooseberries.......	....	....
Horses...............No.	778,000	1938	Cherries................	....	....
Mules................No.	137,000	1938	Custard Apples..........	....	....
Donkeys..............No.	863,000	1938	Figs....................	....	....
Pigs.................No.	948,000	1938	Grapes............vines	164,765,856	1937
Ostriches............No.	40,000	1938	Grapefruit.........trees	321,290	1937
Chickens (E).........No.	9,347,000	1937	Granadillas.............	....	....
Ducks (E)............No.	315,000	1937	Gravas..................	....	....
Geese (E)............No.	162,000	1937	Lemons............trees	180,987	1937
Turkeys (E)..........No.	241,000	1937	Limes...................	....	....
Wool............1000 lbs.	207,903	1938	Lichis..................	....	....
Mohair..........1000 lbs.	3,234	1938	Loganberries............	....	....
Butter..........1000 lbs.	43,284	1938	Loquats.................	....	....
Cheese..........1000 lbs.	12,462	1938	Mangoes...........trees	266,597	1937
Honey...........1000 lbs.	1,144		Melons..................	....	....
Field Crops			Nectarines........trees	92,450	....
Wheat...........1000 lbs.	643,000	1938	Naartjes (Tangerines) trees	295,791	1937
Barley (Grain only)1000 lbs.	56,899	1938	Olives..................	....	....
Oats (Grain only)..1000 lbs.	189,946	1938	Oranges...........trees	4,409,413	1937
Rye.............1000 lbs.	36,114	1938	Pawpaws (Papayas).......	....	....
Kaffir-corn.....1000 lbs.	229,156	1938	Peaches...........trees	4,055,540	1937
Mealies (corn)..1000 lbs.	3,842,550	1938	Pears.............trees	1,110,635	1937
Potatoes (E)....1000 lbs.	382,932	1938	Persimmons..............	....	....
Groundnuts (E)..1000 lbs.	21,253	1938	Pineapples..............	....	....
Onions (E).....1000 lbs.	32,683	1937	Pomegranates............	....	....
Sweet Potatoes (E)1000 lbs.	73,616	1937	Plums.....⎱........trees	1,197,797	1937
Peas............1000 lbs.	5,967	1937	Prunes....⎰		
Beans...........1000 lbs.	38,305	1937	Quince..................	....	....
Alfalfa.................	....	....	Raspberries.............	....	....
Chicory.................	....	....	Strawberries............	....	....
Spineless Cactus........	....	....	Tea.....................	....	....
Sisal...................	....	....	Tomatoes................	....	....
Miscellaneous vegetables...	....	....	Fruit trees (No.'s not shown above).........	2,220,481	1937
			Miscellaneous		
			Wattles.................	....	....
			Eucalyptus..............	....	....

Source of data: Summarized from *Official Yearbook for the Union of South Africa*, No. 20 (1939).
E = European production only.

TABLE 2
PRINCIPAL AGRICULTURAL PRODUCTS IN EACH REGION (1936-37)

Region No.	Region and district	Pastoral Product	Number 1,000 head	Field crops Product	Number 1,000 morgen	Fruit and nut trees Product	Number 1,000 trees
	CAPE PROVINCE						
I	*Southwest* Bredasdorp, Bellville, Caledon, Cape Ceres, Hopefield, Malmesbury, Paarl, Piquetberg, Riversdale, Simons Town, Somerset West, Stellenbosch, Swellendam, Tulbagh, Wellington, Worcester, Wynberg.	Cattle	119	Wheat	361	Orange	200
		Horses	32	Barley	22	Other Citrus	66
		Mules	52	Oats	150	Apple	947
		Pigs	113	Rye	28	Apricot	1,358
		Poultry	896	Mealies	2	Peach and nectarine	1,045
		Woolled sheep	1,538	Potatoes	3	Pear	806
		Non-woolled sheep	48	Beans (dried)	1	Plum	881
		Angora goats	3	Vegetables	5	Quince	143
		Other goats	153	Lucerne	5	Nut	96
				Tobacco	1	Cherry and other	52
						Vines	119,233
II	*Northwest* Britstown, Calvinia, Carnarvon, Clanwilliam, Fraserburg, Hopetown, Kenhardt, Namaqualand, Prieska, Van Rhynsdorp, Sutherland, Victoria West, Williston.	Cattle	68	Wheat	60	Orange	269
		Horses	19	Barley	3	Other Citrus	12
		Mules	9	Oats	9	All deciduous	157
		Donkeys	63	Rye	13	Nut	7
		Pigs	10	Mealies	2	Vines	3,188
		Poultry	124	Lucerne	9		
		Woolled sheep	2,982				
		Non-woolled sheep	1,695				
		Angora goats	5				
		Other goats	784				
III	*South Coast* Albany, Alexandria, Bathurst, George, Humansdorp, Knysna, Mossel Bay, Port Elizabeth, Uitenhage.	Cattle	233	Wheat	27	Orange	740
		Horses	11	Barley	5	Grapefruit	164
		Mules	6	Oats	10	Other citrus	31
		Donkeys	22	Mealies	22	Apple	247
		Pigs	26	Potatoes	4	Other deciduous	123
		Poultry	518	Beans (dried)	1	Nut	48
		Woolled sheep	637	Vegetables	2	Vines	205
		Non-woolled sheep	89	Lucerne	5		
		Angora goats	73	Tobacco	1		
		Other goats	122				
IV	*South Karroo* Aberdeen, Calitzdorp, Jansenville, Ladismith, Laingsburg, Montagu, Oudtshoorn, Prince Albert, Robertson, Steytlerville, Uniondale, Willowmore.	Cattle	50	Wheat	27	Orange	69
		Horses	10	Barley	3	Other citrus	7
		Mules	8	Oats	4	Apple	490
		Donkeys	35	Mealies	4	Apricot	115
		Pigs	16	Potatoes	1	Peach and nectarine	155
		Poultry	220	Beans	2	Other deciduous	188
		Woolled sheep	1,035	Lucerne	26	Vines	31,918
		Non-woolled sheep	446	Tobacco	1		
		Angora goats	347	Spineless cactus	4		
		Other goats	315				
V	*Central Karroo* Beaufort West, Graaff-Reinet, Middelburg, Murraysburg.	Cattle	24	Wheat	6	All citrus	14
		Horses	6	Oats	1	All deciduous	146
		Mules	2	Mealies	2	Vines	238
		Donkeys	14	Lucerne	12		
		Pigs	3	Spineless cactus	1		
		Poultry	50				
		Woolled sheep	1,508				
		Non-woolled sheep	248				
		Angora goats	33				
		Other goats	76				

Appendix

TABLE 2 (continued)

Region No.	Region and district	Pastoral		Field crops		Fruit and nut trees	
		Product	Number 1,000 head	Product	Number 1,000 morgen	Product	Number 1,000 trees
	CAPE PROVINCE (continued)						
VI	*North Karroo* Colesberg, De Aar, Hanover, Philipstown, Richmond, Venterstad.	Cattle	25	Wheat	4	All deciduous	30
		Horses	7	Lucerne	4		
		Mules	1	Spineless cactus	1		
		Donkeys	11				
		Pigs	2				
		Poultry	42				
		Woolled sheep	1,582				
		Non-woolled sheep	137				
		Angora goats	3				
		Other goats	22				
VII	*East Karroo* Bedford, Cradock, Maraisburg, Pearston, Somerset East, Steynsburg.	Cattle	56	Wheat	6	All citrus	28
		Horses	10	Barley	1	All deciduous	266
		Mules	3	Oats	3		
		Donkeys	14	Mealies	4		
		Pigs	5	Lucerne	13		
		Poultry	92	Spineless cactus	1		
		Woolled sheep	1,874				
		Non-woolled sheep	140				
		Angora goats	118				
		Other goats	89				
VIII	*Bechuanaland* Gordonia, Kuruman, Mafeking, Taungs, Vryburg.	Cattle	429	Wheat	11	Orange	197
		Horses	29	Mealies	58	Other citrus	1
		Mules	5	Kaffir-corn	16	Peach and nectarine	128
		Donkeys	95	Cowpeas	7	All other deciduous	39
		Pigs	24	Lucerne	2	Vines	8,421
		Poultry	196				
		Woolled sheep	429				
		Non-woolled sheep	488				
		Angora goats	3				
		Other goats	403				
IX	*Griqualand West* Barkly West, Hay, Herbert, Kimberley.	Cattle	139	Wheat	1	All deciduous	105
		Horses	24	Mealies	2	Vines	255
		Mules	2	Lucerne	1		
		Donkeys	29	Spineless cactus	1		
		Pigs	5				
		Poultry	64				
		Woolled sheep	478				
		Non-woolled sheep	854				
		Angora goats	4				
		Other goats	286				
X	*Border* Adelaide, Cathcart, Fort Beaufort, Glen Grey, Keiskammahoek, Kingwilliamstown, Komgha, Middeldrift, East London, Peddie, Queenstown, Sterkstroom, Stockenstrom, Stutterheim, Tarka, Victoria East.	Cattle	506	Wheat	11	Orange	365
		Horses	29	Barley	4	Other citrus	31
		Mules	1	Oats	16	Apple	92
		Donkeys	12	Rye	1	All other deciduous	103
		Pigs	43	Mealies	41	Tropical and semitropical	25
		Poultry	531	Kaffir-corn	2		
		Woolled sheep	2,921	Potatoes	1		
		Non-woolled sheep	36	Beans	2		
		Angora goats	24	Vegetables	1		
		Other goats	264	Lucerne	4		
				Cactus	1		

Table 2 (continued)

Region No.	Region and district	Pastoral		Field crops		Fruit and nut trees	
		Product	Number	Product	Number	Product	Number
			1,000 head		1,000 morgen		1,000 trees
	CAPE PROVINCE (continued)						
XI	*Northeast* Albert, Aliwal North, Barkly East, Elliot, Herschel, Indwe, Lady Grey, Maclear, Molteno, Wodehouse.	Cattle...... Horses...... Mules....... Donkeys..... Pigs......... Poultry...... Woolled sheep Non-woolled sheep...... Angora goats. Other goats..	237 19 1 11 13 212 2,738 26 11 36	Wheat....... Barley....... Oats......... Rye......... Mealies...... Lucerne..... Grasses......	80 2 20 7 33 5 2	All deciduous	95
XII	*Transkei* Bizana, Butterworth, Elliotdale, Engcobo, Flagstaff, Idutywa, Kentani, Libode, Lusikisiki, Matatiele, Mount Ayliff, Mount Currie, Mount Fletcher, Mount Frere, Mqanduli, Ngqeleni, Nqamakwe, Port St. Johns, Qumbu, St. Marks, Tabankulu, Tsolo, Tsomo, Umtata, Umzimkulu, Willowvale, Xalanga.	Cattle...... Horses...... Donkeys..... Pigs......... Poultry...... Woolled sheep Angora goats. Other goats..	1,731 127 14 177 1,194 3,041 29 895	Wheat....... Barley....... Oats......... Rye......... Mealies...... Cultivated grasses..... Other cultivated crops.	13 1 16 3 31 14 4	All citrus.... All deciduous	21 51
	NATAL						
XIII	*Highveld* Babanango, Bergville, Dundee, Klipriver, Newcastle, Paulpietersburg, Utrecht, Vryheid.	Cattle...... Horses...... Mules and donkeys.... Pigs......... Poultry...... Woolled sheep Non-woolled sheep...... Angora goats. Other goats..	576 32 23 27 515 1,202 39 6 195	Oats........ Mealies...... Kaffir-corn... Potatoes..... Cowpeas..... Cultivated grasses.....	6 83 4 1 4 4	All deciduous	100
XIV	*Middleveld* Alfred, Camperdown, Emtonjaneni, Estcourt, Helpmekaar, Impendhle, Ixopo, Kranskop, Lion's River, Mahlabatini, Msinga, New Hanover, Ngotshe, Nkandhla, Nongoma, Nqutu, Pietermaritzburg, Polela, Richmond, Umvoti, Underberg, Weenen.	Cattle...... Horses...... Mules and donkeys.... Pigs......... Poultry...... Woolled sheep Non-woolled sheep...... Angora goats. Other goats..	1,248 49 66 71 1,137 725 150 3 689	Oats........ Rye......... Mealies...... Kaffir-corn... Potatoes..... Beans........ Cowpeas..... Grasses...... Other cultivated crops.	9 3 107 4 3 3 4 16 3	Orange...... Other citrus.. All deciduous Nut......... Tropical and semitropical	195 26 125 23 7

Appendix

TABLE 2 (continued)

Region No.	Region and district	Pastoral		Field crops		Fruit and nut trees	
		Product	Number	Product	Number	Product	Number
			1,000 head		1,000 morgen		1,000 trees
	NATAL (continued)						
XV	*Coast* Durban, Eshowe, Hlabisa, Inanda, Ingwavuma, Lower Tugela, Lower Umfolosi, Mapumulo, Mtunzini, Ndwedwe, Pinetown, Port Shepstone, Ubombo, Umlazi, Umzinto.	Cattle...... Horses...... Mules and donkeys..... Pigs......... Poultry...... Woolled sheep Non-woolled sheep...... Angora goats. Other goats..	635 85 118 117 2,395 1,935 239 9 1,078	Oats........ Rye......... Mealies...... Kaffir-corn.. Potatoes..... Beans....... Cowpeas..... Vegetables... Grasses...... Other cultivated crops. Sugar cane...	16 3 198 8 4 5 8 2 21 175 85	Orange...... Naartje...... All other citrus..... Nut......... Tropical and semitropical	77 151 44 29 103
	TRANSVAAL						
XVI	*East Highveld* Belfast, Bethal, Carolina, Ermelo, Middelburg, Piet Retief, Standerton, Volksrust, Wakkerstroom, Witbank.	Cattle...... Horses...... Mules and donkeys.... Pigs......... Poultry...... Woolled sheep Non-woolled sheep...... Angora goats. Other goats..	807 71 28 69 937 2,438 19 2 163	Wheat....... Oats........ Rye......... Mealies...... Potatoes..... Beans....... Cowpeas..... Grasses......	14 26 3 416 8 11 2 48	All citrus.... Apple....... Peach and nectarine... All other deciduous .. Nut.........	67 77 254 91 29
XVII	*Central Highveld* Benoni, Boksburg, Brakpan, Brits, Germiston, Heidelberg, Johannesburg, Klerksdorp, Potchefstroom, Pretoria, Roodepoort, Rustenburg, Springs, Ventersdorp, Vereeniging.	Cattle...... Horses...... Mules and donkeys.... Pigs......... Poultry...... Woolled sheep Non-woolled sheep...... Other goats..	970 29 77 97 1,380 547 135 119	Wheat....... Oats........ Mealies...... Kaffir-corn.. Potatoes..... Beans....... Cowpeas..... Vegetable.... Lucerne..... Grasses...... Tobacco.....	38 6 401 14 4 4 3 3 4 27 7	Orange...... Other citrus.. Apple....... Apricot...... Peach and nectarine... Plum and prune...... All other deciduous .. Nut......... Tropical and semitropical	408 39 289 87 1,105 83 384 29 8
XVIII	*West Highveld* Bloemhof, Christiana, Lichtenburg, Marico, Schweizer Reneke, Wolmaransstad.	Cattle...... Horses...... Mules and donkeys.... Pigs......... Poultry...... Woolled sheep Non-woolled sheep...... Goats.......	429 27 81 37 485 805 88 56	Wheat....... Mealies...... Kaffir-corn... Beans....... Cowpeas.....	7 344 54 2 4	All citrus.... Peach and nectarine... All other deciduous ..	75 147 39
XIX	*Lowveld* Barberton, Letaba, Lydenburg, Nelspruit, Pietersburg, Pilgrims Rest, Potgietersrust, Waterberg, Zoutpansberg.	Cattle...... Horses...... Mules and donkeys.... Pigs......... Poultry...... Woolled sheep Non-woolled sheep...... Goats.......	970 7 137 98 1,121 234 181 513	Wheat....... Barley...... Mealies...... Kaffir-corn... Potatoes..... Beans....... Cowpeas..... Vegetables... Tobacco..... Groundnuts..	16 3 123 14 2 3 5 5 5 27	Orange...... Grapefruit... Lemon...... Naartje...... Peach and nectarine... All other deciduous .. Nut......... Tropical and semitropical	1,657 90 67 40 143 171 63 890

Appendix

TABLE 2 (continued)

Region No.	Region and district	Pastoral Product	Number (1,000 head)	Field crops Product	Number (1,000 morgen)	Fruit and nut trees Product	Number (1,000 trees)
	ORANGE FREE STATE						
XX	*Northeast* Bethlehem, Frankfort, Harrismith, Heilbron, Lindley, Reitz, Senekal, Vrede, Winburg.	Cattle Horses Mules and donkeys Pigs Poultry Woolled sheep Non-woolled sheep Angora goats Other goats	972 103 11 63 1,081 3,183 26 27 8	Wheat Oats Rye Mealies Kaffir-corn Potatoes Beans Cowpeas Grasses	194 68 6 709 6 3 2 3 36	Apple Peach and nectarine All other deciduous Nut	102 296 97 9
XXI	*Northwest* Bothaville, Hoopstad, Kroonstad, Ventersburg, Vredefort.	Cattle Horses Mules and donkeys Pigs Poultry Woolled sheep Non-woolled sheep Goats	403 34 25 38 590 1,172 13 6	Wheat Oats Mealies Kaffir-corn Cowpeas Lucerne Grasses	5 4 503 6 5 5	Peach and nectarine All other deciduous	83 50
XXII	*Southeast* Bethulie, Dewetsdorp, Edenburg, Ficksburg, Fouriesburg, Ladybrand, Reddersburg, Rouxville, Smithfield, Thaba 'Nchu, Trompsburg, Wepener, Zastron.	Cattle Horses Mules and donkeys Pigs Poultry Woolled sheep Non-woolled sheep Angora goats Other goats	349 32 12 26 343 2,632 54 6 4	Wheat Oats Rye Mealies Potatoes Cowpeas Lucerne Grasses	211 16 17 160 7 3 5 8	Apple Peach and nectarine All other deciduous Nut	108 224 106 9
XXIII	*Southwest* Bloemfontein, Boshof, Brandfort, Fauresmith, Jacobsdal, Philippolis.	Cattle Horses Mules and donkeys Pigs Poultry Woolled sheep Non-woolled sheep Goats	213 38 38 16 261 2,127 234 24	Wheat Oats Rye Mealies Kaffir-corn Cowpeas	6 3 3 77 7 3	Peach and nectarine All other deciduous Nut	145 108 6

Source of data: *Report on Agricultural and Pastoral Production, 1936-37, Agricultural Census* No. 17 (U. G. No. 18, 1939).

Appendix

TABLE 3
NUMBER AND SIZE OF FARMS AND HOLDINGS OCCUPIED BY EUROPEANS—1936-37

Region*	Owned by Occupier		Occupied by Renter†		Managed Farms		Total all Farms		Area under crops (Morgen)	Area under orchards, vineyards and plantations (banana and pineapple)	Area under timber	Land actually under irrigation
	Number	1,000 Morgen	Number	1,000 Morgen	Number	1,000 Morgen	Number	1,000 Morgen				
1. Southwest (C)	5,217	2,808	1,789	1,202	318	313	7,324	4,322	582,854	63,396	12,109	45,594
2. Northwest (C)	3,280	15,760	1,516	4,756	263	1,725	5,059	22,242	98,843	3,192	356	28,567
3. South Coast (C)	2,815	1,744	1,030	387	211	189	4,056	2,321	83,643	10,523	5,584	19,243
4. South Karroo (C)	2,908	4,207	832	1,009	185	429	3,925	5,646	74,876	12,278	1,183	56,629
5. Central Karroo (C)	861	3,143	196	452	86	385	1,143	3,980	23,254	1,138	547	17,185
6. North Karroo (C)	646	2,361	223	615	91	281	960	3,257	11,167	148	295	7,984
7. East Karroo (C)	1,218	1,883	302	388	126	189	1,646	2,460	29,014	2,101	367	21,006
8. Bechuanaland (C)	1,997	4,244	1,590	2,227	283	1,115	3,870	7,585	96,558	4,044	375	18,500
9. Griqualand West (C)	1,067	2,521	518	849	193	655	1,778	4,026	5,977	596	66	3,463
10. Border (C)	2,671	1,630	827	409	273	230	3,771	2,269	90,322	4,063	2,601	17,482
11. Northeast (C)	2,064	1,601	940	551	264	210	3,268	2,362	152,812	520	4,577	9,727
12. Transkei (C)	868	429	384	168	274	109	1,526	706	80,883	484	5,324	3,540
13. Natal Highveld (N)	1,890	1,424	642	418	283	259	2,815	2,100	106,562	653	29,184	5,586
14. Natal Middleveld (N)	2,613	1,656	855	463	293	321	3,761	2,439	157,882	2,042	148,016	8,084
15. Natal Coast (N)	2,163	485	1,434	95	180	102	3,777	682	185,781	2,671	25,343	8,735
16. East Highveld (T)	5,334	2,979	2,214	1,033	590	619	8,138	4,630	543,763	6,484	76,706	21,896
17. Central Highveld (T)	8,790	3,257	4,113	1,401	514	552	13,417	5,211	517,500	11,376	21,665	62,838
18. West Highveld (T)	3,510	2,014	1,349	818	258	236	5,117	3,069	416,834	1,604	4,525	7,955
19. Lowveld (T)	3,666	3,422	1,497	1,583	539	1,245	5,702	6,249	1,032,555	15,621	46,751	42,786
20. Northeast (O)	5,745	3,042	2,763	1,113	563	384	9,071	4,539	214,379	2,595	15,596	7,903
21. Northwest (O)	3,188	1,821	1,036	577	369	274	4,593	2,671	531,983	744	7,399	6,310
22. Southeast (O)	3,318	2,362	1,110	566	291	225	4,719	3,153	433,817	2,408	6,086	24,505
23. Southwest (O)	3,683	2,827	1,040	679	395	487	5,118	3,993	105,135	1,276	3,434	12,564
Total Cape Province	25,612	42,332	10,147	13,013	2,567	5,831	38,326	61,175	1,330,203	102,483	33,384	248,920
Total Natal	6,666	3,566	2,931	975	756	681	10,353	5,222	450,225	9,179	202,543	22,405
Total Transvaal	21,300	11,762	9,173	4,834	1,901	2,653	32,374	19,158	1,692,276	31,272	149,647	135,475
Total Orange Free State	15,934	10,052	5,949	2,935	1,618	1,369	23,501	14,356	2,103,490	7,023	32,515	51,282
Total Union	69,512	67,621	28,200	21,757	6,842	10,533	104,554	99,912	5,576,194	149,957	418,089	458,082

*Abbreviations: (C) = Cape Province; (N) = Natal; (T) = Transvaal; (O) = Orange Free State.
†Farms rented on a cash and a share basis.
Source of data: *Report on Agricultural and Pastoral Production, 1936-1937. Agricultural Census No. 17, pp. 10-17.*

TABLE 4

REGIONAL DISTRIBUTION OF PRINCIPAL TYPES OF LIVESTOCK—1936–37—OWNED BY EUROPEANS AND NATIVES

Region*	Number 1,000's Omitted									Per Cent of Total						
	Cattle	Horses, mules, and donkeys†	Pigs	Poultry	Woolled sheep	Non-woolled sheep	Angora‡ and other goats	Cattle	Horses, mules, and donkeys	Pigs	Poultry	Woolled sheep	Non-woolled sheep	Goats‡
1. Southwest (C)	119	96	113	896	1,538	48	156	1.06	5.64	11.32	7.04	4.29	.92	2.55
2. Northwest (C)	68	91	9	124	2,982	1,695	789	.61	5.36	.90	.97	8.32	32.60	12.91
3. South Coast (C)	233	38	26	518	636	89	195	2.08	2.24	2.60	4.07	1.78	1.71	3.19
4. South Karroo (C)	50	53	16	220	1,035	446	662	.45	3.12	1.60	1.73	2.89	8.58	10.83
5. Central Karroo (C)	24	22	3	50	1,508	248	109	.22	1.29	.30	.39	4.21	4.77	1.78
6. North Karroo (C)	25	19	5	42	1,582	138	25	.22	1.12	.50	.33	4.41	2.66	.41
7. East Karroo (C)	56	27	2	92	1,874	140	207	.50	1.59	.20	.72	5.23	2.69	3.39
8. Bechuanaland (C)	429	129	24	196	429	488	405	3.84	7.59	2.40	1.54	1.20	9.39	6.63
9. Griqualand West (C)	139	55	5	64	478	854	290	1.24	3.24	.50	.50	1.33	16.43	4.75
10. Border (C)	506	42	42	531	2,921	36	288	4.52	2.47	4.20	4.17	8.15	.69	4.71
11. Northeast (C)	237	31	13	212	2,738	26	47	2.12	1.82	1.30	1.67	7.64	.50	.77
12. Transkei (C)	1,731	141	177	1,194	3,041	1	924	15.47	8.31	17.72	9.38	8.49	.02	15.13
13. Highveld (N)	576	55	27	515	1,202	39	201	5.15	3.24	2.70	4.04	3.36	.75	3.29
14. Middleveld (N)	1,248	116	71	1,137	725	150	693	11.15	6.83	7.11	8.93	2.02	2.89	11.34
15. Coast (N)	635	33	19	743	8	50	193	5.68	1.94	1.90	5.84	.02	.96	3.16
16. East Highveld (T)	807	99	69	937	2,438	19	165	7.21	5.83	6.91	7.36	6.80	.36	2.70
17. Central Highveld (T)	970	106	97	1,380	547	135	120	8.67	6.24	9.71	10.84	1.53	2.60	1.96
18. West Highveld (T)	429	108	37	485	805	56	513	3.84	6.35	3.70	3.81	2.25	1.71	8.40
19. Lowveld (T)	972	144	100	1,121	234	181	32	8.69	8.48	10.01	8.80	.65	3.48	.52
20. North east (O)	402	114	63	1,081	3,183	26	6	3.58	6.71	6.31	8.49	8.88	.50	.10
21. Northwest (O)	60	60	38	590	1,172	13	10	.54	3.53	3.81	4.63	3.27	.25	.16
22. Southeast (O)	349	44	27	343	2,632	54	24	3.12	2.59	2.70	2.69	7.34	1.04	.40
23. Southwest (O)	213	76	16	262	2,127	234		1.90	4.47	1.60	2.06	5.94	4.50	.40
Total Cape Province	3,617	744	435	4,139	20,762	4,209	4,097	32.33	43.79	43.54	32.51	57.94	80.96	67.05
Total Natal	2,459	204	117	2,395	1,935	239	1,087	21.98	12.01	11.71	18.81	5.40	4.60	17.79
Total Transvaal	3,176	457	303	3,923	4,024	424	854	28.39	26.90	30.33	30.81	11.23	8.15	13.98
Total Orange Free State	1,936	294	144	2,276	9,114	327	72	17.30	17.30	14.42	17.87	25.43	6.29	1.18
Total South Africa	11,188	1,699	999	12,733	35,835	5,199	6,110	100.00	100.00	100.00	100.00	100.00	100.00	100.00

*Abbreviations: (C) = Cape Province; (N) = Natal; (T) = Transvaal; (O) = Orange Free State.
†In the Northwest region there are 19,000 horses and 72,000 mules and donkeys; in Bechuanaland region 29,000 horses and 100 mules and donkeys; in the Transkei 127,000 horses and only 14,000 mules and donkeys; in the Lowveld (T) 7,000 horses and 137,000 mules and donkeys; in the Northeast (O) 103,000 horses and only 11,000 mules and donkeys.
‡The following regions have over 50,000 Angora goats: South Coast, 73,000; South Karroo, 347,000; East Karroo, 118,000. These three regions have 77.30 per cent of all Angora goats in the Union of South Africa.
Source of data: Based on data from *Agricultural and Pastoral Production, 1936–1937*, Agricultural Census No. 17, pp. 45–62.

Appendix

TABLE 5
REGIONAL DISTRIBUTION OF PRINCIPAL GROUPS OF FIELD CROPS IN UNION OF SOUTH AFRICA—1936-37

Region*	1,000 Morgen under						Per cent of Total					
	Wheat	Barley, rye and oats	Maize and kaffir-corn‖	Sugar cane	Other crops†	Fodder grasses‡	Wheat	Barley, rye and oats	Maize and kaffir-corn	Sugar cane	Other crops†	Fodder grasses‡
1. Southwest (C)	361	200	3	....	11	5	32.79	39.29	.09	......	5.53	1.69
2. Northwest (C)	60	25	2	....	1	11	5.45	4.91	.06	......	.50	3.72
3. South Coast (C)	27	16	22	....	8	6	2.45	3.14	.68	......	4.02	2.03
4. South Karroo (C)	27	8	4	....	5	30	2.45	1.57	.12	......	2.51	10.13
5. Central Karroo (C)	6	2	2	....	....	13	.54	.39	.06	......	......	4.39
6. North Karroo (C)	4	1	1	....	§	5	.37	.20	.03	......	......	1.69
7. East Karroo (C)	6	4	4	....	§	14	.54	.79	.12	......	......	4.73
8. Bechuanaland (C)	11	§	74	....	9	3	1.00	......	2.27	......	4.52	1.01
9. Griqualand West (C)	1	§	2	....	§	2	.09	......	.06	......	......	.68
10. Border (C)	12	21	44	....	7	6	1.09	4.13	1.35	......	3.51	2.03
11. Northeast (C)	80	29	34	....	2	8	7.27	5.70	1.04	......	1.01	2.70
12. Transkei (C)	13	20	31	....	2	14	1.18	3.93	.95	......	1.01	4.73
13. Highveld (N)	1	7	87	....	6	4	.09	1.37	2.66	......	3.01	1.35
14. Middleveld (N)	1	12	111	....	14	18	.09	2.36	3.40	......	7.04	6.08
15. Coast (N)	§	§	9	170	5	1	......	......	.28	100.00	2.51	.34
16. East Highveld (T)	13	29	418	....	23	58	1.18	5.70	12.80	......	11.56	19.59
17. Central Highveld (T)	38	8	415	....	21	32	3.45	1.57	12.71	......	10.55	10.81
18. West Highveld (T)	7	1	398	....	7	2	.64	.20	12.18	......	3.52	.68
19. Lowveld (T)	16	5	137	....	47	3	1.45	.98	4.19	......	23.62	1.01
20. Northeast (O)	194	75	715	....	9	37	17.62	14.73	21.89	......	4.52	12.50
21. Northwest (O)	5	5	509	....	6	6	.45	.98	15.59	......	3.02	2.03
22. Southeast (O)	211	34	161	....	12	14	19.17	6.68	4.93	......	6.03	4.73
23. Southwest (O)	7	7	83	....	4	4	.64	1.38	2.54	......	2.01	1.35
Total Cape Province	608	326	223	....	45	117	55.22	64.05	6.83	......	22.61	39.53
Total Natal	2	19	207	170	25	23	.18	3.73	6.34	100.00	12.56	7.77
Total Transvaal	74	43	1,368	....	98	95	6.72	8.45	41.88	......	49.25	32.09
Total Orange Free State	417	121	1,468	....	31	61	37.88	23.77	44.95	......	15.58	20.61
Total Union	1,107	509	3,266	170	199	296	100.00	100.00	100.00	100.00	100.00	100.00

*Abbreviations: (C) = Cape Province; (N) = Natal; (T) = Transvaal; (O) = Orange Free State.
†Other crops include potatoes, onions, cowpeas, beans, tobacco, groundnuts (peanuts), and all other crops (excluding cereals, sugar cane, cultivated fodder grasses).
‡Fodder grasses include lucerne (alfalfa), teff grass, spineless cactus, and other grasses cultivated for feed.
§Less than 500 morgen.
‖Kaffir-corn accounts for only 131,000 morgen out of the total of 3,266,000.
Source of data: *Report on Agricultural and Pastoral Production, 1936-1937*, Agricultural Census No. 17, pp. 20-43, 106.

Appendix

TABLE 6
REGIONAL DISTRIBUTION OF PRINCIPAL CLASSES OF FRUITS IN UNION OF SOUTH AFRICA—1936-37

Region*	All citrus† (1,000 trees)	All‡ deciduous fruit (1,000 trees)	Nuts§ (1,000 trees)	Mango, pawpaw, avocado (1,000 trees)	Vines (1,000's)	Pineapple plantations (morgen)	Banana plantations (morgen)	Citrus	Deciduous	Nut	Mango, pawpaw, avocado	Vines	Pineapples	Bananas
								\multicolumn{7}{c}{PERCENTAGE}
1. Southwest (C)	287	5,284	96	*	119,233			5.51	43.70	22.38		72.37		
2. Northeast (C)	281	160	7	*	3,188			5.40	1.32	1.63		1.94		
3. South Coast (C)	935	370	48	1	205		98	17.96	3.06	11.19	0.10	0.12		2.35
4. South Karroo (C)	76	949	44		31,918	2,809		1.46	7.85	10.26		19.37	63.71	
5. Central Karroo (C)	14	146	5		238			0.27	1.21	1.17		0.14		
6. North Karroo (C)	1	30	1					0.02	0.25	0.23				
7. East Karroo (C)	28	266	8					0.54	2.20	1.86				
8. Bechuanaland (C)	198	167	1	*				3.80	1.35	0.23				
9. Griqualand West (C)	6	105	2		8,421			0.12	0.87	0.47		5.11		
10. Border (C)	396	195	10	25	255	570	232	7.60	1.61	2.33	2.40	.16	12.93	5.56
11. Northeast (C)	1	195	1					0.02	1.61	0.23				
12. Transkei (C)	21	51	3	4		13	49	0.40	0.42	0.70	0.38		0.29	1.17
13. Highveld (N)	18	100	2	1		2	1	0.35	0.83	0.47	0.10		0.05	0.02
14. Middleveld (N)	221	125	23	7		13	6	4.24	1.03	5.36	0.67		0.29	0.14
15. Coast (N)	272	18	29	103		945	3,662	5.22	0.15	6.76	9.88		21.43	87.71
16. East Highveld (T)	67	422	29			3	2	1.29	3.49	6.76	0.29		0.07	.05
17. Central Highveld (T)	447	1,748	29	8				8.58	14.46	6.76	0.77			
18. West Highveld (T)	75	226	3	*				1.44	1.87	0.70				
19. Lowveld (T)	1,854	314	63	890		54	125	35.61	2.60	14.68	85.41		1.23	3.00
20. Northeast (O)	3	495	9					0.06	4.10	2.10				
21. Northwest (O)	1	133	1					0.02	1.10	0.23				
22. Southeast (O)	1	438	9					0.02	3.62	2.10				
23. Southwest (O)	4	253	6					0.07	2.09	1.40				
Total Cape Province	2,244	7,818	226	30	163,983	3,392	379	43.10	64.66	52.68	2.88	99.53	76.93	9.08
Total Natal	511	243	54	111	5	960	3,669	9.81	2.01	12.58	10.65	Neg.	21.77	87.87
Total Transvaal	2,443	2,710	124	901	642	57	127	46.92	22.42	28.90	86.47	0.39	1.30	3.05
Total Orange Free State	9	1,319	25		136			0.17	10.91	5.83		0.08		
Total Union	5,207	12,090	429	1,042	164,766	4,409	4,175	100.00	100.00	100.00	100.00	100.00	100.00	100.00

*Abbreviations: (C) = Cape Province; (N) = Natal; (T) = Transvaal; (O) = Orange Free State.
†Citrus fruit includes oranges, lemons, grapefruit, and naartje (tangerines).
‡Deciduous fruit includes apples, apricots, pears, plums and prunes, nectarines, peaches, quinces, and cherries.
§Nuts include walnuts, almonds, pecans, and litchis. Source of data: *Agricultural and Pastoral Production, 1936-1937, Agricultural Census No. 17, pp. 88-104.*

TABLE 7
EMPLOYEES IN THE MINING INDUSTRIES OF UNION OF SOUTH AFRICA, 1910-38

Year	Gold	Diamonds	Coal	All other	Total all branches	European	Non-European	Per cent change 1912=100 European	Per cent change 1912=100 Non-European
1910*	224,347	38,144	23,167	10,841	296,499				
1911	228,875	60,476	24,446	14,707	328,504	38,282	290,222		
1912	231,355	63,041	24,169	16,542	335,107	37,475	297,632	100.0	100.0
1913	221,183	66,332	26,363	15,229	329,107	37,467	291,640	100.0	98.0
1914	202,385	42,077	27,303	14,332	286,097	31,944	254,153	85.2	85.4
1915	229,255	9,325	25,824	14,795	279,199	28,836	250,363	76.9	84.1
1916	238,054	25,907	29,252	17,467	310,680	31,124	279,556	83.1	93.9
1917	216,742	42,071	31,488	18,118	308,419	32,897	275,522	87.8	92.6
1918	211,773	39,501	31,806	12,724	295,804	32,820	262,984	87.6	88.4
1919	203,610	44,877	32,715	10,025	291,227	35,251	255,976	94.1	86.0
1920	207,808	56,922	34,495	9,893	309,118	38,710	270,408	103.3	90.9
1921	202,930	27,276	39,911	8,611	278,728	31,624	247,104	84.4	83.0
1922	186,339	26,694	35,263	7,407	255,703	24,302	231,401	64.8	77.7
1923	208,502	38,121	34,779	9,896	291,298	30,652	260,646	81.8	87.6
1924	210,986	46,595	36,841	11,524	305,946	31,928	274,018	85.2	92.1
1925	208,236	45,665	36,653	13,883	304,437	32,548	271,889	86.9	91.4
1926	215,747	72,041	38,312	18,518	344,618	39,029	305,589	104.1	102.7
1927	221,468	75,581	37,195	19,642	353,886	39,973	313,913	106.7	105.5
1928	231,190	73,607	36,516	19,479	360,792	38,177	322,615	101.9	108.4
1929	227,847	63,391	35,130	23,473	349,841	38,663	311,178	103.2	104.6
1930	236,305	63,297	32,594	20,742	352,938	36,659	316,279	97.8	106.3
1931	244,987	46,402	27,577	14,174	333,140	34,667	298,473	92.5	100.3
1932	253,274	24,078	23,554	10,057	310,963	32,221	278,742	86.0	93.7
1933	270,347	28,230	23,866	12,292	334,735	35,732	299,003	95.3	100.5
1934	299,954	26,387	25,339	15,358	367,038	39,972	327,066	106.7	109.9
1935	333,650	25,346	28,900	17,219	405,115	43,588	361,527	116.3	121.5
1936	361,459	22,120	30,925	26,909	441,413	47,090	394,323	125.7	132.5
1937	369,489	20,370	31,761	31,479	453,099	50,211	402,888	134.0	135.4
1938	386,607	18,722	33,678	35,581	474,588	53,131	421,457	141.8	141.6

Per cent of total employed

Year	Gold	Diamonds	Coal	All other	Total	European	Non-European
1910*	75.7	12.9	7.8	3.6	100.0		
1911	69.7	18.4	7.4	4.5	100.0	11.6	88.4
1912	69.1	18.8	7.2	4.9	100.0	11.2	88.8
1913	67.2	20.2	8.0	4.6	100.0	11.4	88.6
1914	70.7	14.7	9.6	5.0	100.0	11.2	88.8
1915	82.1	3.3	9.3	5.3	100.0	10.3	89.7
1916	76.6	8.4	9.4	5.6	100.0	10.0	90.0
1917	70.3	13.6	10.2	5.9	100.0	10.7	89.3
1918	71.6	13.4	10.7	4.3	100.0	11.1	88.9
1919	69.9	15.4	11.2	3.5	100.0	12.1	87.9
1920	67.2	18.4	11.2	3.2	100.0	12.5	87.5
1921	72.8	9.8	14.3	3.1	100.0	11.3	88.7
1922	72.9	10.4	13.8	2.9	100.0	9.5	90.5
1923	71.6	13.1	11.9	3.4	100.0	10.5	89.5
1924	69.0	15.2	12.0	3.8	100.0	10.4	89.6
1925	68.4	15.0	12.0	4.6	100.0	10.7	89.3
1926	62.6	20.9	11.1	5.4	100.0	11.3	88.7
1927	62.6	21.4	10.5	5.5	100.0	11.3	88.7
1928	64.1	20.4	10.1	5.4	100.0	10.6	89.4
1929	65.1	18.1	10.1	6.7	100.0	11.1	88.9
1930	67.0	17.9	9.2	5.9	100.0	10.4	89.6
1931	73.5	13.9	8.3	4.3	100.0	10.4	89.6
1932	81.5	7.7	7.6	3.2	100.0	10.4	89.6
1933	80.8	8.4	7.1	3.7	100.0	10.7	89.3
1934	81.7	7.2	6.9	4.2	100.0	10.9	89.1
1935	82.4	6.3	7.1	4.2	100.0	10.8	89.2
1936	81.9	5.0	7.0	6.1	100.0	10.7	89.3
1937	81.5	4.5	7.0	7.0	100.0	11.1	88.9
1938	81.5	3.9	7.1	7.5	100.0	11.2	88.8

*Based on six months ended December.
Sources of data: 1910-1911: *Annual Report of the Government Mining Engineer, 1938*, Sec. I, table 1. 1912-1938: *Official Yearbook of the Union of South Africa*, No. 20 (1939), p. 833.

TABLE 8
TREND OF EUROPEAN WAGES* IN MINING INDUSTRY, 1911-38

Year	Gold mining (large)				Diamond mining				Coal mining			
	Number employed	Total wages (1,000 pounds)	Annual wages per employee (pounds)	Per cent change in wages per employee 1911=100	Number employed	Total wages (1,000 pounds)	Annual wages per employee (pounds)	Per cent change in wages per employee 1911=100	Number employed	Total wages (1,000 pounds)	Annual wages per employee (pounds)	Per cent change in wages per employee 1911=100
1911	25,664	8,545	332.9	100.0	4,646	1,234	265.6	100.0	1,232	357	289.8	100.0
1912	24,745	8,196	331.2	99.5	4,658	1,245	267.3	100.6	1,255	386	307.6	106.1
1913	24,020	7,875	327.9	98.5	5,077	1,383	272.4	102.6	1,371	413	301.2	103.9
1914	21,879	7,172	327.8	98.4	3,906	1,023	261.9	98.6	1,350	412	305.2	105.3
1915	22,761	7,555	331.9	99.7	1,029	315	306.1	115.2	1,274	404	317.1	109.4
1916	22,922	8,034	350.5	105.3	1,973	611	309.7	116.6	1,355	455	335.8	115.9
1917	23,015	8,475	368.2	110.6	2,966	947	319.3	120.2	1,463	523	357.5	123.4
1918	23,237	8,881	382.2	114.8	3,393	1,129	332.7	125.3	1,597	649	406.4	140.2
1919	23,621	9,466	400.7	120.4	4,059	1,347	331.9	125.0	1,694	689	406.7	140.3
1920	22,668	11,356	501.0	150.5	4,418	1,819	411.7	155.0	1,818	847	465.9	160.8
1921	21,455	10,641	496.0	149.0	2,699	1,039	385.0	145.0	2,133	994	466.0	160.8
1922	14,430	5,797	401.7	120.7	1,826	511	279.8	105.3	1,590	674	423.9	146.3
1923	18,309	6,805	371.7	111.7	2,585	841	325.3	122.5	1,665	671	403.0	139.1
1924	19,152	7,323	382.4	114.9	2,609	879	336.9	126.8	1,736	690	397.5	137.2
1925	19,971	7,503	375.7	112.9	2,706	912	337.0	126.9	1,737	693	399.0	137.7
1926	20,408	7,654	375.0	112.7	2,938	1,003	341.4	128.5	1,736	708	407.8	140.7
1927	21,420	8,029	374.8	112.6	3,049	1,039	340.8	128.3	1,744	716	410.6	141.7
1928	22,249	8,360	375.8	112.9	3,040	1,048	344.7	129.8	1,714	707	412.5	142.3
1929	22,576	8,480	375.6	112.7	3,127	1,080	345.4	130.0	1,632	684	419.1	144.6
1930	22,635	8,527	376.7	113.2	2,897	1,006	347.3	130.8	1,578	658	417.0	143.9
1931	23,159	8,724	376.7	113.2	2,398	697	290.7	109.5	1,450	593	409.0	141.1
1932	23,964	9,066	378.3	113.6	1,253	310	247.4	93.1	1,354	533	393.6	135.8
1933	25,901	9,696	374.4	112.5	869	207	238.2	89.7	1,351	537	397.5	137.2
1934	29,331	11,224	382.8	115.0	856	232	271.0	102.0	1,423	576	404.8	139.7
1935	32,967	12,772	387.5	116.4	824	263	319.2	120.2	1,624	644	396.6	136.9
1936	36,440	14,330	393.2	118.1	1,009	329	326.1	122.8	1,770	703	397.2	137.1
1937	39,230	15,738	401.2	120.5	1,374	445	323.9	122.0	1,863	757	406.3	140.2
1938	41,739	16,856	403.8	121.3	1,429	467	326.8	123.0	1,931	780	403.9	139.4

*Includes administrative and technical staff.
Source of data: *Annual Report of the Government Mining Engineer*, 1938, Sec. I, table 2, and Sec. II, table 6.

TABLE 9
NUMBER OF NON-EUROPEAN EMPLOYEES AND CASH WAGES* IN THREE MINING INDUSTRIES, 1910-38

Year	Gold mines (large)				Diamond mines				Coal mines			
	Number employed	Total wages (1,000 pounds)	Wages per employee (pounds)	Per cent change in wages per employee 1911=100	Number employed	Total wages (1,000 pounds)	Wages per employee (pounds)	Per cent change in wages per employee 1911=100	Number employed	Total wages (1,000 pounds)	Wages per employee (pounds)	Per cent change in wages per employee 1911=100
1911	201,159	5,743	28.5	100.0	38,750	1,556	40.1	100.0	23,214	485	20.9	100.0
1912	204,609	5,966	29.2	102.5	39,991	1,599	40.0	99.8	22,914	493	21.5	102.9
1913	195,651	5,603	28.6	100.4	40,459	1,649	40.8	101.7	24,992	543	21.7	103.8
1914	179,346	5,361	29.9	104.9	25,739	1,036	40.2	100.2	25,804	580	22.5	107.7
1915	205,424	6,045	29.4	103.2	1,462	37	25.3	63.1	24,550	597	24.3	116.3
1916	213,512	6,268	29.4	103.2	11,422	395	34.6	86.3	27,897	715	25.6	122.5
1917	191,912	5,665	29.5	103.5	18,861	711	37.7	94.0	30,025	760	25.3	121.1
1918	186,798	5,572	29.8	104.6	19,358	720	37.2	92.8	30,209	764	25.3	121.1
1919	178,101	5,517	31.0	108.8	21,938	871	39.7	99.0	31,021	841	27.1	129.7
1920	183,597	6,014	32.8	115.1	23,887	1,034	43.3	108.0	32,677	954	29.2	139.7
1921	179,987	5,965	33.1	116.1	7,710	327	42.4	105.7	37,778	1,102	29.2	139.7
1922	169,636	5,582	32.9	115.4	3,821	174	45.5	113.5	33,673	911	27.1	129.7
1923	187,545	6,387	34.1	119.6	10,603	454	42.8	106.7	33,114	930	28.1	134.4
1924	189,277	6,386	33.7	118.2	13,203	570	43.2	107.7	35,105	979	27.9	133.5
1925	185,708	6,263	33.7	118.2	13,778	616	44.7	111.5	34,916	978	28.0	134.0
1926	192,838	6,461	33.5	117.5	17,521	785	44.8	111.7	36,576	1,035	28.3	135.4
1927	197,638	6,563	33.2	116.5	17,664	758	42.9	107.0	34,451	993	28.0	134.0
1928	206,622	6,879	33.3	116.8	17,521	741	42.3	105.5	34,802	966	27.8	133.0
1929	203,527	6,820	33.5	117.5	17,910	760	42.4	105.7	33,498	946	28.2	134.9
1930	211,751	7,073	33.4	117.2	16,027	675	42.1	105.0	31,016	864	27.9	133.5
1931	219,266	7,293	33.3	116.8	10,032	405	40.4	100.7	26,127	710	27.2	130.1
1932	226,628	7,553	33.3	116.8	2,147	73	34.0	84.8	22,200	587	26.4	126.3
1933	240,213	7,904	32.9	115.4	989	36	36.4	90.8	22,515	599	26.6	127.3
1934	262,081	8,593	32.8	115.1	1,135	43	37.9	94.5	23,916	648	27.1	129.7
1935	285,551	9,511	33.3	116.8	1,782	72	40.4	100.7	27,276	743	27.2	130.1
1936	310,073	10,587	34.1	119.6	2,786	120	43.1	107.5	29,155	802	27.5	131.6
1937	314,378	10,753	34.2	120.0	5,059	223	44.1	110.0	29,898	849	28.4	135.9
1938	329,094	11,409	34.6	121.4	5,115	229	44.8	111.7	31,747	911	28.7	137.3

*Natives employed in the diamond mines are provided with quarters, but not food, in addition to their cash wage. Natives employed in the gold and coal mines are provided with food as well as quarters and also receive free medical care.

Source of data: *Annual Report of the Government Mining Engineer* for 1938, Sec. I, table 2, and Sec. II, table 8.

Appendix

TABLE 10
DETAILED CLASSIFICATION OF INDUSTRIES

Class No.	Class of industry	Types of industry included
I	Raw material (The treatment of raw material, the product of agriculture and pastoral pursuits).	Tallow refining and bone milling, fellmongering and wool scouring, cotton ginning, wattle bark grinding.
II	Stone, clay, etc. (Processes of stone, clay, earthenware, and glass).	Asbestos working, bricks, tiles, pottery, glass, limeworks, cement factories.
III	Wood (Working in wood).	Baskets and wickerwork, brooms and brushes. Carpentry and joinery. Sawmills, cooperages, shop-fitting.
IV	Metals, engineering, etc. (Metal, engineering, machinery and cutlery works).	Brass and copper, cutlery, foundries, galvanized iron tools and plumbing, iron and steel furniture, wire working, electrical engineering.
V	Food, drink, etc. (Preparation, treatment, and preserving of food, drink, condiments, and tobacco).	Bacon and ham curing, butter and cheese factories, bread and biscuit making, confectionery, sugar mills, fruit preserving, breweries, distilleries, tobacco.
VI	Clothing, textiles, etc. (Production of clothing [excluding boots and shoes], textile fabrics, and similar articles).	Tailoring and clothing, dyeing and cleaning, bags and sacks, tarpaulins, textile factories.
VII	Books, printing, etc. (Books, paper, printing and engraving).	Printing, bookbinding, and stationery; bags and cardboard boxes, plate engraving and lithographing.
VIII	Vehicles, etc. (Vehicles, mechanically propelled and otherwise, fittings for and parts of).	Coach and wagon building and blacksmithing, cycle and motor repairing.
IX	Ship building, etc. (Ship and boat building and repairing).	Ship and boat building and repairing.
X	Furniture, etc. (Furniture, bedding and upholstery).	Furniture, cabinet making, mattresses, picture frames.
XI	Chemicals, etc. (Drugs, chemicals, including fertilizers and by-products, paints, varnishes, and allied products).	Drugs, perfumery, disinfectants, explosives and matches, fertilizers, paints, soaps and candles.
XII	Surgical instruments, etc. (Surgical, dental and other scientific instruments and apparatus).	Optician's, dental and surgical.
XIII	Jewelry, etc. (Jewelry, timepieces and plated ware).	Gold and silversmiths, diamond cutting.
XIV	Heat, light, and power.	Electric light and power stations; gas, coke, and tar works.
XV	Leather and leatherware.	Tanneries, boots and shoes, harness and saddlery, bags.
XVI	Building and contracting.	Railroad and road, buildings, irrigation and waterworks.
XVII	Miscellaneous (Other industries).	Musical instruments, rubber goods, taxidermists, toys and sports accessories, starch, pipe making, whaling, film production, fish meal, theatrical properties, buttons, buckles, etc.

Source of data: *Census of Industrial Establishments*, 1936-1937, tables 3 and 4, pp. 5-15.

TABLE 11

GOVERNMENT ASSISTANCE TO FARMERS—1931-32 TO 1938-39
UNION OF SOUTH AFRICA

Nature of Assistance	1931-32 thousand pounds	1932-33 thousand pounds	1933-34 thousand pounds	1934-35 thousand pounds	1935-36 thousand pounds	1936-37 thousand pounds	1937-38 thousand pounds	1938-39 (estimate) thousand pounds	Total thousand pounds
1. Export subsidies (amount paid to exporters of agricultural products)	649	2,584	2,010	1,930	1,734	936	330	50	10,223
2. Interest subsidies (interest rebated)	....	....	345	834	754	674	593	750	3,950
3. Redemption of mealie quota certificates	....	....	....	....	250	51	200	390	891
4. Contribution to maize pool	....	....	550	....	....	....	....	....	550
5. Contribution to wheat pool	....	....	120	33	....	....	....	....	153
6. Contribution to wheat industry control board (for payment of storage losses)	....	....	....	....	....	4	6	....	10
7. Credit and cooperative societies	....	....	650	....	....	....	....	....	650
8. Soil erosion, watershed protection, and eradication of weeds	....	....	9	108	423	374	321	287	1,522
9. Subsidies to farmers for purchase of bulbs	....	....	....	....	10	75	103	100	288
10. Rebates of railway rates	....	....	157	171	164	231	275	261	1,259
11. Subsidy on export charges on fruit (precooling, inspection, shipping, and handling)	....	....	....	....	....	91	105	100	296
12. Agricultural marketing fund	....	....	....	....	....	....	100	....	100
13. Miscellaneous — construction of silos, sheds, etc.; housing and rehabilitation on farms, adjustment of bonds	....	....	....	11	77	160	184	235	637
Total	649	2,584	3,841	3,087	3,412	2,596	2,217	2,173	20,559*

*£17,885,000 of this amount is not refundable by farmers.
Source of data: *The agricultural position and the government's proposals in regard thereto* (Union of South Africa: White Paper, Cape Times Limited, March, 1939), p. 5.

BIBLIOGRAPHY

BOOKS

Frankel, S. Hubert, *Capital investment in Africa* (London, New York and Toronto, Oxford University Press, 1938), 487 pp.

Hailey, (Lord), *An African survey* (London, New York and Toronto, Oxford University Press, 1938), 1837 pp.

Leppan, Hubert D., *The organization of agriculture* (Johannesburg, Central News Agency, 1936), 83 pp.

Nathan, M., *The South African commonwealth* (Johannesburg and Capetown, The Specialty Press of South Africa, Ltd., 1919), 293 pp.

Phillips, Ray E., *The Bantu in the city* (South Africa, The Loveday Press, 1938).

South Africa and science: A handbook (Johannesburg, Hortor's Limited, 1929), 313 pp.

GOVERNMENT PUBLICATIONS

Official Yearbook of the Union of South Africa (Nos. 1-20, Pretoria, published annually by Office of Census and Statistics, Government Printer).

Sixth Census of the Union of South Africa, 1936, Population (Pretoria, Office of Census and Statistics, Government Printer, 1938), Vol. I.

Census of Industrial Establishments, 1936-1937 (Pretoria, Office of Census and Statistics, Government Printer, 1939).

Reports of Agricultural and Pastoral Production, Agricultural Censuses Nos. 13, 14, 15, 16, and 17 (Pretoria, Office of Census and Statistics, Government Printer, 1932, 1934-37, and 1939).

Report of Native Economic Commission, 1930-1932 (published by authority, Pretoria, Government Printer, 1932), U. G. No. 22, 1932, 345 pp.

Report of Native Farm Labour Committee, 1937-1939 (Pretoria, Government Printer, 1939), 95 pp.

Report of the Wine Commission (published by authority, Pretoria, Government Printer, 1937), U. G. No. 25, 1937, 107 pp.

Report of the National Marketing Council, 1938-1939 (published by authority, Pretoria, Government Printer, 1939), U. G. No. 26, 1939, 226 pp.

Annual Report of the Government Mining Engineer for the Calendar Year Ended 31st December, 1938 (Pretoria, Department of Mines, Government Printer, 1939), 156 pp. and 28 tables.

Annual Reports, 1930-1939, Department of Agriculture of South Africa.

Report of the Indian Enquiry Commission, South African Indian Enquiry Commission (London, H. M. Stat. Off., 1914), 40 pp. (Great Britain Parliament. Papers by Command. Cmd. 7265).

Agricultural Statistics (1939), U. S. Dept. of Agriculture, 1937-1939.

Pretorius, W. J., *An economic enquiry into wheat farming in the Western Cape Province* (Bulletin No. 103 of the Union of South Africa Dept. of Agriculture, 1931), 49 pp.

——— *An economic enquiry of the wheat industry in the Union* (Bulletin No. 141 of the Union of South Africa Dept. of Agriculture, 1935), 81 pp.

PAMPHLETS, JOURNALS, ARTICLES

De Villiers, Dr. J. P., "Malnutrition Amongst the Colored People," *Race Relations*, Vol. VI (First Quarter, 1939), No. 1, p. 10.

Fox, F. William, "Diet and Health in South Africa: (2) Malnutrition," Reprint from the *South African Medical Journal*, Vol. X (Jan. 11, 1936), pp. 12-16.

——— "Some Nutritional Problems Amongst the Bantu in South Africa," Reprint from the *South African Medical Journal*, Vol. XIII (Feb. 11, 1939), pp. 87-95.

Frankel, S. H., and S. D. Neumark, "The national income of South Africa" (mimeo.). Report issued in 1940. 45 pp.

Houghton, Hobart D., *Some economic problems of the Bantu in South Africa*, South African Institute of Race Relations, Monograph Series No. 1 (1938), 55 pp.

Randall, R. J., "Some reflections on the financial policy of certain municipalities towards the natives within their boundaries," *The South African Journal of Economics*, Vol. VII (June, 1939), No. 2, 23 pp.

Orenstein, A. J., "Diet of Natives on the Witwatersrand gold mines," *Race Relations*, Vol. VI (First Quarter, 1939), No. 1.

Simons, Henry C., "The requisites of free competition," *American Economic Review*, Vol. XXVI (Supplement, March, 1936), No. 1, pp. 68-76.

Miscellaneous

Anning, C. C. P., "Studies in the nutrition of the people of Benoni" (mimeo.), December 6, 1939, 4 pp. and tables.

Carnegie Commission on the Poor White Problem of South Africa. Report of the Pro Ecclesia Drukkery, Stellenbosch.

Farm Labour in the Orange Free State, South African Institute of Race Relations, Monograph Series No. 2 (April, 1939), 46 pp.

Report on Conference on Nutrition, South African Institute of Race Relations, Vol. VI (First Quarter, 1939), No. 1, 41 pp.; Vol. I (Third Quarter, 1939), No. 3, 131 pp.

Swanepoel, S. J., "Government control in industry" (unpublished thesis), Part II, Chapter I, unpaged.

Forty-Ninth Annual Report (Transvaal Chamber of Mines, 1938), 145 pp.

Annual reports of the Medical Officer of Health, Town and Council of Benoni, Transvaal.

Report of the Nutritional Condition of European School Children in the Union of South Africa, The Department of Public Health (mimeo.), Feb., 1940, 19 pp.

Nutrition Survey: Interim Report, The Department of Public Health (mimeo.), April, 1940, 9 pp.

GLOSSARY

Because of the fact that many of the terms used in South Africa are peculiar to that country, it was considered advisable to include an explanation or definition of unusual terms used in this manuscript.

1. *Afrikaans* is a modified form of the Dutch language. It is one of the two official languages of South Africa; English is the other.

2. *Asiatics* are Natives of Asia and their descendants. In South Africa almost all Asiatics are Indians (from India) with a very small number of Chinese, Japanese, and other Asiatic peoples.

3. *Boer* means farmer. This term is applied generally to the Afrikaans-speaking section of the European population of South Africa. The Afrikaans-speaking section is composed chiefly of persons of Dutch (Holland) and French (Huguenot) extraction.

4. *Colored.* This group consists chiefly of Cape Colored persons (descendants of persons of mixed European and other racial stock), Cape Malays (descendants of slaves imported from the Malayan Archipelago), Bushmen, Hottentots, and all other persons of mixed race.

5. *Europeans,* also called Whites, are persons of *pure* European descent.

6. *Lobola* or *ukalobola* is a Native term used to designate the marriage custom whereby a bridegroom hands over to the father of the bride a stipulated number of cattle (sometimes other livestock are used) as a prelude to marriage. This does not constitute the purchase of a wife, but rather is a compensation to the father for the loss of a useful worker and also a guarantee that the husband will treat his wife well.

7. *Maize,* also known as *mealies,* is the South African term for "corn."

8. *Monetary units.* A pound (£) is equal to $4.866 (parity). In a pound are 20 shillings (20s. or 20/-). A shilling is approximately equal to 25 cents. In a shilling there are 12 pennies (pence or 12d.). A penny is approximately equal to 2 cents.

9. *Morgen* = 2.11654 acres. Farm lands in South Africa are measured in terms of morgen rather than in terms of acres.

10. *Natives* are pure-blooded aboriginals of the *Bantu* race.

11. *Pass Laws.* In South Africa all adult male Natives in certain parts of the country are required by law to carry what amount to identification passes.

12. The *Transkeian Territories* are an area consisting of 27 magisterial districts in the eastern part of the Cape Province, bordering Natal and Basutoland. This area has been preserved for almost exclusive occupation by Natives. It contains about one fifth of all Natives in South Africa.

13. *Union of South Africa*, also called *South Africa* or the *Union*, is one of the members of the British Commonwealth of Nations. It includes four provinces: (1) *Cape of Good Hope*, also called *Cape Province*; (2) *Natal*; (3) *Transvaal*, and (4) the *Orange Free State*.

14. *Woolled sheep*. This term is applied to types of sheep like the Merino, bred mainly for woolled purposes. Non-woolled sheep are types bred chiefly for food purposes and for their skins.

Index

INDEX

Agriculture, Control Policies, 81, 199, 212, 225; efficiency of, 50, 56, 75, 80, 204, 215, 245; natural conditions affecting, 14, 65, 80, 86, 92, 204, 215, 217; shifts in, xi, 18, 52, 67, 75; types of farming, 34, 55, 67, 85
Agricultural Fundamentalism, 210
Aliens Act (1937), 11
Amalgamated Society of Carpenters and Joiners, 181
Anglo-Boer War, 6, 18
Anning, Dr. C. C. P., 239
Asiatics, x, 10, 27, 34, 39, 74, 129, 140, 184, 209, 242

Bantu. *See* Native.
Basutoland. *See* Native Protectorates.
Bechuanaland. *See* Native Protectorates.
Benevolent paternalism, 210
Bi-lingualism, 13, 147, 180
Board of Trade and Industries, 83, 204, 215
Boer, 4, 13, 180
British Empire, relations with, 3, 200, 203, 227
Bushmen, 4, 10, 43

Cape Malays, 4, 10, 43
Carnegie Commission of Enquiry on the Poor White Problem, 18, 240
Carnegie Corporation, viii, xv
Cattle, importance to Natives, 33, 47, 52, 70, 160, 236, 245
Census, 9, 27, 66, 85, 121
Central Cooperative Tobacco Company, 214
Chinese, 19, 39
Civilized Labour Policy, 62, 139, 186, 243
Colored population, x, 27, 41, 74, 91, 93, 129, 140, 155, 184, 209, 241
Colour Bar, 19, 62

Commerce, 140, 181
Cooperative Societies Act (1925), 214
Customs Tariff Act (1925), 203

Dairy Industry Control Board, 221
Dart, Raymond A., 43n, 44n
De Gama, Vasco, 3
Detribalized Natives, 9, 52
De Villiers, Dr. J. P., 242
Diaz, Bartholomew, 3
Dingaan, 5
Domestic Service, 13, 29, 141, 157, 163, 166, 172
Dutch East India Company. *See* Netherlands East India Company.

Economic Self-sufficiency. *See* Self-sufficiency.
Electoral Circles, 10
Electoral College, 10
Electricity, Act (1922), 20, 201; Control Board, 201; Supply Commission, 20, 201
Engine Drivers and Firemen's Association, 182

Factories Act (1918), 61
Farm Labour in the Orange Free State (Report on), 236
Federation of Non-European Trade Unions, 183
Field Crops, 71, 79, 86, 96
Food, as part of Native Wages, 111, 128, 142, 155, 181, 220; changes in food habits, 157, 232
Foreign Trade, 17, 22, 200, 216, 226
Fox, F. William, 234, 237
Franchise. *See* Suffrage.
Frankel, Prof. S. H., 21, 53, 137, 193, 227
French Huguenots, 3, 13
Fruit Crops, 74, 79, 86, 97

Gandhi, Mahatma, 42
General strike, 106

[279]

Government Mining Engineer (Report of), 199
Government Revenue and Expenditures, 189, 196, 225, 247

Hamitic Culture, 45
Hottentots, 4, 10, 43
Houghton, D. Hobart, 16n, 47n
Housing of Natives, as wages in kind, 111, 128, 142, 150, 181

Immigration, xi, 18, 40, 180
Immigration Act (1913), 39
Immigration Quota Act (1930), 11
Imperial Conference, 203
Indenture System, 41
Indian question, 42
Indians. See Asiatics.
Industrial Conciliation Act (1924), 182
Industrial Legislation Commission, 186
Institute of Race Relations, ix, 233, 241
Iron and Steel Industry Act (1928), 20, 202
Iron Moulders Society, 182

Kaffir, 20
Kaffir Wars, 4, 7, 20
Kooperatiewe Wynbouwers Vereeniging, 213

Labor-tenant system, 33, 52, 59, 160, 173, 252
Labor Unions, x, 19, 99, 169, 181, 211, 248
Labour, Department of, 9, 163, 184
Leppan, Hubert D., 221
Livestock and Meat Industries Control Board, 222
Livestock farming, 16, 23, 68, 79, 91, 93, 97
Lobola, 47, 54, 56, 245

Magistrate, 9, 61
Malaria, 31
Manufacturing Industry, general, 34, 174, 181, 202, 227, 248; growth of, 20, 121, 205; location, 132, 199; number employed, 126, 172;
secondary industries, xi, 20, 187, 194, 199, 204; wages in, see Wages.
Marketing Act (1937), 223
Master and Servants Laws, 61
Mealie Control Act (1931), 219
Mealie Industry Control Board, 219
Meat Trade Control Board, 222
Miners Phthisis Act (1925), 165
Mines and Works Act (1925), 61
Mining, coal, 100; diamond, 17, 100, 180; employment in, 105, 108, 172, 206; general, xi, 24, 34, 51, 60, 99, 105, 119, 132, 193, 202, 210, 227; gold, xii, 17, 103, 173, 180, 194, 234, 249; taxation of, see Taxation; wages in, see Wages.

Nathan, M., 43
National Income, 21, 244
Nationalist Party, 200
National Marketing Council, 223
Natives, cultural factors, 7, 19, 39, 44, 54, 149, 169, 243, 250; Protectorates, Reserves, and Locations, 6, 14n, 31, 36, 61; social and economic status of, 51, 115, 145, 152, 167, 197, 235, 244; taxation of, see Taxation; Territories, Reserves, and Locations, 7, 19, 37, 50, 55, 116, 152, 197
Native Affairs, Department of, 7, 50, 142, 245
Native Agriculture, Director of, 50
Native Farm Labour Committee, ix, 30, 57n, 116n, 128n, 141, 159n, 162, 172
Native Economic Commission, 49, 152n, 236n
Native Labor, in Agriculture, 32, 49, 52, 172; Director of, 60, 150; inefficient use of, 32, 37, 148, 245; recruitment of, 32, 60; supply of, 18, 27, 175, 205, 252; working conditions of, xii, 51, 56, 60, 145, 165, 252
Native Labour Regulation Act (1911), 60, 147, 150n
Native Population, 3, 27, 36; location of, 33, 116, 149, 251
Native Service Contract Act (1932), 59

Index

Native (Urban Areas) Act, 147
Native Taxation and Development Act (1925), 59, 195
Negro Hoe Culture, 45
Netherlands East India Company, 3, 43
Neumark, S. D., 21
Nutrition, x, xii, 51, 119, 156, 231, 237, 243

Orange Free State Republic, 5, 40
Orenstein, Dr. A. J., 156

Parliament of Union of South Africa, ix, 8, 218, 234
Patrilineal group, 46
Pass Laws, 57, 147
Phillips, Ray E., 147
Physical Characteristics (South Africa), 14
Polygamy, 48
Poor Whites, 18, 20, 185, 206, 210
Population, 3, 10, 27, 34, 39, 78
Pretorius, W. J., 212, 217
Provincial Governments, 8, 189

Railways, general, 21, 136, 151, 211, 248; employment in, 138; wages in, 140
Randall, R. J., 153
Rations. *See* Food.
Representation of Natives Act, 10
Responsible Government, 5

Segregation, 3, 49, 57, 153, 244
Self-sufficiency, xi, 16, 200, 208, 226
Settlement of Country, 3
Sheep-farming, 68, 91, 97
Sib and Siboko, 45
Simons, Henry C., 249
Slaves, 4
Social problem (general), 42
South Africa Act (1909), 9
South African Indian Inquiry Commission, 42
South African Industrial Federation, 182
South African Iron and Steel Industrial Corporation, 202
South African Native Trust Fund, 191, 196

South African Railways. *See* Railways.
South African Republic, 5, 40
South African Typographical Union, 182
Squatters (Native), 31, 52, 60, 173
State-aided Milk and Butter Scheme, 222, 242
Statistics Act (1914), 66
Suffrage, 9, 40, 221, 243
Sugar Cane Industry, 16, 31, 35, 71, 94, 155, 215, 223
Sugar Industry Control Board, 215
Swanepoel, S. J., 204
Swaziland. *See* Native Protectorates.

Tariff Protection, 20, 203, 212, 226
Taxation, general, 212; of mines, 190, 227, 248; of Natives, 19, 30, 53, 59, 153, 190, 195, 205, 245
Tobacco Control Amendment Act, 215
Tobacco Industry Control Board, 215
Transvaal Chamber of Mines, 115, 182
Transvaal Federation of Trades, 182

Ukalobola. *See* Lobola.
Underprivileged groups, xiii, 225, 245
Union Steel Corporation, 202

Van Rhiebeeck, Jan, 3
Venereal Diseases, 54, 251

Wage and Monetary Economy, 17
Wages, general, 19, 32, 140, 171, 187; in agriculture, 17, 144, 172; in manufacturing, 128, 171, 206; in mining, 110, 171; policy, 19, 179, 183, 206, 245
Wages Act (1937), 61, 182
Wheat Industry Control Board, 218, 225
Wine and Spirits Control Act (1924), 213
Wine Industry, 16, 74, 88, 215, 223
Witch Doctors, 48
Witwatersrand Trade and Labour Council, 182
Workmen's Compensation Act (1936), 164

www.ingramcontent.com/pod-product-compliance
Lightning Source LLC
Chambersburg PA
CBHW021119300426
44113CB00006B/216